LIVING *the* WORD

**Scripture Reflections and Commentaries
for Sundays and Holy Days**

**Laurie Brink, O.P., and
Paul Colloton, O.S.F.S.**

NOVEMBER 27, 2016 THROUGH NOVEMBER 26, 2017   YEAR A

LIVING *the* WORD

Scripture Reflections and Commentaries
for Sundays and Holy Days

Vol. 32   November 27, 2016–November 26, 2017

Published annually

Individual copy: $14.95
2-9 copies: $10.95 per copy;
10-24 copies: $9.95 per copy;
25-99 copies: $8.95 per copy;
100 or more copies: $6.95 per copy

Editor: Alan J. Hommerding
Copy and Production Editor: Marcia T. Lucey
Cover Design and Typesetting: Tejal Patel
Cover Image: Gospel of Matthew (Angel) by Tony Ward
        tonywardarts.com
Director of Publications: Mary Beth Kunde-Anderson

In accordance with c. 827, permission to publish is granted on June 2, 2016, by Most Reverend Francis J. Kane, Vicar General of the Archdiocese of Chicago. Permission to publish is an official declaration of ecclesiastical authority that the material is free from doctrinal and moral error. No legal responsibility is assumed by the grant of this permission.

World Library Publications,
the music and liturgy division of J. S. Paluch Company, Inc.
3708 River Road, Suite 400, Franklin Park, IL 60131-2158
800 566-6150 • fax 888 957-3291
wlpcs@jspaluch.com • www.wlpmusic.com

Printed in the United States of America
WLP 006772 • (ISSN) 1079-4670 • (ISBN) 978-1-58459-840-4

Our liturgy presumes that those who gather for Eucharist, as members of the Body of Christ, are already familiar with the word that they hear proclaimed every Sunday. *Living the Word* is designed to assist individuals, homilists, catechumens, candidates, discussion groups, religious education classes, and similar gatherings to deepen that familiarity with the Sunday scriptures.

Inside this book you will find the readings for each Sunday and holy day from Year A of the liturgical cycle. Each day's readings are preceded by a brief passage intended to suggest a focus or approach to consider while reading these particular scriptures. The readings are followed by a commentary that provides a context for understanding them, making use of biblical scholarship and the Church's longstanding traditions. Then a reflection is offered that expands upon the initial focus and incorporates the fuller understanding from the commentary section. The discussion questions and suggestions for responses that follow are provided as helps to move from reflection to action, inviting those who use this volume to go about truly "living the word."

When reflecting on the scriptures in a group setting or individually, it is best to do so in the context of prayer. Users of this book are encouraged to create an atmosphere that will foster prayerful reflection: in a quiet space, perhaps with lit candle and simple seasonal decoration (incense or soft music may also be appropriate), begin with a prayer and reading of the scriptures aloud for that day, even if you are alone. In a group, encourage members to focus on one word or idea that especially strikes them. Continue with each reading the same way, perhaps taking time to share these ideas with one another.

After you spend some quiet time with the readings, ask yourself how they have changed you, enlightened you, moved you. Move on to the commentary, reflection, and prayer response. Allow the discussion questions to shape your conversation, and try the prayer response on for size. Will you rise to its challenge? Does it give you an idea of something to try in your own life? Share your ideas with someone else, even if you have been preparing alone.

Once you have spent a suitable time in reflection or discussion, you may wish to make a prayerful response to the readings by means of a song or a blessing of someone or something. Pray spontaneously as you think about the texts' meaning for you, or invite people in the group to offer prayers informally.

Finally, challenge yourself, or each other in your group, to take action this week based on your understanding of the readings. You may propose your own prayer for help to undertake this mission or simply stand in a circle and pray the Lord's Prayer. If you are in a group, offer one another a sign of peace before departing. If alone, surprise someone with a sign of peace, either in person, by making a phone call, or offering a simple prayer.

As you repeat this pattern over time, your prayerful reflection can deepen your appreciation of God's word and enable you to live it more fully every day.

Table of Contents

Individual Prayers Before and After Reading Scripture

Speak to me as I read your word, O Lord,
and send your Spirit into my heart.
Guide me today and each day in your service,
for you are the way, the truth, and the life. *Amen!*

or

May the words of my mouth, and the meditations of my heart
be acceptable to you, O Lord, my rock and my redeemer. *Amen!*

❖

God of all graciousness,
I thank you for speaking to me
through your holy word.

Let me put your word into action
today and every day. *Amen!*

or

Blessed are you, Lord God,
maker of heaven and earth,
for sending your Holy Spirit today
to teach me your truth. *Amen!*

Group Prayers Before and After Reading Scripture

Blessed are you, Lord God,
you teach your people by your word.
Open our hearts to your Spirit,
and lead us in the ways of Christ your Son.

All praise and glory be yours for ever. *Amen!*

or

Speak, Lord,
your servants are listening:
You alone have the words of everlasting life. *Amen!*

❖

We praise you, loving God, for sending us your word today.

Grant that we may continue to think and pray on these words,
and to share them with others throughout this day. *Amen!*

or

May this word of life
fill our hearts, be on our lips,
and guide our every thought and deed. *Amen!*

Advent is a time of waiting. As the scriptures describe, a time would come when nations would stream to Jerusalem, yearning to be instructed in the ways of God (Advent 1). The readings from the book of Isaiah poignantly recount the hope and longing for God's visitation. "A shoot shall sprout from the stump of Jesse" envisions an heir to the Davidic kingdom, filled with the Spirit of the Lord, who would rule with justice and set in motion a new peace (Advent 2). The desert would bloom, roadways would be made straight, and the ransomed would return (Advent 3). And all this would be accomplished because God would dwell with God's people (Advent 4).

The second readings are taken from a variety of New Testament texts and reflect the themes of expectancy. Paul's Letter to the Romans reminds us that our salvation is nearer than when we first believed (Advent 1), and both Gentile and Jew are called to be holy (Advent 4). Therefore we should remain in harmony with one another (Advent 2). James also stresses maintaining right relationships among believers (Advent 3).

In much the same way, the Gospel readings anticipate a new day. Jesus warns that the Son of Man will come unexpectedly, so believers had best stay watchful and alert (Advent 1). The nearness of the kingdom of heaven was heralded by John the Baptist, who warned the crowds to repent and be baptized (Advent 2). But despite John's prophetic announcement, he himself seemed to need reassurance that Jesus was indeed "the one who is to come" (Advent 4).

In Advent we wait for two distinct events. First, we await an annual celebration of the birth of Jesus. Second, we await—united with all past and future believers—the *parousia*, Jesus' return, when the reign of heaven will be complete.

As we enter into the Christmas season, we rejoice because in our readings we see both the now and the not-yet of God's reign. Jesus is "God with us" and also "the one who is to come." The Gospel readings are taken from the writings of the evangelist Matthew, so we hear his particular emphasis on Jesus' Jewish roots and the fulfillment of the prophetic promises.

November 27, 2016

FIRST SUNDAY OF ADVENT

Today's Focus: Preparing for That Thief in the Night

Unlike our everyday life, in which we can never fully prepare for crisis or emergency, we are able to prepare spiritually for the time of the Lord's return.

FIRST READING
Isaiah 2:1–5

This is what Isaiah, son of Amoz,
saw concerning Judah and Jerusalem.
    In days to come,
the mountain of the LORD's house
    shall be established as the highest mountain
    and raised above the hills.
All nations shall stream toward it;
    many peoples shall come and say:
"Come, let us climb the LORD's mountain,
    to the house of the God of Jacob,
that he may instruct us in his ways,
    and we may walk in his paths."
For from Zion shall go forth instruction,
    and the word of the LORD from Jerusalem.
He shall judge between the nations,
    and impose terms on many peoples.
They shall beat their swords into plowshares
    and their spears into pruning hooks;
one nation shall not raise the sword against another,
    nor shall they train for war again.
O house of Jacob, come,
    let us walk in the light of the LORD!

PSALM RESPONSE
Psalm 122:1

Let us go rejoicing to the house of the Lord.

SECOND READING
Romans 13:11–14

Brothers and sisters: You know the time; it is the hour now for you to awake from sleep. For our salvation is nearer now than when we first believed; the night is advanced, the day is at hand. Let us then throw off the works of darkness and put on the armor of light; let us conduct ourselves properly as in the day, not in orgies and drunkenness, not in promiscuity and lust, not in rivalry and jealousy. But put on the Lord Jesus Christ, and make no provision for the desires of the flesh.

GOSPEL
Matthew 24:
37–44

Jesus said to his disciples: "As it was in the days of Noah, so it will be at the coming of the Son of Man. In those days before the flood, they were eating and drinking, marrying and giving in marriage, up to the day that Noah entered the ark. They did not know until the flood came and carried them all away. So will it be also at the coming of the Son of Man. Two men will be out in the field; one will be taken, and one will be left. Two women will be grinding at the mill; one will be taken, and one will be left. Therefore, stay awake! For you do not know on which day your Lord will come. Be sure of this: if the master of the house had known the hour of night when the thief was coming, he would have stayed awake and not let his house be broken into. So too, you also must be prepared, for at an hour you do not expect, the Son of Man will come."

❖ *Understanding the Word*

The prophet Isaiah envisions a thoroughly obedient people of God, who "climb the Lord's mountain," Mount Moriah in Jerusalem, the seat of the holy temple. From this abode, God's instructions (the Torah) will not only be understood, they will be followed. Adherence to God's law leads to right relationship among all peoples so that wars end and peace prevails. But Isaiah's vision was future-oriented. He held out to the king and court what Judah could be like if its leadership turned from disobedience and injustice and guided the people properly.

Paul's address to the Christians in Rome echoes Isaiah's future-oriented message, but with greater urgency: "It is the hour . . . our salvation is nearer now" (Romans 13:11). This passage serves as the reason for his earlier instructions about right relationship with authorities and one's neighbors (Romans 13:1ff). The nearness of the day of Jesus Christ's return should prompt all believers to conduct themselves properly and "make no provision for the desires of the flesh" (Romans 13:14).

The Gospel reading is taken from the apocalyptic discourse in Matthew Chapter 24, in which Jesus instructs his disciples privately about the coming end of this age (Matthew 24:3). Calamities and false messiahs will signal the beginning of the labor pains (Matthew 24:8). The temple will be defiled and believers scattered (Matthew 24:15–16). All this precedes the coming of the Son of Man, who will return and gather the elect from the four winds (Matthew 24:31). But the timing of these events is unknown, even to the Son. In today's passage, Jesus invokes the memory of the flood and Noah's preparedness to serve as an example to his disciples. The discrimination between who will be taken and who will remain is based on their readiness for the kingdom. Jesus will use several different examples to emphasize the need to be ready and alert. A thief would not be successful if the householder were awake (Matthew 24:43). The wise maidens brought additional oil for their lamps in anticipation of the bridegroom's delay (Matthew 24:4). The admonition to wait patiently was aimed at the first-century Christians for whom the sense of the immediacy of the *parousia* had faded.

Were you ever robbed? During my senior year of high school I was called home one day because someone broke into our house. My grandfather surprised the robbers and chased them out of the house so quickly that they broke the back door off its hinges. They hit him with the crowbar they used to break into the house so he was hospitalized for observation. He insisted that I sleep at home that night to "protect" the house, which I did but without sleeping. Life changed that day. While we fixed doors and changed safety procedures, we knew it could happen again.

Our readings tell us to be prepared (Matthew 24:44) and "awake from sleep" (Romans 13:11) to be ready for Christ's return. We await something good, the way of God's peace: swords become plowshares, spears become pruning hooks; life without war and God's justice, that is, right relationship with God and all creation. At that time the light that destroys the darkness of terrorism, disease, death, divorce, destruction, addiction, and . . . fill in the blank . . . will appear. I long for that day! We can hasten that day's coming by putting on the armor of light and living the ways of Jesus that we put on in baptism: love, mercy, truth, humility, patience, modesty, and obedience to the Word-made-flesh. St. Francis de Sales taught that by living these little virtues, we could overcome our enemy (see *Introduction to the Devout Life*, Ch. III). Living these virtues prepares us for the Lord's return. Living these virtues makes Christ's presence known. By living these virtues we walk in the light of the Lord and shine with the light that robs darkness of its power. Pick a virtue and live it.

✤ Consider/Discuss

- What darkness do I most fear overtaking my life?
- What virtue will help me put on the armor of light this Advent?

✤ *Living and Praying with the Word*

Come, Lord Jesus; instruct us in your ways that we might wake up to your presence in our world, and by living the little virtues, fill the world with your hope, light, and rejoicing.

December 4, 2016

SECOND SUNDAY OF ADVENT

Today's Focus: Time for a Change

Sometimes we do not like change, but when it comes to living more closely in the image of Christ, things about our lives do need to change. We cannot change our lives without a change of heart first.

FIRST READING
Isaiah 11:1–10

On that day, a shoot shall sprout from the stump of Jesse,
   and from his roots a bud shall blossom.
The spirit of the Lord shall rest upon him:
   a spirit of wisdom and of understanding,
  a spirit of counsel and of strength,
   a spirit of knowledge and of fear of the LORD,
   and his delight shall be the fear of the LORD.
Not by appearance shall he judge,
   nor by hearsay shall he decide,
but he shall judge the poor with justice,
   and decide aright for the land's afflicted.
He shall strike the ruthless with the rod of his mouth,
   and with the breath of his lips he shall slay the wicked.
Justice shall be the band around his waist,
   and faithfulness a belt upon his hips.
Then the wolf shall be a guest of the lamb,
   and the leopard shall lie down with the kid;
the calf and the young lion shall browse together,
   with a little child to guide them.
The cow and the bear shall be neighbors,
   together their young shall rest;
   the lion shall eat hay like the ox.
The baby shall play by the cobra's den,
   and the child lay his hand on the adder's lair.
There shall be no harm or ruin on all my holy mountain;
   for the earth shall be filled with knowledge of the LORD,
   as water covers the sea.
On that day, the root of Jesse,
   set up as a signal for the nations,
the Gentiles shall seek out,
   for his dwelling shall be glorious.

PSALM RESPONSE
Psalm 72:7

Justice shall flourish in his time, and fullness of peace for ever.

SECOND READING
Romans 15: 4–9

Brothers and sisters: Whatever was written previously was written for our instruction, that by endurance and by the encouragement of the Scriptures we might have hope. May the God of endurance and encouragement grant you to think in harmony with one another, in keeping with Christ Jesus, that with one accord you may with one voice glorify the God and Father of our Lord Jesus Christ.

Welcome one another, then, as Christ welcomed you, for the glory of God. For I say that Christ became a minister of the circumcised to show God's truthfulness, to confirm the promises to the patriarchs, but so that the Gentiles might glorify God for his mercy. As it is written:

> *Therefore, I will praise you among the Gentiles*
> *and sing praises to your name.*

GOSPEL
Matthew 3: 1–12

John the Baptist appeared, preaching in the desert of Judea and saying, "Repent, for the kingdom of heaven is at hand!" It was of him that the prophet Isaiah had spoken when he said:

> *A voice of one crying out in the desert,*
> *Prepare the way of the Lord,*
> *make straight his paths.*

John wore clothing made of camel's hair and had a leather belt around his waist. His food was locusts and wild honey. At that time Jerusalem, all Judea, and the whole region around the Jordan were going out to him and were being baptized by him in the Jordan River as they acknowledged their sins.

When he saw many of the Pharisees and Sadducees coming to his baptism, he said to them, "You brood of vipers! Who warned you to flee from the coming wrath? Produce good fruit as evidence of your repentance. And do not presume to say to yourselves, 'We have Abraham as our father.' For I tell you, God can raise up children to Abraham from these stones. Even now the ax lies at the root of the trees. Therefore every tree that does not bear good fruit will be cut down and thrown into the fire. I am baptizing you with water, for repentance, but the one who is coming after me is mightier than I. I am not worthy to carry his sandals. He will baptize you with the Holy Spirit and fire. His winnowing fan is in his hand. He will clear his threshing floor and gather his wheat into his barn, but the chaff he will burn with unquenchable fire."

Isaiah has confidence that a ruler from "the stump of Jesse, " the father of David, will fulfill the Davidic promise and restore national hope and religious fidelity. But throughout his long tenure as a prophet of Jerusalem, he had failed to convince many of the kings to trust that God would protect the kingdom. In today's first reading, Isaiah looks to the future when the Davidic rule, thought only to be a stump, will bring forth a new shoot. The Spirit of God will bestow on this one all the virtues of a just king: wisdom, understanding, counsel, strength, knowledge, and fear of the Lord. These virtues will lead to right action and the administration of justice, which will not only affect Jerusalem and Judah, but the entire created world will be at peace. Even the Gentiles will seek out the holy city.

Part of the reason that Paul wrote to the church at Rome may have been to heal divisions within the Roman Christian community. Romans 14:1—15:6, from which our second reading is taken, addresses the disparity between the strong and the weak. Paul assures the community that the scriptures provide instruction and offer encouragement even though the believers are not under the law of Moses. He then draws from the Greek background of his Gentile readers, invoking a common political motif of unity. The community is "to think in harmony" (Romans 15: 5) and be of "one accord" (Romans 15:6). Similar language is found in First Corinthians where Paul is addressing the schisms among the believers (1 Corinthians 1:10).

The merciful and just messianic king envisioned by Isaiah is complemented by John the Baptist's depiction of a mighty one who is to come. This one will offer judgment: "every tree that does not bear good fruit will be cut down and thrown into the fire" (Matthew 3:10). Dressed in camel's hair, John is presented in the image of Elijah, Israel's prophet whose return would herald the coming end of the age. Jewish apocalyptic expectations anticipated that the reign of heaven would begin with the judgment of sinners. The approach of Pharisees and Sadducees seeking baptism provokes a strong rebuke by John: "You brood of vipers!" (Matthew 3:7). Throughout Matthew's Gospel, the Jewish religious authorities will receive increasing condemnation (Matthew 23:1–26).

❖ *Reflecting on the Word*

When my mother called me "Paul Henry," I knew I had better pay attention. What followed was important. Most often what followed was, "You'd better change your ways, young man." Strong words invite attention and almost demand a response. Such are John's words to the Pharisees and Sadducees, "You brood of vipers!"(Matthew 3:7). Such are Isaiah's words to the Israelites, "On that day" (Isaiah 11:1). The desired response? Produce good fruit, Pharisees and Sadducees. Show the spirit of the LORD, Israelites. Judge by fact, not hearsay. Be just, that is, live in right relationship with God and all creation. Befriend enemies. Keep the most vulnerable safe. Remove ruin and harm from God's holy mountain. These signify that the sprout of Jesse's root, the Messiah, has come. The second reading adds harmony, hospitality, and inclusivity to the list of desired responses.

Words like these can instill fear in us or inhibit us or they can invite us to change our ways. Change offers hope. We can be counted among the gathered wheat rather than the burning chaff. The gifts of the Holy Spirit named in Isaiah today and bestowed in the sacrament of Confirmation do make a notable difference: enemies speak to each other, adversaries join hands, people seek to meet together, love overcomes hatred, revenge gives way to forgiveness, and discord becomes mutual respect, to paraphrase *Eucharistic Prayer II for Reconciliation*. Living these words gives flesh to our psalm response: "Justice shall flourish in his time, and fullness of peace for ever." Hear God use the name your parents used to call for attention. God invites the change that hope, healing, and justice offer. Respond by following the One who has given us the Holy Spirit and the fire of God's love, Jesus Christ.

✜ Consider/Discuss

- What change might God be asking of you in order to live God's justice more clearly this Advent?
- What will help you try to live the words of the Eucharistic Prayer mentioned above?

✜ Living and Praying with the Word

Merciful God, each Advent you renew your call to proclaim the presence of your Son in my life. Deepen your Spirit within me so that I can live in right relationship with you and with all creation.

December 8, 2016

IMMACULATE CONCEPTION OF THE BLESSED VIRGIN MARY

Today's Focus: What's Your Response?

When we hear the word of God, there are a variety of ways we can respond, including not responding at all. But those around us—and God—will know how deeply the word has penetrated.

FIRST READING
Genesis 3: 9–15, 20

After the man, Adam, had eaten of the tree, the LORD God called to the man and asked him, "Where are you?" He answered, "I heard you in the garden; but I was afraid, because I was naked, so I hid myself." Then he asked, "Who told you that you were naked? You have eaten, then, from the tree of which I had forbidden you to eat!" The man replied, "The woman whom you put here with me—she gave me fruit from the tree, and so I ate it." The LORD God then asked the woman, "Why did you do such a thing?" The woman answered, "The serpent tricked me into it, so I ate it."

Then the LORD God said to the serpent:
  "Because you have done this, you shall be banned
    from all the animals
    and from all the wild creatures;
  on your belly shall you crawl,
    and dirt shall you eat
    all the days of your life.
  I will put enmity between you and the woman,
    and between your offspring and hers;
  he will strike at your head,
    while you strike at his heel."
The man called his wife Eve, because she became the mother of all the living.

PSALM RESPONSE
Psalm 98:1a

Sing to the Lord a new song, for he has done marvelous deeds.

SECOND READING
Ephesians 1: 3–6, 11–12

Brothers and sisters: Blessed be the God and Father of our Lord Jesus Christ, who has blessed us in Christ with every spiritual blessing in the heavens, as he chose us in him, before the foundation of the world, to be holy and without blemish before him. In love he destined us for adoption to himself through Jesus Christ, in accord with the favor of his will, for the praise of the glory of his grace that he granted us in the beloved.

In him we were also chosen, destined in accord with the purpose of the One who accomplishes all things according to the intention of his will, so that we might exist for the praise of his glory, we who first hoped in Christ.

15

GOSPEL
Luke 1:26–38
The angel Gabriel was sent from God to a town of Galilee called Nazareth, to a virgin betrothed to a man named Joseph, of the house of David, and the virgin's name was Mary. And coming to her, he said, "Hail, full of grace! The Lord is with you." But she was greatly troubled at what was said and pondered what sort of greeting this might be. Then the angel said to her, "Do not be afraid, Mary, for you have found favor with God. Behold, you will conceive in your womb and bear a son, and you shall name him Jesus. He will be great and will be called Son of the Most High, and the Lord God will give him the throne of David his father, and he will rule over the house of Jacob forever, and of his kingdom there will be no end." But Mary said to the angel, "How can this be, since I have no relations with a man?" And the angel said to her in reply, "The Holy Spirit will come upon you, and the power of the Most High will overshadow you. Therefore the child to be born will be called holy, the Son of God. And behold, Elizabeth, your relative, has also conceived a son in her old age, and this is the sixth month for her who was called barren; for nothing will be impossible for God." Mary said, "Behold, I am the handmaid of the Lord. May it be done to me according to your word." Then the angel departed from her.

 Understanding the Word

The first two chapters of the book of Genesis describe two different stories of creation. In both, the creation of human beings signals a high point in God's generative activities. The tone of peaceful coexistence is abruptly shattered by the intrusion of the serpent, which causes the original couple (both are present in Genesis 3:6) to question God's commands. As punishment for their actions, God places enmity between the serpent and humanity. As the book of Genesis progresses, this enmity will grow, leading to sin, violence, lust, and a variety of vices, causing God to regret having made humankind (Genesis 6:6).

The Letter to the Ephesians hearkens back to the ideal creation—a people without blemish before God. Ephesians proposes that the believers were chosen and destined for adoption. The adoption theme suggests that the community to whom this letter is addressed includes Gentiles (see Galatians 4:5, Ephesians 2:19). Through Christ, the original intention of God is realized "so that we might exist for the praise of his glory" (Galatians 1:12).

Today's feast celebrates the conception of Mary, who, doctrine holds, was preserved from sin at the moment of her conception. Our Gospel reading describes the reason for Mary's sinless state: that she might conceive and bear the Son of the Most High. It seemed fitting that for Jesus to be born without sin, his mother would also have to be without sin. Jesus' sinless nature is likely why Luke does not narrate Jesus' baptism in the Jordan for a remission of sins. Luke's infancy narratives portray two very different responses to Gabriel's announcements. Zechariah questions the angel's credibility when he announces the birth of John (1:19). But Mary ponders not *that* she will conceive, but rather *how* it will occur. She accepts the angel's announcement and offers herself as God's handmaiden.

✥ Reflecting on the Word

Our words give us away. An answer to a question can reveal what we know and how we feel. God asked Adam, "Where are you?" Adam's answer gave away that he had eaten from the tree God had forbidden. Gabriel greeted Mary. Her response revealed her wonderment and fear. Why else would Gabriel have said, "Do not be afraid"? Adam's words, along with those of Eve and the snake, make their disobedience known. Mary's words in dialogue with Gabriel made her obedience possible. Unlike Adam, Eve, and the snake, who passed the buck, Mary's honesty and openness expressed her inner freedom. Conceived free from sin, she could be a worthy vessel for the sinless Savior. We can be free from the ultimate power of sin and that is a source of hope for us, although we know the effects of original sin. Yet even Eve will become "the mother of all the living" (Genesis 3:20), words of hope. God did not abandon our first parents after their original sin. Nothing is impossible for God.

You and I know the effects of original, personal, and corporate sin all too well. Evidence of sin surrounds us and can blind us to the evidence of God's goodness that also surrounds us. God has blessed *us* in Christ. God chose *us* and destines *us* "for the praise of the glory of his grace that he granted *us* in the beloved" (Ephesians 1:6). Do we believe these words? Our response will give us away.

We are full of grace. The Lord *is* with *us* because the Holy Spirit has been given us. Believe! Do not be afraid. Let this belief make a difference in your life, for nothing is impossible with God.

✥ Consider/Discuss

- How does sin keep you from believing that God has chosen you to be holy?
- When has God's mercy freed you to see God present in your life?

✥ Living and Praying with the Word

God, our Father, you fill us with your Holy Spirit and have chosen us in Christ. Help us pray like Mary in dialogue with the angel Gabriel, listening to your voice and speaking from our heart. Overshadow our sin and fear with the forgiving love you shower on us each and every day.

December 11, 2016

THIRD SUNDAY OF ADVENT

Today's Focus: Imagine That!

Today we hear what happens when the reign of God truly breaks into the world. Can we imagine a world or a life that looks like those signs?

FIRST READING
Isaiah 35: 1–6a, 10

The desert and the parched land will exult;
    the steppe will rejoice and bloom.
They will bloom with abundant flowers,
    and rejoice with joyful song.
The glory of Lebanon will be given to them,
    the splendor of Carmel and Sharon;
they will see the glory of the LORD,
    the splendor of our God.
Strengthen the hands that are feeble,
    make firm the knees that are weak,
say to those whose hearts are frightened:
    Be strong, fear not!
Here is your God,
    he comes with vindication;
with divine recompense
    he comes to save you.
Then will the eyes of the blind be opened,
    the ears of the deaf be cleared;
then will the lame leap like a stag,
    then the tongue of the mute will sing.

Those whom the LORD has ransomed will return
    and enter Zion singing,
    crowned with everlasting joy;
they will meet with joy and gladness,
    sorrow and mourning will flee.

PSALM RESPONSE
Isaiah 35:4

Lord, come and save us.

SECOND READING
James 5:7–10

Be patient, brothers and sisters, until the coming of the Lord. See how the farmer waits for the precious fruit of the earth, being patient with it until it receives the early and the late rains. You too must be patient. Make your hearts firm, because the coming of the Lord is at hand. Do not complain, brothers and sisters, about one another, that you may not be judged. Behold, the Judge is standing before the gates. Take as an example of hardship and patience, brothers and sisters, the prophets who spoke in the name of the Lord.

GOSPEL
Matthew 11:
2–11

When John the Baptist heard in prison of the works of the Christ, he sent his disciples to Jesus with this question, "Are you the one who is to come, or should we look for another?" Jesus said to them in reply, "Go and tell John what you hear and see: the blind regain their sight, the lame walk, lepers are cleansed, the deaf hear, the dead are raised, and the poor have the good news proclaimed to them. And blessed is the one who takes no offense at me."

As they were going off, Jesus began to speak to the crowds about John, "What did you go out to the desert to see? A reed swayed by the wind? Then what did you go out to see? Someone dressed in fine clothing? Those who wear fine clothing are in royal palaces. Then why did you go out? To see a prophet? Yes, I tell you, and more than a prophet. This is the one about whom it is written:
   Behold, I am sending my messenger ahead of you;
   he will prepare your way before you.
Amen, I say to you, among those born of women there has been none greater than John the Baptist; yet the least in the kingdom of heaven is greater than he."

❖❖ *Understanding the Word*

The first reading is likely from the period of Israel's Babylonian exile, and was part of a collection of oracles attributed to an unknown prophet preaching in the tradition of Isaiah. The majority of these oracles are found in Chapters 40–55. The vision this prophet announces is one of redemption in which God will save the faithful exiles (Isaiah 35:4). Evidence of God's presence is made manifest in the supernatural responses of nature. The arid wilderness will bloom and rejoice. The fabled beauty of Lebanon and Carmel will now belong to the dry land of the desert and steppe. Some unnamed members are called to strengthen and make firm the returning exiles (Isaiah 35:3). God's presence will not only be evident in nature. Human disabilities will be corrected. The blind will see, the deaf hear, the lame leap, and those without speech sing (Isaiah 35:5). This same verse will be cited by Jesus to describe his own ministry in today's Gospel.

While the Letter of James and the oracle of Isaiah are addressed to two different communities more than five hundred years apart, they both speak with hope of the coming presence of God. James addresses a community in despair because of the delay of the *parousia*. "You too must be patient," he admonishes (James 5:8). This echoes earlier encouragement to endure trials patiently (James 1:2–4). Until the time that Jesus returns, the community is to endure without complaint, taking the lives of the prophets as their guide. The grumbling against others may result from rising doubts about the coming judgment (James 5:9).

The question John sends via his disciples may puzzle some readers who remember John's declaration in Matthew 3:11 that there one was coming who would be mightier than he, followed by his reluctant baptizing of Jesus (Matthew 3:14). Likely, the source of this encounter and Jesus' subsequent pronouncement about John comes from Q, a sayings source shared by Matthew and Luke, but not found in Mark. Jesus answers John's disciples by citing Isaiah 35. Jesus is demonstrating the deeds that portend God's presence among the people: the blind see, the lame walk, the sick are healed, etc. By describing his actions, Jesus is demonstrating that he is the Messiah. No wonder Jesus adds, "And blessed is the one who takes no offense at me" (Matthew 11:6).

✤ Reflecting on the Word

A friend walked me through his newly planted garden to help me see how it would look in spring. He finally stopped and said, "You can't picture any of this, can you?" I couldn't until I saw it in full bloom the following springtime. Then I could understand why he planted the seeds where he had. Then I saw the beauty and bounty that his planting represented. "Tell John what you hear and see," Jesus says to John's disciples. The signs of the Messiah proclaimed by the prophets are beginning to bloom. Look and see! Hear the singing of those once mute and the rejoicing of the crowds who witness these works. The beauty and the bounty of our generous God are all around.

James wrote to a community experiencing hardship, like the exiled Israelites in today's first reading. Isaiah and James exhort people to trust that they will see God's presence in their midst once again, so be patient. That's easier said than done, isn't it? St. Francis de Sales says to be patient with everyone, and most of all with ourselves. Patience means accepting suffering and delay without becoming angry or upset. Easier said than done. Praying for this virtue each day, sometimes often throughout the day, does help. Breathe in the Spirit of God and say, "Give me patience, Lord." Then exhale anger, upset, and impatience. Staring at a garden won't make a shoot spring up any faster; however, giving thanks for the seed, the water, the soil, and the Giver of all life can deepen our trust that the garden will grow. So be patient. Rejoice always. See and be the signs of God's beauty and bounty in our world today.

✤ Consider/Discuss

- If I were one of John's disciples, what signs of God's presence would I name today?
- What helps me live the virtue of patience? What gets in the way of it?

✤ Living and Praying with the Word

Almighty God, we rejoice in the gift of your Son, Jesus Christ. Belonging to him makes even the least of us greater than John the Baptizer. Help me be grateful for that gift each and every day of my life.

December 18, 2016

FOURTH SUNDAY OF ADVENT

Today's Focus: Looking Back to Look Forward

We hear about Jesus' many ancestors in Matthew's Gospel. Surely Jesus knew of these men and women, but he always lived focused on the future, building on what he had inherited from them.

FIRST READING
Isaiah 7:10–14

The LORD spoke to Ahaz, saying: Ask for a sign from the LORD, your God; let it be deep as the netherworld, or high as the sky! But Ahaz answered, "I will not ask! I will not tempt the LORD!" Then Isaiah said: Listen, O house of David! Is it not enough for you to weary people, must you also weary my God? Therefore the LORD himself will give you this sign: the virgin shall conceive, and bear a son, and shall name him Emmanuel.

PSALM RESPONSE
Psalm 24:7c, 10b

Let the Lord enter; he is king of glory.

SECOND READING
Romans 1:1–7

Paul, a slave of Christ Jesus, called to be an apostle and set apart for the gospel of God, which he promised previously through his prophets in the holy Scriptures, the gospel about his Son, descended from David according to the flesh, but established as Son of God in power according to the Spirit of holiness through resurrection from the dead, Jesus Christ our Lord. Through him we have received the grace of apostleship, to bring about the obedience of faith, for the sake of his name, among all the Gentiles, among whom are you also, who are called to belong to Jesus Christ; to all the beloved of God in Rome, called to be holy. Grace to you and peace from God our Father and the Lord Jesus Christ.

GOSPEL
Matthew 1:
18–24

This is how the birth of Jesus Christ came about. When his mother Mary was betrothed to Joseph, but before they lived together, she was found with child through the Holy Spirit. Joseph her husband, since he was a righteous man, yet unwilling to expose her to shame, decided to divorce her quietly. Such was his intention when, behold, the angel of the Lord appeared to him in a dream and said, "Joseph, son of David, do not be afraid to take Mary your wife into your home. For it is through the Holy Spirit that this child has been conceived in her. She will bear a son and you are to name him Jesus, because he will save his people from their sins." All this took place to fulfill what the Lord had said through the prophet:

> Behold, the virgin shall conceive and bear a son,
> and they shall name him Emmanuel,

which means "God is with us."
When Joseph awoke, he did as the angel of the Lord had commanded him and took his wife into his home.

❖ *Understanding the Word*

One of the principles of Catholic biblical study recognizes that we read the Old Testament through a Christological lens. In other words, like the earliest Christians, we attempt to understand Jesus as the Messiah by interpreting scriptures that may foreshadow his coming. Today's first reading is one such text. In its ancient context, Isaiah of Jerusalem is addressing King Ahaz, who fears that the kings of Aram and Ephraim have joined forces and are about to attack Jerusalem. First, Isaiah announces that God will not let this come to pass (Isaiah 7:7), but Ahaz remains in doubt. God offers a sign of confirmation: "the virgin shall conceive, and bear a son, and shall name him Emmanuel" (Isaiah 7:14). Scholars propose that this "sign" in its historical context is not a prophecy, since the Hebrew verb is in the past tense. A maiden *has become* pregnant. This sign is meant to assure Ahaz that God is currently present to him and the people of Judah, thus the child will be called "God with us."

Paul hoped to visit the believers in Rome and solicit support for his mission to Spain (Romans 15:24). Since he had not founded this community, he penned a letter of introduction in which he summarized his understanding of the gospel of God, made manifest in Christ's life, death, and resurrection (Romans 1:3–4). Paul was called to be an apostle to the Gentiles (Romans 1:5), and seems to be addressing a mostly Gentile church at Rome (Romans 1:6–7).

In the Greco-Roman world, great and noble people had to have had auspicious origins. As the early Christian community garnered more Gentile believers, they brought with them their cultural expectations. Both Matthew and Luke include infancy narratives, likely encouraged by the growing interest in Jesus' earthly origins and his pre-public life. While Luke appears to have a source drawn from Mary's perspective, Matthew's portrayal is firmly rooted in Joseph's story. The angel of the Lord appears not to Mary, but to Joseph. The angel clarifies the child's origins, "for it is through the Holy Spirit that this child has been conceived in her" (Matthew 1:20). Matthew then explains the conception of Jesus as the fulfillment of the prophecy set forth in Isaiah 7.

We are fascinated with the lives of great leaders, heroes, heroines, and saints. We read biographies and autobiographies or watch movies that tell their stories. When we like them, we excuse their peccadilloes. When we don't, we use their sins to erase their goodness. Like Isaiah, Paul, and Matthew, we read their stories through the lens of the present.

Matthew describes the backstory to Jesus' birth. Mary, engaged to but not yet living with Joseph, is found to be pregnant. Because Joseph loved her deeply he wanted to keep this quiet. She could be stoned according to the law, so he wanted to divorce her quietly. Then the angel appeared and made clear that the child's conception was of God. Because of his faith in God and in Mary, Joseph did as he was commanded.

Isaiah spoke to a people on the verge of attack to engender trust that God was with them, no matter the outcome. We hear about a virgin who would conceive and bear a son named Emmanuel, God-with-us. See the connection with today's Gospel? The people believed.

Paul wrote his letter to make clear that he was set apart by God, an apostle, chosen to witness the power of God made known in Jesus Christ the Lord. They knew his past as a persecutor, but, faith in Jesus changed his life. His seemingly impossible transformation meant that people would know that God-with-us through him.

This last Advent Sunday reminds us that we come from a long line of people whose faith and trust made clear that God is with us. We are to make Christ's presence known today. Tell the story of how you know God's presence because you follow Jesus. Through you others will see Emmanuel, God-with-us.

❖❖ Consider/Discuss

- Who first told you about Jesus and the difference he made in their lives?
- What concrete signs make clear that God is with you and with us?

❖❖ Living and Praying with the Word

Emmanuel, you have come into our world through people like Mary, Joseph, and Paul, and have made God's presence known through prophets like Isaiah. Make my life a sign of the power of your love that invites others to faith and trust that God is with us still.

December 25, 2016

CHRISTMAS: MASS DURING THE DAY

Today's Focus: The Light That Helps Us See

All the ends of the earth see the saving power of God because God's Light from light—
Jesus Christ—shines for all to see, and for all to be able to see.

FIRST
READING
Isaiah 52:7–10

How beautiful upon the mountains
    are the feet of him who brings glad tidings,
announcing peace, bearing good news,
    announcing salvation, and saying to Zion,
    "Your God is King!"

Hark! Your sentinels raise a cry,
    together they shout for joy,
for they see directly, before their eyes,
    the Lord restoring Zion.
Break out together in song,
    O ruins of Jerusalem!
For the Lord comforts his people,
    he redeems Jerusalem.
The Lord has bared his holy arm
    in the sight of all the nations;
all the ends of the earth will behold
    the salvation of our God.

PSALM
RESPONSE
Psalm 98:3c

All the ends of the earth have seen the saving power of God.

SECOND
READING
Hebrews 1:1–6

Brothers and sisters: In times past, God spoke in partial and various ways to our ancestors through the prophets; in these last days, he has spoken to us through the Son, whom he made heir of all things and through whom he created the universe, who is the refulgence of his glory, the very imprint of his being, and who sustains all things by his mighty word. When he had accomplished purification from sins, he took his seat at the right hand of the Majesty on high, as far superior to the angels as the name he has inherited is more excellent than theirs.

For to which of the angels did God ever say:
    You are my son; this day I have begotten you?
Or again:
    I will be a father to him, and he shall be a son to me?
And again, when he leads the firstborn into the world, he says:
    Let all the angels of God worship him.

In the shorter form of the reading, the passages in brackets are omitted.

GOSPEL
John 1:1–18
or 1:1–5, 9–14

In the beginning was the Word,
   and the Word was with God,
   and the Word was God.
He was in the beginning with God.
All things came to be through him,
   and without him nothing came to be.

What came to be through him was life,
   and this life was the light of the human race;
the light shines in the darkness,
   and the darkness has not overcome it.

[A man named John was sent from God. He came for testimony, to testify to the light, so that all might believe through him. He was not the light, but came to testify to the light.] The true light, which enlightens everyone, was coming into the world.

He was in the world,
   and the world came to be through him,
   but the world did not know him.
He came to what was his own,
   but his own people did not accept him.

But to those who did accept him he gave power to become children of God, to those who believe in his name, who were born not by natural generation nor by human choice nor by a man's decision but of God.

And the Word became flesh
   and made his dwelling among us,
   and we saw his glory,
   the glory as of the Father's only Son,
   full of grace and truth.

[John testified to him and cried out, saying, "This was he of whom I said, 'The one who is coming after me ranks ahead of me because he existed before me.' " From his fullness we have all received, grace in place of grace, because while the law was given through Moses, grace and truth came through Jesus Christ. No one has ever seen God. The only Son, God, who is at the Father's side, has revealed him.]

❖ Understanding the Word

The first reading is taken from Second Isaiah (Chapters 40–55), a collection of oracles dated to the Exile. Jerusalem, having suffered God's wrath for its failure to uphold God's covenant (Isaiah 51:17), will see its enemies suffer the same fate (Isaiah 51:23). As Chapter 52 opens, Jerusalem is called to awaken and shake off her bonds of captivity (Isaiah 52:1–2). Now her sentinels anxiously await the messenger who will bring good news announcing salvation. God will return to Zion, having comforted and redeemed her. The oracle anticipates the joyous return of a holy and ritually clean people who live in peace (Isaiah 52:11).

The second reading is taken from Hebrews, a late first-century sermon once attributed to Paul. In it, the redemptive actions of the Son are heralded. Whereas in the past God had spoken in partial ways through the prophets, God is now speaking through the Son who has been appointed heir of all things (Hebrews 1:1–2). Hebrews echoes John's Prologue. Through Jesus the universe was created and in him we see the refulgence of God's glory. The author describes Jesus having "accomplished purification from sins," a sacrificial understanding of Jesus' death that is developed more fully in Hebrews 9.

The Gospel of John lacks an infancy narrative, but roots Jesus' origins to a time before the creation of the world. Jesus is the pre-existent word (*logos* in Greek, a term with deep philosophical undertones). All of creation exists through this word, and his life will become the light of human beings. The elevated tone of John's Prologue suggests roots in the Jewish wisdom tradition, but with a decidedly Christian twist. Jesus Christ is the incarnation of God, the Word-become-flesh. He shares in the divinity of God, yet he has taken on the human condition totally. Jesus' divine connection to the Father will be shared with his disciples, those who remain in him and love one another, two key motifs throughout the Gospel of John.

❖ Reflecting on the Word

Christmas celebrates the light of God's Word-made-flesh. Light comes in many forms. Some light is direct. Others are a mere reflection of another source. The glow of a candle, lights on a highway, motion detectors, and lamps in our homes lessen darkness, offer comfort, provide guidance, calm fears, and help us see. Lights in church tell us God is here.

Jesus, the Word, is the light that no darkness can overcome; but at times it seems as though darkness is overcoming the light. While these words on this page were being written, a series of terrorist attacks changed the lives of many and more senseless shootings took place in our cities. News reports often pay more attention to darkness than the lights of people who hold a dying stranger, welcome others into their homes, and protest the violence. These sisters and brothers testify to the power of light, like John the Baptist. They help us see glimpses of God-with-us. Their actions announce glad tidings and bear the good news that the light of Christ is stronger. Small deeds speak loudly. Our words and deeds give birth to Jesus each day. They testify that the seemingly impossible can happen, that is, God's light grows stronger when our actions and presence reflect that God is here.

Celebrate Christmas as people of hope who give praise and thanks for Jesus Christ. Restore peace by offering comfort and hope in actions that make God's glory known. Let the light of our lives match the lights that decorate our trees and homes to lessen darkness, offer comfort, give guidance, calm fears, and help all see that God is here. That's how all the ends of the earth can see the saving power of God, even where darkness seems stronger on any given day.

❖ Consider/Discuss

- When have you experienced the Light of Christ as stronger than darkness in your life?
- What is one way that you can testify to the power of the Christ-light this Christmas?

❖ Living and Praying with the Word

Luminous God, you took on our flesh in the Word, Jesus Christ, so that we might know your nearness in concrete ways. Help us live in ways that testify to the power of your light so that others can see your face today and come to believe that no darkness can overcome it.

December 30, 2016

THE HOLY FAMILY OF JESUS, MARY, AND JOSEPH

Today's Focus: Divine Dreams

There are dreamers all throughout the Bible. In a way, the Bible is a book of God's dreams; dreams born of love, dreams for a time to come in which all know and share in the divine dream.

FIRST READING
Sirach 3:2–6, 12–14

God sets a father in honor over his children;
  a mother's authority he confirms over her sons.
Whoever honors his father atones for sins,
  and preserves himself from them.
When he prays, he is heard;
  he stores up riches who reveres his mother.
Whoever honors his father is gladdened by children,
  and, when he prays, is heard.
Whoever reveres his father will live a long life;
  he who obeys his father brings comfort to his mother.

My son, take care of your father when he is old;
  grieve him not as long as he lives.
Even if his mind fail, be considerate of him;
  revile him not all the days of his life;
kindness to a father will not be forgotten,
  firmly planted against the debt of your sins
  —a house raised in justice to you.

PSALM RESPONSE
Psalm 128:1

Blessed are those who fear the Lord and walk in his ways.

In the shorter form of the reading, the passage in brackets is omitted.

SECOND READING
Colossians 3:12–21 or 3:12–17

Brothers and sisters: Put on, as God's chosen ones, holy and beloved, heartfelt compassion, kindness, humility, gentleness, and patience, bearing with one another and forgiving one another, if one has a grievance against another; as the Lord has forgiven you, so must you also do. And over all these put on love, that is, the bond of perfection. And let the peace of Christ control your hearts, the peace into which you were also called in one body. And be thankful. Let the word of Christ dwell in you richly, as in all wisdom you teach and admonish one another, singing psalms, hymns, and spiritual songs with gratitude in your hearts to God. And whatever you do, in word or in deed, do everything in the name of the Lord Jesus, giving thanks to God the Father through him.

[Wives, be subordinate to your husbands, as is proper in the Lord. Husbands, love your wives, and avoid any bitterness toward them.

Children, obey your parents in everything, for this is pleasing to the Lord. Fathers, do not provoke your children, so they may not become discouraged.]

Matthew 2:
13–15, 19–23

When the magi had departed, behold, the angel of the Lord appeared to Joseph in a dream and said, "Rise, take the child and his mother, flee to Egypt, and stay there until I tell you. Herod is going to search for the child to destroy him." Joseph rose and took the child and his mother by night and departed for Egypt. He stayed there until the death of Herod, that what the Lord had said through the prophet might be fulfilled,
Out of Egypt I called my son.

When Herod had died, behold, the angel of the Lord appeared in a dream to Joseph in Egypt and said, "Rise, take the child and his mother and go to the land of Israel, for those who sought the child's life are dead." He rose, took the child and his mother, and went to the land of Israel. But when he heard that Archelaus was ruling over Judea in place of his father Herod, he was afraid to go back there. And because he had been warned in a dream, he departed for the region of Galilee. He went and dwelt in a town called Nazareth, so that what had been spoken through the prophets might be fulfilled,
He shall be called a Nazorean.

❖ Understanding the Word

The foundation of Israelite society was the *beit* Av, or House of the Father (Genesis 24–38), and the fifth commandment assured that one's parents remained objects of respect and care (Exodus 20:12; Deuteronomy 5:16). The reading from Sirach is an exposition on the reason for the commandment. God has placed parents in roles of honor over their children, and anyone who follows this commandment "stores up riches" and "when he prays, is heard." Sirach is part of Wisdom literature, which provided life lessons directed at ensuring success and avoiding failure. Part of being successful in Israelite understanding meant caring for your aged and infirm parents.

While the commandments govern the actions of Israel, Christ should control the hearts of believers, according to the Letter to the Colossians. The mantle of a Christian is a virtuous life filled with heartfelt compassion, kindness, humility, gentleness, and patience (Colossians 3:12). Attending to the word of Christ through liturgical actions will support one's efforts (Colossians 3:16). Like Sirach, Colossians describes what leads to a successful life: proper order in society. Wives, husbands, children, and fathers are directed to follow their ordained paths. The letter further states that slaves should also obey their earthly masters (Colossians 3:22). Scholars recognize that the author of Colossians 3:18–24 is following the standard codes established in Greco-Roman society of the time to assure the best management of the household. A contemporary reading of these codes should take this into account.

Like his namesake in Genesis, the Joseph found in today's Gospel reading is directed by God through dreams. First, he was told to take Mary as his wife

29

(Matthew 1:20). Now by a dream, Joseph is told to flee to Egypt because of Herod's murderous plans (Matthew 2:13). An angel will appear in a dream and direct him back to Israel (Matthew 2:20). For fear that Herod's son, Archelaus, would continue his father's vengeful rule, Joseph is directed in a final dream to go to Galilee (Matthew 2:22). Matthew, more than the other evangelists, includes numerous scripture citations and allusions to firmly connect the Jesus of Nazareth with the prophecies of the Old Testament.

✠ Reflecting on the Word

In the 1960s the Everly Brothers released a song that began "Dream, dream, dream, dream, dream." Today's Gospel is filled with dreams. An angel tells Joseph to flee to Egypt with Mary and Jesus; an angel tells Joseph to take Mary and Jesus to Israel, where it is now safe; an angel warns Joseph to go to Galilee because Israel wasn't as safe as previously thought. Dreams are a window to the heart, revealing what we value or fear, or in what we believe.

Whatever our family looks like, we have dreams for those we love, especially for our children. The first reading describes God's dream for family life: parents, *honor* your children; children *revere* your parents and be *kind* to them, even if their minds fail. Sirach's dream seeks basic respect. Paul's dream includes compassion, kindness, humility, gentleness, patience, forgiveness, love, peacefulness, and gratitude, tied with a bow that is the word of Christ. These values are needed for true obedience, from *ob audire*, to listen to. Listen to the voice of spouses, parents, children, and God. Speak your reality respectfully. Submit to these virtues by means of honest dialogue. Healthy relationships of give and take require this kind of respectful dialogue.

To be holy families we need to live the virtues. St. Francis de Sales wrote that we ought to love everyone with great love, but should have no friendships except for those that communicate the things of virtue (see the *Introduction to the Devout Life*, III, p. 19). Which of the virtues named in Sirach's and Paul's dreams invite your deep listening? What virtues do you need for you to hear God's voice and live in ways that will make your relationships holy because they are grounded in the Lord Jesus Christ? Do you—like Joseph—listen for and listen to the angels?

✠ Consider/Discuss

- What are my dreams for those who are family to me?
- What virtue might help repair the relationships through which those dreams have been broken or shattered?

✠ Living and Praying with the Word

God our Father, you invite us to experience the holiness that Jesus, Mary, and Joseph shared. Heal dysfunction in my relationships with family and friends. Give me a grateful heart, a heart for relationships that are holy. Help me listen to your Son Jesus and to your Holy Spirit, to become more whole this day.

January 1, 2017

MARY, THE HOLY MOTHER OF GOD

Today's Focus: Holy Cardio

Today we celebrate Mary, who held God's mysteries and pondered them in her heart, and whose heart would be pierced in sorrow. Like Mary, we need to train our hearts to be given wholly to God.

FIRST READING
Numbers 6: 22–27

The LORD said to Moses: "Speak to Aaron and his sons and tell them: This is how you shall bless the Israelites. Say to them:
The LORD bless you and keep you!
The LORD let his face shine upon you, and be gracious to you!
The LORD look upon you kindly and give you peace!
So shall they invoke my name upon the Israelites, and I will bless them."

PSALM RESPONSE
Psalm 67:2a

May God bless us in his mercy.

SECOND READING
Galatians 4:4–7

Brothers and sisters: When the fullness of time had come, God sent his Son, born of a woman, born under the law, to ransom those under the law, so that we might receive adoption as sons. As proof that you are sons, God sent the Spirit of his Son into our hearts, crying out, "Abba, Father!" So you are no longer a slave but a son, and if a son then also an heir, through God.

GOSPEL
Luke 2:16–21

The shepherds went in haste to Bethlehem and found Mary and Joseph, and the infant lying in the manger. When they saw this, they made known the message that had been told them about this child. All who heard it were amazed by what had been told them by the shepherds. And Mary kept all these things, reflecting on them in her heart. Then the shepherds returned, glorifying and praising God for all they had heard and seen, just as it had been told to them. When eight days were completed for his circumcision, he was named Jesus, the name given him by the angel before he was conceived in the womb.

✤ Understanding the Word

The reading from Numbers, known as the "priestly blessing," recounts the blessing the Aaronite priests were to say over the people of Israel. Though placed back into the period of Moses and Aaron, the prayer likely was used at the end of worship services in the temple. The blessing invites the presence of God ("let his face shine upon you" [Numbers 6:25]) to dwell among the people. In poetic form, it states that God's blessing will keep the people, God's presence will be gracious, and when God's attention is directed toward Israel, there will be peace. In response to this blessing, the Israelites were to bear God's name, making them a sign of God's presence, grace, and peace (Numbers 6:27).

Countering rival evangelists, Paul reminds the Galatians that they are no longer bound by the law of Moses. The Torah had served the Jewish people as a guide, but with the coming of Christ that law was no longer necessary. The Father had sent the Son to be born of a woman, under the law, so as to release those under the law. As people baptized into Christ, the Galatians are now adopted children of God who have received the Spirit of God, enabling them to call God "Abba."

Where Matthew introduces magi from the East as the first visitors to the Christ child, Luke has shepherds. Matthew means to show the universal dimensions of Jesus' birth, while Luke emphasizes the lifting up of the lowly (Luke 1:52). In today's reading, the shepherds share the message made known to them by the angels and all are amazed. The Greek word *thaumazo* means to marvel or wonder at, and becomes the frequent response of the crowds toward Jesus' teaching and miracles (Luke 8:25; 11:14). Mary is said to treasure or preserve (*suntereo*) these things in her heart. A similar word is used of Mary's actions in Luke 2:19, where she keeps these things in her heart. Mary's response to the prophetic announcements and angelic encounters demonstrates that unlike the crowds who only marvel, she takes it all to heart, the foundational stance of a believer (Luke 8:15; 24:32).

✤ Reflecting on the Word

How is your heart? To answer that question for myself, I had an MRI to discover whether widening in a major artery could become an aneurism. I'm grateful that it's just part of my aging and that my physical heart health is good. In today's Gospel people were amazed by what the shepherds shared with Mary, and she "kept all these things, reflecting on them in her heart" (Luke 2:19). Another translation says that Mary treasured and pondered these things. Mary offers an example for how to maintain spiritual heart health: Take time to listen to God's voice, ponder what you hear, and treasure God's nearness, even when challenged to change your ways. Remember, even Mary's heart was pierced at times.

Mary listened to God's voice and honestly spoke from her heart. Because of this she was free to say yes to God, who dwells with us through Jesus Christ. Their Spirit was "sent into our hearts, crying out, 'Abba, Father!' " (Galatians 4:6). The Spirit cries out for us when we know not what to say. The Spirit opens our hearts, clearing them of any blockage that would keep us from knowing God's blessing, shining face, graciousness, and peace. New Year's Day is a good time to ponder the previous calendar year and the year ahead. What do we keep in our heart from both exercises? What do we treasure? What needs to be released? Pray the first reading to feel God's blessing in your life. Cry out in gratitude for God's keeping you. Ask for God's peace. Let this spiritual MRI treasure the good, reflect on the bad, and empower you to live in ways that reveal the presence of Jesus in your life. Be heart-healthy in all ways.

❖ Consider/Discuss

- Where is God's blessing clear in your life?
- Describe how you speak heart to heart with God.

❖ Living and Praying with the Word

Abba, Father, I often focus on your absence more than your presence. Let Mary be my guide so that I take time to reflect on life in ways that treasure what is good and release what gets in the way of my experiencing your blessing.

January 8, 2017

EPIPHANY OF THE LORD

Today's Focus: Many Epiphanies

An epiphany is a moment of revelation, a moment that can occur when something long expected finally happens, or when something completely unexpected breaks into our lives.

FIRST READING
Isaiah 60:1–6

Rise up in splendor, Jerusalem! Your light has come,
  the glory of the Lord shines upon you.
See, darkness covers the earth,
  and thick clouds cover the peoples;
but upon you the Lord shines,
  and over you appears his glory.
Nations shall walk by your light,
  and kings by your shining radiance.
Raise your eyes and look about;
  they all gather and come to you:
your sons come from afar,
  and your daughters in the arms of their nurses.

Then you shall be radiant at what you see,
  your heart shall throb and overflow,
for the riches of the sea shall be emptied out before you,
  the wealth of nations shall be brought to you.
Caravans of camels shall fill you,
  dromedaries from Midian and Ephah;
all from Sheba shall come
  bearing gold and frankincense,
  and proclaiming the praises of the Lord.

PSALM RESPONSE
Psalm 72:11

Lord, every nation on earth will adore you.

SECOND READING
Ephesians 3: 2–3a, 5–6

Brothers and sisters: You have heard of the stewardship of God's grace that was given to me for your benefit, namely, that the mystery was made known to me by revelation. It was not made known to people in other generations as it has now been revealed to his holy apostles and prophets by the Spirit: that the Gentiles are coheirs, members of the same body, and copartners in the promise in Christ Jesus through the gospel.

GOSPEL
Matthew 2:
1–12
When Jesus was born in Bethlehem of Judea, in the days of King Herod, behold, magi from the east arrived in Jerusalem, saying, "Where is the newborn king of the Jews? We saw his star at its rising and have come to do him homage." When King Herod heard this, he was greatly troubled, and all Jerusalem with him. Assembling all the chief priests and the scribes of the people, he inquired of them where the Christ was to be born. They said to him, "In Bethlehem of Judea, for thus it has been written through the prophet:

And you, Bethlehem, land of Judah,
  are by no means least among the rulers of Judah;
since from you shall come a ruler,
  who is to shepherd my people Israel."

Then Herod called the magi secretly and ascertained from them the time of the star's appearance. He sent them to Bethlehem and said, "Go and search diligently for the child. When you have found him, bring me word, that I too may go and do him homage." After their audience with the king they set out. And behold, the star that they had seen at its rising preceded them, until it came and stopped over the place where the child was.

They were overjoyed at seeing the star, and on entering the house they saw the child with Mary his mother. They prostrated themselves and did him homage. Then they opened their treasures and offered him gifts of gold, frankincense, and myrrh. And having been warned in a dream not to return to Herod, they departed for their country by another way.

✢ Understanding the Word

Wealth in the ancient Mediterranean world was centered around trade and therefore those cities with harbors or located on trade routes acquired massive riches. Jerusalem, some forty miles east of the nearest seaport of Joppa and about an equal distance from major caravan routes, had little hope of accruing bounty from trade. But the poem from Second Isaiah depicts a marvelously altered reality. After suffering her long exile, Jerusalem will rise up in splendor, her light reflecting God's presence with her. To her will the nations stream. Her children will return. And the riches of the sea from the West, and the caravans from the East will bring their wealth to her in praise of God (Isaiah 60:5, 6).

The short reading from Ephesians captures the theme of the letter: the Gentiles are coheirs and copartners in the promise of Christ Jesus. Paul has suffered and been imprisoned because of his testimony to the Gentiles (Ephesians 3:1), but he is compelled. He has been commissioned by God's grace and given a revelation (Ephesians 3:2). Though the Letter to the Ephesians comes two decades after Paul's martyrdom, it continues to depict the Gentile mission as part of the mystery hidden for ages in God (Ephesians 3:9).

Today's Gospel reading from Matthew presents us with the quintessential Gentiles seeking the Jewish king. The word *magos* originally referred to a member of the Persian priestly class. It later took on the connotation of those who engage in Eastern philosophy and science—magicians and astrologers. Matthew's magi report that they have seen a star rising. In popular understanding, such a phenomenon signaled a significant birth. But this star is unusual. It directs the magi to Bethlehem, where they pay homage to baby Jesus and present him with gifts befitting a king—gold, frankincense, and myrrh. They are warned in a dream not to return to Herod, so they go home by a different route. The introduction of the "wise" men from the East bearing riches foreshadows the inclusion of the Gentiles into the developing Christian faith.

❖ Reflecting on the Word

Epiphany celebrates the appearance of a star that led three foreign magi to Jesus, Mary, and Joseph. An epiphany can also be a sudden, intuitive perception or insight into the meaning of something, usually initiated by some simple or commonplace occurrence or experience. New stars are common occurrences. The magi chose to follow this new star and were changed. I have had epiphanies through common experiences like talking with someone, engaging in everyday tasks, and enjoying nature's beauty. What about you?

The feast of the Epiphany celebrates God's all-inclusive love. Any limits we try to place on it do not hold. The magi were Gentiles, not Jews. Yet they listened to God in dreams, paid homage to Jesus, and gave Jesus gifts befitting a monarch. Isaiah tells Jerusalem, the center for Israelite faith, that God's glory would shine upon her and all nations. Paul tells the Ephesians that "the Gentiles are coheirs, members of the same body, and copartners in the promise in Christ Jesus through the gospel" (Ephesians 3:6). The early church struggled with the fact that God was not limited by the experience and expectations of the Jewish Christians. Many tend to limit where God works, with whom, and how. Today's feast offers the essential insight that we cannot limit God's love. That insight is challenging, when someone I judge unworthy shows me how to live my faith, or when someone of another faith tradition lives God's love in ways that I fail, like the Muslims who stood hand-in-hand around a church to protect their Christian sisters and brothers. Epiphanies comes in many forms. The feast of the Epiphany asks us to open our eyes to see God's presence where we might least expect.

❖ Consider/Discuss

- Describe an epiphany that came to you through some simple or commonplace experience.
- Where has the presence of God surprised you and stretched your understanding?

❖ Living and Praying with the Word

We prayed, "Lord, every nation on earth will adore you," yet we can resist your presence in those whom we fear or misunderstand. Open our eyes to see you wherever and in whomever you make yourself known so that we can do you homage by offering the gifts of our acceptance and belief.

January 9, 2017

BAPTISM OF THE LORD

Today's Focus: Beloved Daughters and Sons

The Spirit of God and the voice of God name Jesus in the Jordan as "Beloved Son." In Baptism, that same Spirit bound us all to the one Body of Christ, making us each a beloved daughter or son.

FIRST READING
Isaiah 42:1–4, 6–7

Thus says the LORD:
Here is my servant whom I uphold,
  my chosen one with whom I am pleased,
upon whom I have put my spirit;
  he shall bring forth justice to the nations,
not crying out, not shouting,
  not making his voice heard in the street.
A bruised reed he shall not break,
  and a smoldering wick he shall not quench,
until he establishes justice on the earth;
  the coastlands will wait for his teaching.

I, the LORD, have called you for the victory of justice,
  I have grasped you by the hand;
I formed you, and set you
  as a covenant of the people,
  a light for the nations,
to open the eyes of the blind,
  to bring out prisoners from confinement,
  and from the dungeon, those who live in darkness.

PSALM RESPONSE
Psalm 29:11b

The Lord will bless his people with peace.

SECOND READING
Acts 10:34–38

Peter proceeded to speak to those gathered in the house of Cornelius, saying: "In truth, I see that God shows no partiality. Rather, in every nation whoever fears him and acts uprightly is acceptable to him. You know the word that he sent to the Israelites as he proclaimed peace through Jesus Christ, who is Lord of all, what has happened all over Judea, beginning in Galilee after the baptism that John preached, how God anointed Jesus of Nazareth with the Holy Spirit and power. He went about doing good and healing all those oppressed by the devil, for God was with him."

GOSPEL
Matthew 3:
13–17

Jesus came from Galilee to John at the Jordan to be baptized by him. John tried to prevent him, saying, "I need to be baptized by you, and yet you are coming to me?" Jesus said to him in reply, "Allow it now, for thus it is fitting for us to fulfill all righteousness." Then he allowed him. After Jesus was baptized, he came up from the water and behold, the heavens were opened for him, and he saw the Spirit of God descending like a dove and coming upon him. And a voice came from the heavens, saying, "This is my beloved Son, with whom I am well pleased."

❖ *Understanding the Word*

Today's first reading is part of a series of poems called the Servant Songs (42:1–4; 49:1–6; 50:4–11; 52:13 — 53:12). Some scholars propose that a historical individual is to be understood, while others suggest that the servant is Israel personified. Though the identity of this servant is debated, his mission is clear. He is to bring forth justice to the nations (Isaiah 42:1), will not tire or grow weary until he accomplish his task, and "the coastlands wait for his teaching" (Isaiah 42:4). Verses 6–7 more obviously address the exiles themselves, who as a people covenanted to God will be a light to the nations.

In Acts 10, from which today's second reading is taken, we are introduced to an unusual Gentile. Cornelius the centurion is described as a devout God-fearer (one who prayed in the synagogue with Jews and upheld the ethical demands of Judaism). In response to a command from an angel, Cornelius sends for Peter, who has had his own vision. Peter addresses those gathered in Cornelius's house and announces, "In truth, I see that God shows no partiality" (Acts 10:34). Peter's vision had assured him that all animals were clean and thus he could enter a Gentile's home. Now in the presence of this Gentile, Peter comes to even greater insight about the impartiality of God.

John's baptism was a baptism for the repentance of sins. As the early Christians reflected on Jesus' identity, they had difficulty with the sinless Jesus approaching John for such a baptism. Luke handles this dilemma by simply not depicting the actual baptism: "After all the people had been baptized and Jesus also had been baptized . . . " (Luke 3:21). Matthew inserts a dialogue between John and Jesus in which John recognizes Jesus' true nature. "John tried to prevent him, saying, 'I need to be baptized by you' " (Matthew 3:14). Jesus explains that this baptism serves to fulfill righteousness, thus deflecting the question of sin. As Jesus emerges from the water, the heavens open and he sees the Spirit of God descending upon him. Mark depicts this as a private experience: "You are my Son" (Mark 1:11). But for Matthew, it is public. The voice from the cloud speaks to the crowd. "This is my beloved Son" (Matthew 3:17).

While planning their mother's funeral one of her children said, "I hope you're not offended, but Mom said that I was her favorite." The other siblings looked at each other and started laughing. "Mom told each of us that." Their mother showed no partiality, yet each of her children felt special and beloved.

Peter proclaims, "In truth, I see that God shows no partiality" (Acts 10:34). Previous visions opened him to see that "in every nation whoever fears [God] and acts uprightly is acceptable" (Acts 10:35), whether Jew or Gentile Christian. The Spirit of God descended upon each of us when we were baptized, so each of us can hear God call us "my beloved" son or daughter. Like Jesus, each of us is God's beloved. Unlike Jesus we are adopted children of God, not the Son of God.

Having grasped us by the hand and formed us in the womb, God makes us people of justice and peace. Biblical justice is egalitarian, giving according to our gifts and taking according to our needs. Both can enable us to give sight to those blind to God's presence in our midst, freedom to those imprisoned by narrowness and fear, and light to those enveloped in darkness. Like God's servant in Isaiah we do not shout out or break the bruised reed. We follow the example of Jesus, who submitted to God with open arms on the cross. We sing, "When the Holy Spirit comes to us, we receive the power of God" (We Receive Power, James V. Marchionda, op, World Library Publications, ©1995). The Holy Spirit has come to us. We received power as God's beloved to live the life of the Spirit in justice and peace and without partiality.

❖ Consider/Discuss

- When have you felt like God's beloved daughter or son?
- Where does showing partiality keep you from seeing all people as children of God?

❖ Living and Praying with the Word

God of our Lord Jesus Christ, you are the creator of all of us. We are your handiwork. Fill me with an awareness of your Holy Spirit that I might see all people the way you do. Empower me to follow the example of your Son and servant, Jesus Christ.

Introduction to Ordinary Time I

The majority of our first readings are taken from the book of Isaiah and are designed to reflect elements of the Gospel readings. On their own account, these readings portray God's continual care of Israel, despite its failures. The theme of light is woven throughout the readings, as Israel is prophesied to become a light to the nations, a light of hope and restoration. A remnant will remain, a people poor and humble before God, who will become the seed of a new faithful generation. The readings for the Sixth and Seventh Sundays interrupt our reading of the prophets. Sirach reminds us that the choice is ours. We can keep the commandments, trust in God, and do good, or we can choose not to. Leviticus focuses those commandments: We are to be holy because God is holy, and we are to love our neighbor as ourselves.

It's fitting in Ordinary Time that we read through First Corinthians as our second Sunday reading, for the letter from the Apostle Paul describes the struggles of believers to live their faith in "ordinary time." Likely composed between 54–56 A.D. while the apostle was living in Ephesus, First Corinthians is the first of several letters (Second Corinthians is a composite of at least five letter fragments) that we have between Paul and the church he founded in Greece. The theme of his letter is clearly stated in 1 Corinthians 1:10: "I urge . . . that you all agree . . . and that there be no divisions among you." Throughout the letter, Paul reminds the church community that they have been sanctified (1 Corinthians 6:11), a sanctification rooted in Christ (1 Corinthians 1:30). God has called them to fellowship (1 Corinthians 1:9), both Jews and Greeks alike (1 Corinthians 1:24). They are God's holy temple (1 Corinthians 3:17), the holy ones who will judge the world (1 Corinthians 6:2). Paul addresses disturbances in the Corinthian community: divisions and rival groups (1 Corinthians 1:10–17; 3:1–4:5; 11:18), immorality (1 Corinthians 5:1–13), litigious action (1 Corinthians 6:1–8), disregard for the weaker Christian (8:11), liturgical abuses (1 Corinthians 11:17–22), and resurrection (chapter 15).

This year we will read through the Gospel according to Matthew. Traditionally, the early church used this Gospel exclusively. It was seen as a manual for the church because only Matthew uses the word *ekklesia* or church. The author whom tradition has named Matthew endeavored to demonstrate Jesus' credentials as Israel's true Messiah by presenting him as the supreme teacher and interpreter of the Mosaic Torah—the principles that provided Matthew's Jewish Christian community with ethical guidance. Matthew follows Mark's order in which he places five teaching blocks:

Sermon on the Mount (4:23 — 7:29)

Missionary discourse (10:1 — 11:1)

Parables speech to Israel and disciples (13:1 — 58)

Community order and discipline (18:1 — 35)

The millennial discourse (24:1 — 25:46)

Scholars propose that Matthew is purposely creating a comparison between Jesus and Moses, and that the five sections are meant to parallel the five books of Moses known as the Torah. Many of our Gospel readings for the first eight Sundays are taken from the Sermon on the Mount.

January 15, 2017

SECOND SUNDAY IN ORDINARY TIME

Today's Focus: Who Am I?

Today, as John the Baptist calls Jesus the "Lamb of God," we are set on a journey toward Ash Wednesday to discover who Jesus is—and who we are as well.

FIRST READING
Isaiah 49:3, 5–6

The LORD said to me: You are my servant,
  Israel, through whom I show my glory.
Now the LORD has spoken
  who formed me as his servant from the womb,
that Jacob may be brought back to him
  and Israel gathered to him;
and I am made glorious in the sight of the LORD,
  and my God is now my strength!
It is too little, the LORD says, for you to be my servant,
  to raise up the tribes of Jacob,
  and restore the survivors of Israel;
I will make you a light to the nations,
  that my salvation may reach to the ends of the earth.

PSALM RESPONSE
Psalm 40:8a, 9a

Here am I, Lord; I come to do your will.

SECOND READING
1 Corinthians 1:1–3

Paul, called to be an apostle of Christ Jesus by the will of God, and Sosthenes our brother, to the church of God that is in Corinth, to you who have been sanctified in Christ Jesus, called to be holy, with all those everywhere who call upon the name of our Lord Jesus Christ, their Lord and ours. Grace to you and peace from God our Father and the Lord Jesus Christ.

GOSPEL
John 1:29–34

John the Baptist saw Jesus coming toward him and said, "Behold, the Lamb of God, who takes away the sin of the world. He is the one of whom I said, 'A man is coming after me who ranks ahead of me because he existed before me.' I did not know him, but the reason why I came baptizing with water was that he might be made known to Israel." John testified further, saying, "I saw the Spirit come down like a dove from heaven and remain upon him. I did not know him, but the one who sent me to baptize with water told me, 'On whomever you see the Spirit come down and remain, he is the one who will baptize with the Holy Spirit.' Now I have seen and testified that he is the Son of God."

The first reading is part of the book of Isaiah attributed to an anonymous exilic prophet writing in the tradition of Isaiah of Jerusalem. In this reading, he describes his call to be a prophet to Israel. Chosen before his birth, Second Isaiah will be made glorious before God and have God's strength as his own. The message of the prophet will serve as a light to the nations. The encouragement and strength with which the prophet has been gifted will be sorely needed, for his ministry will result in much personal suffering and finally death (Isaiah 53:3–9).

In the second reading, we hear Paul's opening salutation in his First Letter to the Corinthians. Paul will carry on a lengthy correspondence with this Greco-Roman city in Achaia (southern Greece). The mixed community of Gentiles and Jews struggled mightily with integrating their new faith with their Greco-Roman surroundings. In today's reading, Paul uses a standard letter format but enhances it with unique Christian themes in order to strengthen the believers. He reminds them that they have been "sanctified" and "called to be holy," and as the letter will develop Paul will describe what such a sanctified and holy life should resemble.

The Gospel presents John's version of John the Baptist's first encounter with Jesus. John uses four descriptions to identify Jesus. These titles then foreshadow events to unfold throughout the Gospel. Jesus is the Lamb of God, understood in the first-century context to be a sacrificial animal, hearkening back to the Passover (Exodus 12). He is one who existed before, stated clearly in the Prologue, but then revealed by Jesus himself in his "I am" statements (6:35, 48; 8:12, 58; 9:5; 10:9, 11; 11:25; 14:6; 15:1). Jesus is the one upon whom the Spirit descends and remains with until Jesus returns it to his Father (John 19:30). Jesus promises to send this same Spirit to his disciples (14:16–17). Finally, John recognizes that Jesus is the Son of God. Jesus will make this known when he declares that he and the Father are one (10:30).

❖ *Reflecting on the Word*

When someone asks, "Who are you?" how do you respond? I am Paul Henry Colloton, son of Betty Jane and Paul, grandson of Henry. I am a Catholic Christian. I am a musician, liturgist, teacher, preacher, spiritual companion, and guide. I am a priest of the Oblates of St. Francis de Sales who was a Dominican. I am a sinner in need of God's mercy. Who are you?

Today's readings answer this implied question. Israel is God's servant, formed in his mother's womb to be a light to the nations. Paul is an apostle of Jesus Christ and a preacher who proclaims God's call to holiness. John is the baptizer who points out the Lamb of God and testifies that Jesus is the Son of God. Jesus is the Lamb and Son of God, existed before John, will come after him, and ranks ahead of him. The Spirit descends and remains on Jesus.

As we begin Ordinary Time we are asked, "Who are you?" Baptism makes each of us a servant of God, called to be a light to our world. Each of us is a disciple of Jesus Christ. We are called to be holy, that is, called to be whole and grounded in the truth of both our gifts and our weaknesses. In ordinary ways we can testify that Jesus is the Son of God if we listen for the voice of the Holy Spirit in prayer, others, and world events. Who are you? Take some time to answer this question in light of today's readings and then respond with the psalmist, "Here am I, Lord; I come to do your will."

❖ Consider/Discuss

- Write and share your answer to the question "Who are you?"
- How does my faith in Jesus Christ affect my answer?

❖ Living and Praying with the Word

Loving God, you formed me in my mother's womb and in baptism anointed me to be your servant. May I respond to your love each day by the ways in which I seek your will and then live it, even when that is difficult.

January 22, 2017

THIRD SUNDAY IN ORDINARY TIME

Today's Focus: Factions Lead to Fractions

There is no denying that the world, our society, our church, are all in a state of factionalism. For Christians, fiercely belonging to a faction often means that we can only share a fraction of the gospel.

FIRST READING
Isaiah 8:23 — 9:3

First the LORD degraded the land of Zebulun and the land of Naphtali; but in the end he has glorified the seaward road, the land west of the Jordan, the District of the Gentiles.

Anguish has taken wing, dispelled is darkness:
 for there is no gloom where but now there was distress.
The people who walked in darkness
 have seen a great light;
upon those who dwelt in the land of gloom
 a light has shone.
You have brought them abundant joy
 and great rejoicing,
as they rejoice before you as at the harvest,
 as people make merry when dividing spoils.
For the yoke that burdened them,
 the pole on their shoulder,
and the rod of their taskmaster
 you have smashed, as on the day of Midian.

PSALM RESPONSE
Psalm 27:1a

The Lord is my light and my salvation.

SECOND READING
1 Corinthians 1:10–13, 17

I urge you, brothers and sisters, in the name of our Lord Jesus Christ, that all of you agree in what you say, and that there be no divisions among you, but that you be united in the same mind and in the same purpose. For it has been reported to me about you, my brothers and sisters, by Chloe's people, that there are rivalries among you. I mean that each of you is saying, "I belong to Paul," or "I belong to Apollos," or "I belong to Cephas," or "I belong to Christ." Is Christ divided? Was Paul crucified for you? Or were you baptized in the name of Paul? For Christ did not send me to baptize but to preach the gospel, and not with the wisdom of human eloquence, so that the cross of Christ might not be emptied of its meaning.

GOSPEL
Matthew
4:12–23 or
4:12–17

When Jesus heard that John had been arrested, he withdrew to Galilee. He left Nazareth and went to live in Capernaum by the sea, in the region of Zebulun and Naphtali, that what had been said through Isaiah the prophet might be fulfilled:

Land of Zebulun and land of Naphtali,
the way to the sea, beyond the Jordan,
Galilee of the Gentiles,
the people who sit in darkness have seen a great light,
on those dwelling in a land overshadowed by death
light has arisen.

From that time on, Jesus began to preach and say, "Repent, for the kingdom of heaven is at hand."

[As he was walking by the Sea of Galilee, he saw two brothers, Simon who is called Peter, and his brother Andrew, casting a net into the sea; they were fishermen. He said to them, "Come after me, and I will make you fishers of men." At once they left their nets and followed him. He walked along from there and saw two other brothers, James, the son of Zebedee, and his brother John. They were in a boat, with their father Zebedee, mending their nets. He called them, and immediately they left their boat and their father and followed him.

He went around all of Galilee, teaching in their synagogues, proclaiming the gospel of the kingdom, and curing every disease and illness among the people.]

❖❖ *Understanding the Word*

The united kingdom of David and Solomon did not survive another generation. The two kingdoms that emerged, Israel in the north and Judah in the south, witnessed constant invasions from more powerful nations. In 721 B.C., Assyria destroyed the northern kingdom and set its sights on Judah. Listening to Isaiah's instructions, the king of Judah trusted that God would protect Jerusalem, and the Assyrian assault of 701 B.C. was thwarted (2 Kings 19:1–7). Today's reading may be describing the aftermath of that victory when "the people who walked in darkness have seen a great light" (Isaiah 9:1).

As the Corinthians attempted to integrate their new faith with their Greco-Roman culture, they argued about appropriate behavior and fought about whose gifts of the Spirit were most important (1 Corinthians 12). We hear about this schism in our second reading. Chloe's people (probably a Corinthian house church) sent a report to Paul, who may have been residing in Ephesus at the time. The schism has at its roots a fight over status ("I belong to Paul . . . . I belong to Apollos"), as the Corinthians claimed superiority based on who baptized them (1 Corinthians 1:13). In the body of the letter to follow, Paul will demonstrate his thesis: that believers are to "be united in the same mind and in the same purpose" (1 Corinthians 1:10) lest "the cross of Christ . . . be emptied of its meaning" (1 Corinthians 1:17).

Through the Gospel of Matthew, the evangelist will demonstrate that Jesus is the fulfillment of scripture. To strengthen his presentation, Matthew will turn to the first Testament. Of the sixty-five references to the Old Testament in Matthew, forty-three are verbal citations. In today's Gospel, Matthew cites our first reading from Isaiah. Through Matthew's Christological lens, he saw that the Isaiah passage not only spoke about a historical experience but also prophesied a future one. Jesus is the one who will renew "a land overshadowed by death" (Matthew 4:16). As the Gospel continues, Jesus will not effect this change on his own. Immediately after arriving in Capernaum, Jesus seeks disciples to join him in his mission: "Come after me, and I will make you fishers of men" (Matthew 4:19).

❖ Reflecting on the Word

"The people who sit in darkness have seen a great light" (Matthew 4:16). That light was needed in Isaiah's time, in Matthew's time, and even in Paul's time after Jesus walked the earth. It is still needed today. Pope Francis reflects on this need, reminding us that when we are faced with tragic events, we sometimes feel crushed, even asking, "Why?" Humanity's evil can appear to be an abyss or loveless void, containing no goodness or life. We ourselves cannot fill the emptiness; only God can. (See the pope's homily from the Mass proclaiming St. Gregory of Narek a Doctor of the Church, April 12, 2015.)

God uses us to fill the world's abyss with the light of Christ. We become instruments of light by heeding Jesus' call to repent, which means reorienting our lives to live the way of Jesus. He offers hope and life. Rather than viewing the world through glasses of doom and gloom, Christ helps us see that change is possible. Evil does not have the last word. Rather than playing the game that divided the Corinthians—"My baptizer is better than yours"—we focus on Christ into whom we were all baptized. Rather than being self-centered, we seek the greater good that alone can transform our world. Rather than thinking that I am in charge, we submit to the One who really is and can fill the emptiness that evil deepens. For us it is impossible, but not for God made known in Jesus Christ, our light and our salvation. Sit in Christ's light. Give your darkness to him to lessen. Recharged, spread that light as the fishers of people we are called to be.

❖ Consider/Discuss

- What darkness feels overwhelming to you?
- Where do you see the light of Christ calling you out of darkness to be a marvelous light?

❖ Living and Praying with the Word

Generous God, I want to believe that I will see your bounty in the land of the living, both in heaven and here on earth. Give me courage not only to see your light but also to become your light that brings rejoicing, peace, and hope to our world.

January 29, 2017

FOURTH SUNDAY IN ORDINARY TIME

Today's Focus: An "A" Attitude

The Beatitudes in today's Gospel reading show us how to orient ourselves and to give ourselves an attitude toward living that is truly Christ-like.

FIRST READING
Zephaniah 2:3; 3:12–13

Seek the LORD, all you humble of the earth,
    who have observed his law;
seek justice, seek humility;
    perhaps you may be sheltered
    on the day of the LORD's anger.

But I will leave as a remnant in your midst
    a people humble and lowly,
who shall take refuge in the name of the LORD:
    the remnant of Israel.
They shall do no wrong
    and speak no lies;
nor shall there be found in their mouths
    a deceitful tongue;
they shall pasture and couch their flocks
    with none to disturb them.

PSALM RESPONSE
Matthew 5:3

Blessed are the poor in spirit; the kingdom of heaven is theirs!

SECOND READING
1 Corinthians 1:26–31

Consider your own calling, brothers and sisters. Not many of you were wise by human standards, not many were powerful, not many were of noble birth. Rather, God chose the foolish of the world to shame the wise, and God chose the weak of the world to shame the strong, and God chose the lowly and despised of the world, those who count for nothing, to reduce to nothing those who are something, so that no human being might boast before God. It is due to him that you are in Christ Jesus, who became for us wisdom from God, as well as righteousness, sanctification, and redemption, so that, as it is written, "Whoever boasts, should boast in the Lord."

GOSPEL
Matthew 5:1–12a

When Jesus saw the crowds, he went up the mountain, and after he had sat down, his disciples came to him. He began to teach them, saying:

"Blessed are the poor in spirit,
    for theirs is the kingdom of heaven.
Blessed are they who mourn,
    for they will be comforted.
Blessed are the meek,
    for they will inherit the land.

Blessed are they who hunger and thirst for righteousness,
>   for they will be satisfied.
Blessed are the merciful,
>   for they will be shown mercy.
Blessed are the clean of heart,
>   for they will see God.
Blessed are the peacemakers,
>   for they will be called children of God.
Blessed are they who are persecuted for the sake of
>   righteousness,
>   for theirs is the kingdom of heaven.
Blessed are you when they insult you and persecute you and utter every kind of evil against you falsely because of me. Rejoice and be glad, for your reward will be great in heaven."

❖ Understanding the Word

During the sixth century B.C., the prophet Zephaniah railed against the apostasy of Judah, describing a coming conflagration (Zephaniah 1:2–6) that would wipe clean despoiled Jerusalem, leaving only a remnant of those humble before God. Throughout the Old Testament, the "humble and lowly" are under God's particular protection, since they have no other sources of help. The remnant of which the prophet Zephaniah speaks is the faithful of Israel, who have done no wrong and have humbly followed God's will. In response, they will be at peace, which for an agrarian society is best portrayed as pasturing and couching their flocks with no one to disturb them (Zephaniah 3:13).

As the First Letter to the Corinthians continues, Paul lampoons the Corinthians' pridefulness: "Not many of you were wise by human standards, not many were powerful, not many were of noble birth" (1 Corinthians 1:26). Having deflated their egos, he now explains why weakness is a blessing. The wisdom of this world cannot compare to the true wisdom from God (1 Corinthians 1:30), which has been made manifest in Christ Jesus. Far from being disparaging, the motif of "foolishness," found throughout First Corinthians (1:18, 21, 23, 25; 2:14, 3:19), is used to explain the message of the cross, "a stumbling block to Jews and foolishness to Gentiles" (1 Corinthians 1:23).

Matthew has situated five distinct teaching blocks within his Gospel to replicate the five books of Moses. In today's reading, we begin the first such section in which Jesus reinterprets the law in a new way: "You have heard it said . . . but I say to you" (5:21). The setting of a mountain is meant to mirror Moses' giving of the law from Mount Sinai, further establishing the comparison between Jesus and Moses. Matthew makes various editorial changes to his Q source. He adds "in spirit" to his beatitude about the poor. This may indicate that his community was not economically poor, but rather spiritually so. The Beatitudes make reference to Old Testament themes of justice, peace, and care for the neighbor to connect Matthew's community with biblical Israel. The Beatitudes are future-oriented, depicting the eschatological blessings that await those who suffer in this world.

The first two steps of a twelve-step program are to admit both our powerlessness and our need for a power greater than ourselves to restore us to sanity. In other words, we cannot heal ourselves. We need to abandon our desire for control and recognize our utter dependence upon someone or something greater than ourselves. For Christians this can mean recognizing that we are utterly dependent upon God and mutually dependent upon each other. The Beatitudes, attitudes for being disciples of Jesus, say something similar. Blessed are the poor in spirit (the powerless); those meek enough to let go of our egos; and those who hunger and thirst for a clean heart, that is, sanity through right relationship with God. Freed from self-focus we can pay attention to those who mourn, or those we've hurt, and the divisions in our lives. We can feel with others and become compassionate and merciful peacemakers. Living these attitudes is no small task.

Like the Corinthians, we need to stop thinking we are powerful, noble, wise, or better than others. My Aunt Sophia called this nose-out-of-joint attitude "nose trouble." It is only when we admit our weakness, lowliness, and need for God and one another that the journey of healing begins. That's the power of Christ's death and resurrection. In humility, take refuge in the name of the Lord and try God's way when our own attempts have failed or not been long-lasting.

Blessed are we when we admit this need. Blessed are we when we relinquish our egos and seek the strength, wisdom, healing, and sanity that come from God alone. Blessed are we when we seek the Lord and are surprised at the comfort, satisfaction, and glimpses of God we find.

✦ Consider/Discuss

- When has trying to control my life not been enough to bring the change and healing I seek and need?
- When has the self-surrender of turning my life over to God given me strength in weakness and raised me up when I felt lowly?

✦ Living and Praying with the Word

Almighty God, I long to see your face. I long to experience the freedom you promise even when all is going badly. Thank you for your healing touch and the call to follow your Son, Jesus. May his attitudes for living become my attitudes more and more each day.

February 5, 2017

FIFTH SUNDAY IN ORDINARY TIME

Today's Focus: Do Good, Then Do Better

Though few of us are called to do grand and publicly glorious things for Christ, each of us is called upon to bring some goodness into the world, and to do a little bit better at that every day.

FIRST READING
Isaiah 58:7–10

Thus says the Lord:
    Share your bread with the hungry,
        shelter the oppressed and the homeless;
    clothe the naked when you see them,
        and do not turn your back on your own.
    Then your light shall break forth like the dawn,
        and your wound shall quickly be healed;
    your vindication shall go before you,
        and the glory of the Lord shall be your rear guard.
    Then you shall call, and the Lord will answer,
        you shall cry for help, and he will say: Here I am!
    If you remove from your midst
        oppression, false accusation and malicious speech;
    If you bestow your bread on the hungry
        and satisfy the afflicted;
    then light shall rise for you in the darkness,
        and the gloom shall become for you like midday.

PSALM RESPONSE
Psalm 112:4a

The just man is a light in darkness to the upright.

SECOND READING
1 Corinthians 2:1–5

When I came to you, brothers and sisters, proclaiming the mystery of God, I did not come with sublimity of words or of wisdom. For I resolved to know nothing while I was with you except Jesus Christ, and him crucified. I came to you in weakness and fear and much trembling, and my message and my proclamation were not with persuasive words of wisdom, but with a demonstration of Spirit and power, so that your faith might rest not on human wisdom but on the power of God.

GOSPEL
Matthew
5:13–16
Jesus said to his disciples: "You are the salt of the earth. But if salt loses its taste, with what can it be seasoned? It is no longer good for anything but to be thrown out and trampled underfoot. You are the light of the world. A city set on a mountain cannot be hidden. Nor do they light a lamp and then put it under a bushel basket; it is set on a lampstand, where it gives light to all in the house. Just so, your light must shine before others, that they may see your good deeds and glorify your heavenly Father."

❖ Understanding the Word

The first reading today is taken from yet another anonymous prophet writing in the tradition of Isaiah of Jerusalem. Third Isaiah is thought to be prophesying after the Exile. The joyous return to the land was soon dampened when the people discovered the monumental task of rebuilding their ruined city. Infighting and lethargy thwarted attempts to rebuild the temple and reestablish religious and cultural practices. Today's reading offers a very simple plan to help heal the people wounded by exile, so that they become again a people worthy of God. Sharing food with the hungry, sheltering the oppressed and homeless, clothing the naked—these actions of mercy will be as a soothing balm. Then "your wound shall quickly be healed" (Isaiah 58:8).

The Apostle Paul, by his own admission, was not a grand orator (1 Corinthians 2:4) and in fact, his opponents used his weakness against him (2 Corinthians 10:10). And yet, he was exceedingly successful (Romans 15:17–19). The singularity of his message (Jesus Christ crucified) and the power of the Spirit formed him into a fitting vessel (2 Corinthians 4:7). Paul acknowledges his weakness in order to stress that the Corinthians' belief is not the result of Paul's persuasive speech but of God's power.

The Sermon on the Mount is continued in today's Gospel reading. These three short analogies describe how the disciples are to behave, and serve as a transition from the third-person address of the eight beatitudes to the first-person address of the rest of the sermon. The disciples are to be like salt, which serves only one purpose and without that it is useless. The disciples are lights of the world (reminiscent of the light described in Matthew 4:16 and Isaiah 9:1–2). They show the world that the shadow of death is abated, but only if they remain unhidden. Finally, the disciples have a personal mission. They are to give light to "all in the house" (Matthew 5:15). Their illumination for the world may have represented the Gentile mission in Matthew's day, while the light at home could signal the mission to the Jews.

I have to admit that when I hear Jesus' call to be salt and light and do good deeds that glorify our heavenly Father, I can feel overwhelmed. It is a tall task, especially when I compare myself to saints like Blaise, whom we celebrated a few days ago, or Valentine, whom we'll celebrate in about a week. But when I hear Jesus' words in the context of the first reading, I am less overwhelmed and more empowered. I don't have to do great things or be the brightest bulb in the bunch. I simply need to share the gifts God has given to me. I can clothe people with love and care. I can pay attention to those around me. I can listen to the needs of the world and refuse to turn my back on others. I can do what I can, nothing more but nothing less. That's Paul's message to the Corinthians. When we share what God has given us every day, Christ's light will shine, we will be salt that flavors the world with God's presence, and we glorify God.

St. Francis de Sales advised the Curé of Get, a priest he counseled, to do what he was doing and do it better if he could. In that way he would see the glory of God. The same is true for us. We don't need to do extraordinary things to be Christ's light in our world. We simply need to use our God-given gifts, whatever our way of life. Then people will see the presence of God that lessens the darkness of evil and oppression in our world.

✦ Consider/Discuss

- What are the gifts that God has given me?
- How does God give light to the world and draw flavor out of my sisters and brothers through my witness?

✦ Living and Praying with the Word

Holy God, you choose the weak and make them strong in bearing witness to you. Thank you for the gifts you have given me, even those places where my need for you is more than evident. Help me use them to bring your light to the world and free those who are oppressed in any way.

February 12, 2017

SIXTH SUNDAY IN ORDINARY TIME

Today's Focus: More

It is tempting to try and figure out the bare minimum that we can do and still think we are a follower of Christ. But he always challenges us to do more than the minimum, to stay away from the Tempter who leads us down that path.

FIRST READING
Sirach 15:15–20

If you choose you can keep the commandments,
    they will save you;
    if you trust in God, you too shall live;
he has set before you fire and water;
    to whichever you choose, stretch forth your hand.
Before man are life and death, good and evil,
    whichever he chooses shall be given him.
Immense is the wisdom of the Lord;
    he is mighty in power, and all-seeing.
The eyes of God are on those who fear him;
    he understands man's every deed.
No one does he command to act unjustly,
    to none does he give license to sin.

PSALM RESPONSE
Psalm 119:1b

Blessed are they who follow the law of the Lord!

SECOND READING
1 Corinthians 2:6–10

Brothers and sisters: We speak a wisdom to those who are mature, not a wisdom of this age, nor of the rulers of this age who are passing away. Rather, we speak God's wisdom, mysterious, hidden, which God predetermined before the ages for our glory, and which none of the rulers of this age knew; for, if they had known it, they would not have crucified the Lord of glory. But as it is written:
    What eye has not seen, and ear has not heard,
    and what has not entered the human heart,
    what God has prepared for those who love him,
this God has revealed to us through the Spirit.

For the Spirit scrutinizes everything, even the depths of God.

GOSPEL
Matthew 5:
17–37 or
5:20–22a,
27–28,
33–34a, 37

Jesus said to his disciples: ["Do not think that I have come to abolish the law or the prophets. I have come not to abolish but to fulfill. Amen, I say to you, until heaven and earth pass away, not the smallest letter or the smallest part of a letter will pass from the law, until all things have taken place. Therefore, whoever breaks one of the least of these commandments and teaches others to do so will be called least in the kingdom of heaven. But whoever obeys and teaches these commandments will be called greatest in the kingdom of heaven.] I tell you, unless your righteousness surpasses that of the scribes and Pharisees, you will not enter the kingdom of heaven.

"You have heard that it was said to your ancestors,
You shall not kill; and whoever kills will be liable to judgment.
But I say to you, whoever is angry with his brother will be liable to judgment; [and whoever says to brother, 'Raqa,' will be answerable to the Sanhedrin; and whoever says, 'You fool,' will be liable to fiery Gehenna. Therefore, if you bring your gift to the altar, and there recall that your brother has anything against you, leave your gift there at the altar, go first and be reconciled with your brother, and then come and offer your gift. Settle with your opponent quickly while on the way to court. Otherwise your opponent will hand you over to the judge, and the judge will hand you over to the guard, and you will be thrown into prison. Amen, I say to you, you will not be released until you have paid the last penny.]

"You have heard that it was said,
You shall not commit adultery.
But I say to you, everyone who looks at a woman with lust has already committed adultery with her in his heart. [If your right eye causes you to sin, tear it out and throw it away. It is better for you to lose one of your members than to have your whole body thrown into Gehenna. And if your right hand causes you to sin, cut it off and throw it away. It is better for you to lose one of your members than to have your whole body go into Gehenna.

"It was also said,
Whoever divorces his wife must give her a bill of divorce.
But I say to you, whoever divorces his wife—unless the marriage is unlawful—causes her to commit adultery, and whoever marries a divorced woman commits adultery.]

"Again you have heard that it was said to your ancestors,
Do not take a false oath,
but make good to the Lord all that you vow.
But I say to you, do not swear at all; [not by heaven, for it is God's throne; nor by the earth, for it is his footstool; nor by Jerusalem, for it is the city of the great King. Do not swear by your head, for you cannot make a single hair white or black.] Let your 'Yes' mean 'Yes,'and your 'No' mean 'No.' Anything more is from the evil one."

Wisdom literature (Job, Psalms, Proverbs, Ecclesiastes, Song of Songs, Wisdom, and Ben Sira) is a collection of texts that present God's revelation not primarily in historical events but in the ordinariness of life. The goal of such wisdom is practical. How are we to live, love, and prosper in the face of the challenges of life? Jewish Wisdom theology held that God was the prime author of ordered creation, so fear of the Lord was the beginning of wisdom. Writing in the second century B.C., Ben Sira, from whose writings our first reading is taken, attempts to counter the influence of Hellenism (Greek culture). He reminds the Jews of his day that the traditions of Israel and not Greek philosophy and culture were the foundations of true wisdom. The choice is simple: keep the commandments and be saved.

Paul's eschatological biases are showing in today's second reading. Like many first-century Jews and early Christians, Paul believed that the current evil age would be ended when the Messiah came (Jewish perspective) or the Son of Man returned (Christian understanding). Through this lens, we see that the "wisdom of this age" and "rulers of this age" likely refer to the cosmic powers that are ultimately responsible for the crucifixion of "the Lord of glory" (1 Corinthians 2:8). But Paul preaches against this evil age, proclaiming God's wisdom, a mystery hidden from the rulers of this age but available to believers.

Following the Beatitudes (Matthew 5:1–11) and two parables (Matthew 5:12–16), Jesus turns to questions about the law and the prophets in today's Gospel reading. Jesus assures his disciples that his intent is not to abolish the law, but to fulfill it (Matthew 5:17). He proposes six reinterpretations of scripture that address murder (vv. 21–26), adultery (vv. 27–30), divorce (vv. 31–32), the taking of oaths (vv. 33–37), retaliation (vv. 38–42), and treatment of the enemy (vv. 43–48). In order to enter the kingdom of heaven, the disciples are to possess right-eousness that exceeds that of the scribes and Pharisees (Matthew 5:20), whom Matthew critiques as the very purveyors of inadequate interpretations (Matthew 15:4; 16:12; 23:15).

❖ Reflecting on the Word

When I was a teacher, young children often asked, "Teacher, what can I do to help you and to learn?" Older students asked, "What must I do to pass?" Jesus' teaching seems to answer "What can I do to follow God's ways?" rather than "What must I do?" What's the difference? The second question is about minimal requirements. The first question is about the maximal benefits involved with turning one's life over to God. Jesus asks for more. Not merely "Do not kill," but do not harbor what leads to killing in your hearts. Make amends. Reconcile with your opponent. Not merely "Do not commit adultery," but be faithful in your heart. Try to work things out, don't just give up. Respect others. Do not objectify anyone. The basics can be difficult enough to live, but the "more" that Jesus asks is a greater challenge.

The readings make clear that we have choices: between life and death, good and evil, right and wrong, and giving good example or leading others astray. Choices have consequences. Those responsible for Jesus' death would not see that he did not abolish the law and the prophets. He asked people to live them more intensely. They had him crucified when his words and way became too great a threat. New ways of looking at things can threaten us. We saw that in the Synod on the Family in 2014 and 2015. The "more" is challenging. However, when we want to do all we can to live God's ways, we will see the mystery of God present even when we fall, lifting us up to a newness of life that is prepared for those who love God.

❖ Consider/Discuss

- Which of Jesus' teachings in today's Gospel do you find to be most challenging?
- Which of them do you find most affirming?

❖ Living and Praying with the Word

Instruct me, O Lord, in your ways. Free me to seek you, even when you ask more of me than I think I am able to give. Help me be an example that invites others to you rather than leads them away.

February 19, 2017

SEVENTH SUNDAY IN ORDINARY TIME

Today's Focus: The Law of Love

To love one's enemies may be the most difficult teaching of Jesus, the one that leads us many times to act in direct contradiction to the wisdom of the world. Yet that is at the heart of his message.

FIRST READING
Leviticus 19:1–2, 17–18

The LORD said to Moses, "Speak to the whole Israelite community and tell them: Be holy, for I, the LORD, your God, am holy.

"You shall not bear hatred for your brother or sister in your heart. Though you may have to reprove your fellow citizen, do not incur sin because of him. Take no revenge and cherish no grudge against any of your people. You shall love your neighbor as yourself. I am the LORD."

PSALM RESPONSE
Psalm 103:8a

The Lord is kind and merciful.

SECOND READING
1 Corinthians 3:16–23

Brothers and sisters: Do you not know that you are the temple of God, and that the Spirit of God dwells in you? If anyone destroys God's temple, God will destroy that person; for the temple of God, which you are, is holy.

Let no one deceive himself. If any one among you considers himself wise in this age, let him become a fool, so as to become wise. For the wisdom of this world is foolishness in the eyes of God, for it is written:
God catches the wise in their own ruses,
and again:
The Lord knows the thoughts of the wise,
  that they are vain.
So let no one boast about human beings, for everything belongs to you, Paul or Apollos or Cephas, or the world or life or death, or the present or the future: all belong to you, and you to Christ, and Christ to God.

GOSPEL
Matthew 5:38–48

Jesus said to his disciples: "You have heard that it was said,
  An eye for an eye and a tooth for a tooth.
But I say to you, offer no resistance to one who is evil. When someone strikes you on your right cheek, turn the other one as well. If anyone wants to go to law with you over your tunic, hand over your cloak as well. Should anyone press you into service for one mile, go for two miles. Give to the one who asks of you, and do not turn your back on one who wants to borrow.

"You have heard that it was said,
You shall love your neighbor and hate your enemy.
But I say to you, love your enemies and pray for those who persecute you, that you may be children of your heavenly Father, for he makes his sun rise on the bad and the good, and causes rain to fall on the just and the unjust. For if you love those who love you, what recompense will you have? Do not the tax collectors do the same? And if you greet your brothers only, what is unusual about that? Do not the pagans do the same? So be perfect, just as your heavenly Father is perfect."

❖❖ Understanding the Word

The first reading from Leviticus is often been cited as the distillation of the entire Torah: Be holy since God is holy, and love your neighbor as yourself (Matthew 22:35–40). Occasionally, Leviticus 19:1 has been misread as "be holy as I am holy, " mandating a human impossibility, since human beings cannot achieve divine holiness. Rather, the text calls us to separate ourselves for God. The Hebrew word that we translate as "holy" is *qadosh*, which means "to be separate for God." In other words, we are to dedicate ourselves to God. In a personal place of holiness, we are then to exhibit divine behavior—love of neighbor. The act of love bears witness to the reality of one's holiness.

The theme of holiness continues in the second reading in which Paul compares the Corinthians to the temple of God. By virtue of their baptism, the Spirit of God now dwells within them. This radical imagery would have had a profound effect on the Jewish Christians for whom the temple of Jerusalem was the most holy site. Likewise the Gentile believers were surrounded by pagan temples, each of which claimed to house a god. Now Paul is saying that the believers themselves are the embodiment of these temples. "The temple of God, which you are, is holy" (1 Corinthians 3:17). No wonder Paul engages the motif of foolishness, since what Paul is preaching is absurd to non-believers. "Everything belongs to you . . . and you to Christ, and Christ to God" (1 Corinthians 3:23).

In today's Gospel, we hear the crescendo of Jesus' reinterpretation of the law, which culminates with "love your enemies" (Matthew 5:44). This passage illustrates the law of retribution (Matthew 5:38) in light of the command to love one's enemies (Matthew 5:44). Jesus tells his disciples to offer no resistance to the evil one, and in fact, to respond with generosity even if struck or sued or solicited (Matthew 5:38–39a). The verses that follow present a series of actions to which a disciple is to respond with non-retaliation, and are paralleled in Luke 6:29–30. Matthew 5:39b–42 depicts four different settings: a violent personal insult, a scene from debtor's court, impressment into service, and an encounter with a beggar or someone in need of a loan. Matthew's verses decrease in severity, moving from a violent slap in verse 39b to a request for aid in verse 42. If the disciple is slapped, sued, extorted, or solicited from, he or she is to respond not with any kind of retaliation, but by refusing to escalate the situation any further. Jesus' reasoning for this ethical injunction: because the disciples are to be "children of (their) heavenly father" (Matthew 5:45).

Reflecting on the Word

"Offer no resistance to one who is evil" (Matthew 5:19). Does Jesus know what he is asking? Living like that can lead to my demise. But that's exactly what Jesus did when he was arrested and when he stood before Pilate and when his executioners struck and ridiculed him. He walked his talk. While he died on the cross, resurrection and new life came from the actions of those who had acted in an evil way toward him. These words challenge us, and challenge they ought. Yet, if we're honest, resistance and retaliation have not ended or lessened evil. They put it at bay for a while, but it rises even stronger than before, like the terrorism and violence evident in every part of our world, when force is lifted.

Jesus asks us for more. Go two miles, hand over your cloak, do not ignore those in need, love your enemies. Tough love sets limits, creates boundaries, and challenges behavior in order to invite change, not to seek revenge. Pope Francis lives Jesus' teaching that only love can reduce hate and rob evil of its power. Force may be necessary at times, but evil is reduced only as long as the force lasts. Without deeper change evil returns once the force is gone.

Being holy, for God is holy, means to love God, St. Francis de Sales taught. To love God we must love our neighbor. As the temples in whom God's Spirit dwells, we love God when we respect all God's children. This can be difficult enough in the face of goodness. In the face of evil it is my greatest challenge. How do Jesus' words challenge you? Where have you tried them and been surprised?

Consider/Discuss

- What have resistance and retaliation really gained for you?
- Where has a non-resistant response surprised you?

Living and Praying with the Word

Holy God, you call us to be holy for you are holy. Holiness means we live the way of Jesus. This comforts us at times, and challenges us deeply at other times. Open my mind and heart to your Spirit within so that my struggle to walk Jesus' talk makes what seems impossible possible and worth the effort.

February 26, 2017

EIGHTH SUNDAY IN ORDINARY TIME

Today's Focus: Anxiety Attack

There is a way in which our living in anxiety is a statement that we don't trust in God. Complete trust in God doesn't mean life won't have difficulties, but it does mean they can be faced calmly, with faith.

FIRST READING
Isaiah 49:14–15

Zion said, "The LORD has forsaken me;
    my LORD has forgotten me."
Can a mother forget her infant,
    be without tenderness for the child of her womb?
Even should she forget,
    I will never forget you.

PSALM RESPONSE
Psalm 62:6a

Rest in God alone, my soul.

SECOND READING
1 Corinthians 4:1–5

Brothers and sisters: Thus should one regard us: as servants of Christ and stewards of the mysteries of God. Now it is of course required of stewards that they be found trustworthy. It does not concern me in the least that I be judged by you or any human tribunal; I do not even pass judgment on myself; I am not conscious of anything against me, but I do not thereby stand acquitted; the one who judges me is the Lord. Therefore do not make any judgment before the appointed time, until the Lord comes, for he will bring to light what is hidden in darkness and will manifest the motives of our hearts, and then everyone will receive praise from God.

GOSPEL
Matthew 6:24–34

Jesus said to his disciples: "No one can serve two masters. He will either hate one and love the other, or be devoted to one and despise the other. You cannot serve God and mammon.

"Therefore I tell you, do not worry about your life, what you will eat or drink, or about your body, what you will wear. Is not life more than food and the body more than clothing? Look at the birds in the sky; they do not sow or reap, they gather nothing into barns, yet your heavenly Father feeds them. Are not you more important than they? Can any of you by worrying add a single moment to your life-span? Why are you anxious about clothes? Learn from the way the wild flowers grow. They do not work or spin. But I tell you that not even Solomon in all his splendor was clothed like one of them.

If God so clothes the grass of the field, which grows today and is thrown into the oven tomorrow, will he not much more provide for you, O you of little faith? So do not worry and say, 'What are we to eat?' or 'What are we to drink?'or 'What are we to wear?' All these things the pagans seek. Your heavenly Father knows that you need them all. But seek first the kingdom of God and his righteousness, and all these things will be given you besides. Do not worry about tomorrow; tomorrow will take care of itself. Sufficient for a day is its own evil."

❖ Understanding the Word

This brief first reading from Second Isaiah is a poignant and tender word of consolation from God to the exiles, who feared they had been forgotten. Zion or Jerusalem is often used to refer to all of the people of Israel. In Isaiah 49, the prophet likens God's faithfulness to that of a mother who could never forget her infant or be without tenderness for her child (v. 15). As the passage continues, the metaphor for God becomes that of a redeemer who brings Zion's lost children home (vv.22–23).

Throughout his apostolic ministry, Paul continually had to demonstrate his credentials, since his call came "as one untimely born" and he had persecuted the church of God (1 Corinthians 15:8). In today's second reading, Paul announces his role (as servant of Christ and steward of the mystery of God) but offers no supporting evidence. In fact, he eschews human judgment of any kind (1 Corinthians 4:3), since it is the Lord who will judge (1 Corinthians 4:4). Paul's prior actions among the Corinthians testify to his trustworthiness (1 Corinthians 4:15–16).

In Matthew's Sermon on the Mount, Jesus now turns to issues of right behavior before God, drawing out in more detail the meaning of "give us this day our daily bread" (Matthew 6:11). A disciple must choose whom he or she will serve: God or mammon. The latter is an Aramaic loan word with an uncertain etymology, perhaps deriving from "to trust" or "to believe in." It came to signify possessions, money, and resources. The disciple is to "trust" that God will provide for his or her needs (Matthew 6:25), just as God has cared for all of creation (Matthew 6:26, 28). To pray for one's daily bread and then say, "What are we to eat?" proves the disciple unfit for the kingdom of God.

Picturing God as a tender mother unable to forget her infant is one of my favorite images in scripture, most likely because I was raised by a single mother who sacrificed much for my grandfather and me. She died when I was thirteen. She was forty. While we had our ups and downs, I could rely on her love, even when she seemed absent. I felt most safe when she came home from work, when we were together. I worried when she was late or gone for an extended period of time. I had to learn how to live without her. But worry only drained my energy and faith. It was turning to God in prayer, voicing my concerns and letting them go, that freed me to find strength by sensing God's continual presence. That's where I found hope, security, and peace as a child and do today.

St. Francis de Sales taught that with the exception of sin, anxiety is the greatest evil we can experience. It distracts us, robs us of energy, and leads us to trust what is not God (mammon) more than God. God alone is our rock. Anxiety weakens our immunity to the Evil One, who gains access to our minds and hearts in ways that chip away at faith. Living without worry and anxiety is easier said than done, but not impossible. Close your eyes. Imagine yourself in your mother's or father's arms, whichever relationship is more comforting. Take a deep breath. Pray, "Rest in God alone, my soul." Then exhale and pray, "Take my worries and anxieties from me, God." Breathe again and pray, "Rest in God alone, my soul." Now pray as you exhale, "Give me this day my daily bread."

❖ Consider/Discuss

- What has worry or anxiety gained for you in life?
- Have prayer and trust in God offered peace even in the midst of difficulty? How?

❖ Living and Praying with the Word

Strong and tender God, hold me in your arms today and every day. Make me aware that I always live in your presence. Help me to turn to you in times of need and thank you in times of blessing.

Notes

The season of Lent serves as a forty-day period of preparation, leading us to our ultimate feast, the celebration of Easter. The readings chosen for this season attempt to answer two questions: why do we need salvation and who is this Jesus who comes to save us? The first and second readings attempt to answer the first question, while the Gospel readings attend to the second.

The balance of the relationship between God and the first couple is permanently upset when Adam and Eve fall prey to the serpent's testing (First Sunday). This primal rupture becomes the foundation for Paul's understanding of Jesus as the new Adam (First Sunday). In stark contrast to the original disobedience, Abram responds without hesitation to God's invitation to leave his family for a land yet to be revealed (Second Sunday). Almost as if in response to what would await Abram, First Timothy reminds believers to bear the hardship of the gospel (Second Sunday). Both Abram and the community of First Timothy are to trust God's abiding presence, something the wandering Israelites frequently failed to do (Third Sunday). On numerous occasions, they complain to Moses about their hunger and thirst, and each time Moses effects positive results through God's power. The second reading for the Third Sunday is taken from Romans, in which Paul reminds the community that while they were still sinners, Christ died for them. As Moses guided the people in the desert, so too will David lead his people in the way of God (Fourth Sunday). Ephesians challenges believers to live worthy lives as "children of the light," for they are to be pleasing to the Lord (Fourth Sunday). The first reading from Genesis introduced the origin of humanity's estrangement from God, which led to their mortality. The reading from Ezekiel (Fifth Sunday) envisions a reversal of that state so that dry bones are brought to life. So Romans 8 can celebrate the knowledge that if the spirit of God dwells within us, we too will rise (Fifth Sunday).

The Gospel readings paint a portrait of an extraordinary human being, who though tested repeatedly by the devil never sides against God (First Sunday). We are given a glimpse of the glory that awaits Jesus in the story of the Transfiguration (Second Sunday). The characteristics of a true disciple are depicted in the story of the Samaritan woman (Third Sunday) and the man born blind (Fourth Sunday). The Samaritan woman recognizes Jesus as both prophet and Messiah. The man whose sight is restored stands in contradiction to the Pharisees, who are blind to Jesus' true identity. With the raising of Lazarus from the dead, Martha and Mary come to the full knowledge of who Jesus is—the resurrection and the life (Fifth Sunday).

March 5, 2017

FIRST SUNDAY OF LENT

Today's Focus: Good and Good for You

The fruit of the tree in Eden was good, but the eating of it wasn't a good thing for Adam and Eve. In Christ we can discern both what is good and what will be good for us.

FIRST READING
*Genesis 2:7–9;
3:1–7*

The LORD God formed man out of the clay of the ground and blew into his nostrils the breath of life, and so man became a living being.

Then the LORD God planted a garden in Eden, in the east, and placed there the man whom he had formed. Out of the ground the LORD God made various trees grow that were delightful to look at and good for food, with the tree of life in the middle of the garden and the tree of the knowledge of good and evil.

Now the serpent was the most cunning of all the animals that the LORD God had made. The serpent asked the woman, "Did God really tell you not to eat from any of the trees in the garden?" The woman answered the serpent: "We may eat of the fruit of the trees in the garden; it is only about the fruit of the tree in the middle of the garden that God said, 'You shall not eat it or even touch it, lest you die.' " But the serpent said to the woman: "You certainly will not die! No, God knows well that the moment you eat of it your eyes will be opened and you will be like gods who know what is good and what is evil." The woman saw that the tree was good for food, pleasing to the eyes, and desirable for gaining wisdom. So she took some of its fruit and ate it; and she also gave some to her husband, who was with her, and he ate it. Then the eyes of both of them were opened, and they realized that they were naked; so they sewed fig leaves together and made loincloths for themselves.

PSALM RESPONSE
Psalm 51:3a

Be merciful, O Lord, for we have sinned.

In the shorter form of the reading, the passage in brackets is omitted.

SECOND
READING
Romans
5:12–19 or
5:12, 17–19

Brothers and sisters: Through one man sin entered the world, and through sin, death, and thus death came to all men, inasmuch as all sinned—[for up to the time of the law, sin was in the world, though sin is not accounted when there is no law. But death reigned from Adam to Moses, even over those who did not sin after the pattern of the trespass of Adam, who is the type of the one who was to come.

But the gift is not like the transgression. For if by the transgression of the one, the many died, how much more did the grace of God and the gracious gift of the one man Jesus Christ overflow for the many. And the gift is not like the result of the one who sinned. For after one sin there was the judgment that brought condemnation; but the gift, after many transgressions, brought acquittal.] For if, by the transgression of the one, death came to reign through that one, how much more will those who receive the abundance of grace and of the gift of justification come to reign in life through the one Jesus Christ. In conclusion, just as through one transgression condemnation came upon all, so, through one righteous act, acquittal and life came to all. For just as through the disobedience of the one man the many were made sinners, so, through the obedience of the one, the many will be made righteous.

GOSPEL
Matthew 4:
1–11

At that time Jesus was led by the Spirit into the desert to be tempted by the devil. He fasted for forty days and forty nights, and afterwards he was hungry. The tempter approached and said to him, "If you are the Son of God, command that these stones become loaves of bread." He said in reply, "It is written:

> One does not live on bread alone,
> but on every word that comes forth
> from the mouth of God."

Then the devil took him to the holy city, and made him stand on the parapet of the temple, and said to him, "If you are the Son of God, throw yourself down. For it is written:

> He will command his angels concerning you
> and with their hands they will support you,
> lest you dash your foot against a stone."

Jesus answered him, "Again it is written,
> You shall not put the Lord, your God, to the test."

Then the devil took him up to a very high mountain, and showed him all the kingdoms of the world in their magnificence, and he said to him, "All these I shall give to you, if you will prostrate yourself and worship me." At this, Jesus said to him, "Get away, Satan! It is written:

> The Lord, your God, shall you worship
> and him alone shall you serve."

Then the devil left him and, behold, angels came and ministered to him.

The first eleven chapters of the book of Genesis, from which our first reading is taken, are a collection of etiological (origin) stories, designed to explain how creation came about, why God made humans (Genesis 1:26–27), why human lives are so short (Genesis 3:22–24), why we speak in different languages (Genesis 11:9), etc. These stories helped pre-modern people to understand the world around them, in particular how a good God could allow evil. Today's reading answers that question by describing the encounter between the serpent and the first couple. The desire of humanity to be like gods caused Adam and Eve to transgress God's law, which had tragic consequences. They were banished from the Garden of Eden, and with them the sin of disobedience was carried out into the world.

By the time Paul is writing his Letter to the Romans, the story of Adam and Eve had been so thoroughly theologized that Adam came to represent the one by whom "sin entered the world, and through sin, death" (Romans 5:12). Paul interprets the sin of Adam as redounding on all of humanity. But Jesus Christ's obedience to God has the opposite effect. "For if by the transgression of the one, the many died, how much more did the grace of God and the gracious gift of the one man Jesus Christ overflow for the many" (Romans 5:15). In Paul's understanding, Jesus Christ became the new Adam (1 Corinthians 15:45), thus returning believers to a state of righteousness (Romans 5:19).

Adam and Eve had a serpent, but in today's Gospel reading, the antagonist is called "the devil" (Matthew 4:1, 5, 8,11) and "Satan" (Matthew 4:10). In the New Testament, Satan is the ruler of the demonic realm (Matthew 12:26), bent on the destruction of all that is good (Mark 4:15). The cosmic encounter between Satan and Jesus foreshadows the resistance Jesus will meet in the human realm. The temptations of hunger, idolatry, and power resemble the testing of Israel during the wanderings in the wilderness and its settlement in the land. To each, Jesus responds with citations from the book of Deuteronomy (8:3; 6:16; 6:13), demonstrating that unlike the children of Israel, Jesus as the true Son is wholly obedient to God.

❖ Reflecting on the Word

The tree in the middle of the garden was enticing, "good for food, pleasing to the eyes, and desirable for gaining wisdom" (Genesis 3:8). Adam and Eve only wanted the good. How many people wish that we were gods at times? They ate and their eyes were opened. They were creatures, not gods, nor God. Trying to be something other than who they were filled them with shame, feeling bad about who we are. Healthy guilt, on the other hand, means feeling bad about what we did. Shame is destructive. Guilt can give life. We can learn what is truly good, pleasing, and desirable, rather than what only appears to be.

Satan tempts Jesus by offering what the Evil One cannot deliver: true food, ultimate authority, and true worship. At first sight what is offered appears to be good. However, only God can satisfy our deepest hungers. That is why we are to trust and not test God. Only God is worthy of our worship. Jesus saw through these offers because he knew the One who alone can satisfy us and is worthy of our worship and trust. Forty days and nights of fasting deepened his understanding of who he and God are. That knowledge freed him to accept death on the cross, where we receive the gift of justification.

Lent asks, "Have we put our trust in what only appears to be good, pleasing, and desirable, or in the One who alone can satisfy our hungry hearts?" Open your eyes to see who we are, children of God who belong to Jesus Christ. May our Lenten journey renew our identity so that we can discover what is really good, desirable, and life-giving.

❖ Consider/Discuss

- Where do you place trust in people, things, or ways of being other than God?
- Where has admitting your sin opened your eyes to let God's mercy fill you, free you, and change your life?

❖ Living and Praying with the Word

Open my eyes, Lord, to see beyond appearances into the heart. May I fast from what only appears to be good and pleasing so that I can find you deep within all who make you known. Help me accept the gift of being your child, your creature, and your beloved.

March 12, 2017

SECOND SUNDAY OF LENT

Today's Focus: Leaving the Mountaintop, Not the Light

Though the experience of the Transfiguration was dazzling, the followers of Christ had to come to learn that no matter where they were, Christ their Light always remained with them, even when leaving the mountaintop.

FIRST READING
Genesis 12:1–4a

The Lord said to Abram: "Go forth from the land of your kinsfolk and from your father's house to a land that I will show you.

"I will make of you a great nation,
and I will bless you;
I will make your name great,
so that you will be a blessing.
I will bless those who bless you
and curse those who curse you.
All the communities of the earth
shall find blessing in you."

Abram went as the Lord directed him.

PSALM RESPONSE
Psalm 33:22

Lord, let your mercy be on us, as we place our trust in you.

SECOND READING
2 Timothy 1: 8b–10

Beloved: Bear your share of hardship for the gospel with the strength that comes from God.

He saved us and called us to a holy life, not according to our works but according to his own design and the grace bestowed on us in Christ Jesus before time began, but now made manifest through the appearance of our savior Christ Jesus, who destroyed death and brought life and immortality to light through the gospel.

GOSPEL
Matthew 17: 1–9

Jesus took Peter, James, and John his brother, and led them up a high mountain by themselves. And he was transfigured before them; his face shone like the sun and his clothes became white as light. And behold, Moses and Elijah appeared to them, conversing with him. Then Peter said to Jesus in reply, "Lord, it is good that we are here. If you wish, I will make three tents here, one for you, one for Moses, and one for Elijah." While he was still speaking, behold, a bright cloud cast a shadow over them, then from the cloud came a voice that said, "This is my beloved Son, with whom I am well pleased; listen to him." When the disciples heard this, they fell prostrate and were very much afraid. But Jesus came and touched them, saying, "Rise, and do not be afraid." And when the disciples raised their eyes, they saw no one else but Jesus alone.

As they were coming down from the mountain, Jesus charged them, "Do not tell the vision to anyone until the Son of Man has been raised from the dead."

❖ Understanding the Word

Our first reading is taken from the book of Genesis, chapter 12. While the previous eleven chapters depicted a mythic past belonging to all humanity, chapter 12 describes the call and response of a particular people, represented by their patriarch Abram. We are not told why Abram is singled out, but God invites him to leave kith and kin and travel to a land yet to be revealed. As surety, God makes Abram a three-fold promise of land (Genesis 12:1), nationhood (Genesis 12:2), and blessing (Genesis 12:2). The promise will include numerous descendants (Genesis 13:16; 15:4–5; 17:5). Despite his advancing age, Abram trusts in God, who credits his faith as righteousness (Genesis 15:6).

The second reading is taken from Second Timothy, which is doubly pseudonymous, purporting to have been written by Paul to his protégé Timothy, but long after their deaths. The early second-century writer hopes to encourage his community to bear their "share of hardship for the gospel" (2 Timothy 1:8), indicating either a literal or spiritual struggle among the believers. They are to be encouraged because through no effort on their part, the grace has been bestowed on them in Christ Jesus even before time began (2 Timothy 1:9). This grace has been manifested in Christ's resurrection and appearance so that immortality awaits the faithful (2 Timothy 1:10).

The Gospel recounts the Transfiguration of Jesus and serves three functions in the Gospel of Matthew. First, it confirms Jesus' identity (Matthew 1:23) as God's Son (Matthew 3:17) by means of the heavenly apparition of Moses (Israel's greatest prophet) and Elijah (the prophet whose return would signal the end-times), and by the direct statement by the voice from the cloud (Matthew 17:5). Second, it foreshadows Jesus' resurrection: "Do not tell the vision to anyone until the Son of Man has been raised from the dead" (Matthew 17:9). And finally, it reminds Matthew's community (and today's readers) not to dwell on the mountain of Transfiguration (Matthew 17:4) so as to avoid the Passion (Matthew 17:12), but to "Rise, and . . . not be afraid" (Matthew 17:7) of what awaits true disciples.

❖ Reflecting on the Word

St. Francis de Sales said that those who go, stay and those who stay, go. A part of those who have touched our lives remains when they move on. Part of us stays with them when they go on their way, for good and for ill.

Peter, James, and John glimpse Jesus' glory on the Transfiguration mount. The presence of Elijah and Moses and the voice of God clarify that Jesus is the promised Son of Man. They have a glimpse of Resurrection glory. They want to stay in this positive experience. Who wouldn't? And although Jesus returns them to daily life, they are changed. That glimpse remains with them and probably helped them through some tough times. I wonder how often they returned to that mountain in their minds and hearts.

God asks Abram, an old man, to take his kin to a land promised but unknown. He trusts God's promises and goes. I wonder how often he hearkened back to the home that he, Sarah, and their kin left. His deep faith and trust in God remained with him on the way.

Lent invites us to leave life as we have known it and embrace the way of the gospel more fully. Life's journey includes times of blessing and times of hardship. We can sometimes wish we had remained as we were. Our journey will take the best of life with us and open us to the healing, hope, and light the gospel offers. Are we willing to leave the familiar, like Peter, James, John, and Abram, to find Christ in daily life, whether easy or difficult? What goes along with us on the journey and what do we leave behind?

✤ Consider/Discuss

- What experiences of Jesus do we wish would be as strong as they once were?
- Where have we found new life because we accepted the invitation to live the gospel more clearly in daily life by releasing something or someone?

✤ Living and Praying with the Word

Holy God, baptism has made us your beloved daughters and sons. Free us to answer your call, wherever it leads. Help us to put our trust in you on the peaks and in the valleys of life.

March 19, 2017

THIRD SUNDAY OF LENT

Today's Focus: The Water of Life

The most common substance on earth—water—is also the most precious. It is no wonder that the stories of our salvation feature it so frequently.

FIRST READING
Exodus 17:3–7

In those days, in their thirst for water, the people grumbled against Moses, saying, "Why did you ever make us leave Egypt? Was it just to have us die here of thirst with our children and our livestock?" So Moses cried out to the LORD, "What shall I do with this people? A little more and they will stone me!" The LORD answered Moses, "Go over there in front of the people, along with some of the elders of Israel, holding in your hand, as you go, the staff with which you struck the river. I will be standing there in front of you on the rock in Horeb. Strike the rock, and the water will flow from it for the people to drink." This Moses did, in the presence of the elders of Israel. The place was called Massah and Meribah, because the Israelites quarreled there and tested the LORD, saying, "Is the LORD in our midst or not?"

PSALM RESPONSE
Psalm 95:8

If today you hear his voice, harden not your hearts.

SECOND READING
Romans 5:1–2, 5–8

Brothers and sisters: Since we have been justified by faith, we have peace with God through our Lord Jesus Christ, through whom we have gained access by faith to this grace in which we stand, and we boast in hope of the glory of God.

And hope does not disappoint, because the love of God has been poured out into our hearts through the Holy Spirit who has been given to us. For Christ, while we were still helpless, died at the appointed time for the ungodly. Indeed, only with difficulty does one die for a just person, though perhaps for a good person one might even find courage to die. But God proves his love for us in that while we were still sinners Christ died for us.

In the shorter form of the reading, the passages in brackets are omitted.

GOSPEL
*John 4:5–42 or
4:5–15, 19b–26,
39a, 40–42*
Jesus came to a town of Samaria called Sychar, near the plot of land that Jacob had given to his son Joseph. Jacob's well was there. Jesus, tired from his journey, sat down there at the well. It was about noon.

A woman of Samaria came to draw water. Jesus said to her, "Give me a drink." His disciples had gone into the town to buy food. The Samaritan woman said to him, "How can you, a Jew, ask me, a Samaritan woman, for a drink?"—For Jews use nothing in common with Samaritans.—Jesus answered and said to her, "If you knew the gift of God and who is saying to you, 'Give me a drink,' you would have asked him and he would have given you living water." The woman said to him, "Sir, you do not even have a bucket and the cistern is deep; where then can you get this living water? Are you greater than our father Jacob, who gave us this cistern and drank from it himself with his children and his flocks?" Jesus answered and said to her, "Everyone who drinks this water will be thirsty again; but whoever drinks the water I shall give will never thirst; the water I shall give will become in him a spring of water welling up to eternal life." The woman said to him, "Sir, give me this water, so that I may not be thirsty or have to keep coming here to draw water."

[Jesus said to her, "Go call your husband and come back." The woman answered and said to him, "I do not have a husband." Jesus answered her, "You are right in saying, 'I do not have a husband.' For you have had five husbands, and the one you have now is not your husband. What you have said is true." The woman said to him, Sir, ["I can see that you are a prophet. Our ancestors worshiped on this mountain; but you people say that the place to worship is in Jerusalem." Jesus said to her, "Believe me, woman, the hour is coming when you will worship the Father neither on this mountain nor in Jerusalem. You people worship what you do not understand; we worship what we understand, because salvation is from the Jews. But the hour is coming, and is now here, when true worshipers will worship the Father in Spirit and truth; and indeed the Father seeks such people to worship him. God is Spirit, and those who worship him must worship in Spirit and truth." The woman said to him, "I know that the Messiah is coming, the one called the Christ; when he comes, he will tell us everything." Jesus said to her, "I am he, the one speaking with you."

[At that moment his disciples returned, and were amazed that he was talking with a woman, but still no one said, "What are you looking for?" or "Why are you talking with her?" The woman left her water jar and went into the town and said to the people, "Come see a man who told me everything I have done. Could he possibly be the Christ?" They went out of the town and came to him. Meanwhile, the disciples urged him, "Rabbi, eat." But he said to them, "I have food to eat of which you do not know." So the disciples said to one another, "Could someone have brought him something to eat?" Jesus said to them, "My food is to do the will of the one who sent me and to finish his work. Do you not say, 'In four months the harvest will be here'? I tell you, look up and see the fields ripe for the harvest. The reaper is already receiving payment and gathering crops for eternal life, so that the sower and reaper can rejoice together. For here the saying is verified that 'One sows and another reaps.' I sent you to reap what you have not worked for; others have done the work, and you are sharing the fruits of their work."]

Many of the Samaritans of that town began to believe in him because of the word of the woman who testified, "He told me everything I have done." When the Samaritans came to him, they invited him to stay with them; and he stayed there two days. Many more began to believe in him because of his word, and they said to the woman, "We no longer believe because of your word; for we have heard for ourselves, and we know that this is truly the savior of the world."

❖ Understanding the Word

The portrait painted in Exodus of the wandering Israelites is none too flattering. They grumble against Moses because the water source is bitter (Exodus 15:24). They complain that they are hungry and miss "the fleshpots of Egypt" (Exodus 16:3). In today's reading, they are quarreling with Moses again over their thirst (Exodus 17:3). Despite God's miraculous rescue of the people from the Egyptians, the Israelites require additional assurances of God's presence. In response, God directs Moses to take witnesses from among the elders and to travel to Horeb, where God will be stationed. With the staff given to him by God, Moses strikes the rock and water pours forth. Apparently the water traveled back to the people at Rephidim via a wadi or dry riverbed (Exodus 17:1). The place was named Massah ("quarreling") and Meribah ("testing") as a reminder of the people's doubt, "Is the LORD in our midst or not?" (Exodus 17:7).

The reading from Paul's Letter to the Romans reads as an explanation of 1 Corinthians 13:13—"So faith, hope, love remain, these three; but the greatest of these is love." As Paul explains, salvation in Christ awaits the believer who first has "faith" (Romans 5:1) in Jesus Christ, who has secured peace between God and us. Therefore, we can "hope" to stand before the glory (understood as "presence") of God (Romans 5:2). But the root of our faith and hope is not based on our own actions. Rather, the source is God's "love," made manifest through Christ's sacrifice (Romans 5:8) that is poured into our hearts (Romans 5:5). Indeed, the "greatest of these is love."

In order to understand the significance of Jesus' interaction with the Samaritan woman in today's Gospel, we need to turn to the chapter before. In John 3:1–21, Nicodemus is introduced as a man of the Pharisees and ruler of the Jews (John 3:1), and a teacher of Israel (John 3:10) whose primary trait is misunderstanding (John 3:4, 9). He is attracted by the signs that Jesus produces (John 3:2), but fails to grasp Jesus' teaching. But the Samaritan woman is presented without any significant credentials (John 4:9), nor does she see Jesus produce any signs. Rather, she and Jesus engage in a theological conversation that leads her to see Jesus as "a prophet" (John 4:19) and wonder if he is the "messiah" (John 4:25, 29). For the first time in John's Gospel, Jesus responds, "I am," the same self-designation used for God in Exodus 3:14.

❖ Reflecting on the Word

A canticle from Isaiah sings that we shall draw water joyfully from the well-springs of salvation (Isaiah 12:3). Water bookends our readings and our lives of faith. The Israelites grumble in their thirst. Moses cries out to God in exasperation. God gives the people water from a rock. An extraordinary event makes known that the LORD is in their midst.

Jesus gives a Samaritan woman more than water by ordinary means—dialogue and presence. The story is not ordinary. Why? Jews considered Samaritans to be less than human. Men did not speak to women in public. But Jesus spoke to this Samaritan woman in a public place. His request, "Give me a drink," put himself in need of her and began a conversation that satisfied her deeper thirsts for God and acceptance. Transformed, she returned to the people she tried to avoid and shared her experience. She led the people she tried to avoid to Jesus. Their encounter with him transformed them. They came to know that the Savior, the Lord, was in their midst.

When we were baptized the Holy Spirit was given to us and we became one with Jesus Christ. By his gift of self on the cross, Jesus gave us living water and offered us the wellsprings of salvation. God quenches our thirst when we are willing to be vulnerable, like the woman, and empty ourselves of whatever keeps us from believing that God's love can transform us. Reflect on that love. Give thanks for the times that Christ has quenched your thirst and empowered you to bring his presence to others. Ordinary acts can open up the wellsprings of salvation for us and for others. Extraordinary!

❖ Consider/Discuss

- When have you wondered whether or not the Lord was in your midst?
- How has being vulnerable freed you to be honest with God, yourself, or another and quenched your deepest longing?

❖ Living and Praying with the Word

Loving God, your love for us is so great that Jesus died for us while we were sinners. Help us believe in your love. Let the living water poured out on us in baptism quench our thirst and empower us to proclaim that you are here, in our midst.

March 26, 2017

FOURTH SUNDAY OF LENT

Today's Focus: A More Precious Vision

As our Lenten journey progresses, we strive to improve the manner in which we "see" with our hearts, hoping that, in the light of Christ, we can truly come to see the world as God does.

FIRST READING
1 Samuel 16: 1b, 6–7, 10–13a

The LORD said to Samuel: "Fill your horn with oil, and be on your way. I am sending you to Jesse of Bethlehem, for I have chosen my king from among his sons."

As Jesse and his sons came to the sacrifice, Samuel looked at Eliab and thought, "Surely the Lord's anointed is here before him." But the LORD said to Samuel: "Do not judge from his appearance or from his lofty stature, because I have rejected him. Not as man sees does God see, because man sees the appearance but the LORD looks into the heart." In the same way Jesse presented seven sons before Samuel, but Samuel said to Jesse, "The LORD has not chosen any one of these." Then Samuel asked Jesse, "Are these all the sons you have?" Jesse replied, "There is still the youngest, who is tending the sheep." Samuel said to Jesse, "Send for him; we will not begin the sacrificial banquet until he arrives here." Jesse sent and had the young man brought to them. He was ruddy, a youth handsome to behold and making a splendid appearance. The LORD said, "There—anoint him, for this is the one!" Then Samuel, with the horn of oil in hand, anointed David in the presence of his brothers; and from that day on, the spirit of the LORD rushed upon David.

PSALM RESPONSE
Psalm 23:1

The Lord is my shepherd; there is nothing I shall want.

SECOND READING
Ephesians 5: 8–14

Brothers and sisters: You were once darkness, but now you are light in the Lord. Live as children of light, for light produces every kind of goodness and righteousness and truth. Try to learn what is pleasing to the Lord. Take no part in the fruitless works of darkness; rather expose them, for it is shameful even to mention the things done by them in secret; but everything exposed by the light becomes visible, for everything that becomes visible is light. Therefore, it says:

"Awake, O sleeper,
and arise from the dead,
and Christ will give you light."

In the shorter form of the reading, the passages in brackets are omitted.

GOSPEL
John 9:1–41 or
9:1, 6–9, 13–17,
34–38

As Jesus passed by he saw a man blind from birth. [His disciples asked him, "Rabbi, who sinned, this man or his parents, that he was born blind?" Jesus answered, "Neither he nor his parents sinned; it is so that the works of God might be made visible through him. We have to do the works of the one who sent me while it is day. Night is coming when no one can work. While I am in the world, I am the light of the world." When he had said this,] he spat on the ground and made clay with the saliva, and smeared the clay on his eyes, and said to him, "Go wash in the Pool of Siloam"—which means Sent—. So he went and washed, and came back able to see.

His neighbors and those who had seen him earlier as a beggar said, "Isn't this the one who used to sit and beg?" Some said, "It is," but others said, "No, he just looks like him." He said, "I am." [So they said to him, "How were your eyes opened?" He replied, "The man called Jesus made clay and anointed my eyes and told me, 'Go to Siloam and wash.' So I went there and washed and was able to see." And they said to him, "Where is he?" He said, "I don't know."]

They brought the one who was once blind to the Pharisees. Now Jesus had made clay and opened his eyes on a sabbath. So then the Pharisees also asked him how he was able to see. He said to them, "He put clay on my eyes, and I washed, and now I can see." So some of the Pharisees said, "This man is not from God, because he does not keep the sabbath." But others said, "How can a sinful man do such signs?" And there was a division among them. So they said to the blind man again, "What do you have to say about him, since he opened your eyes?" He said, "He is a prophet."

[Now the Jews did not believe that he had been blind and gained his sight until they summoned the parents of the one who had gained his sight. They asked them, "Is this your son, who you say was born blind? How does he now see?" His parents answered and said, "We know that this is our son and that he was born blind. We do not know how he sees now, nor do we know who opened his eyes. Ask him, he is of age; he can speak for himself." His parents said this because they were afraid of the Jews, for the Jews had already agreed that if anyone acknowledged him as the Christ, he would be expelled from the synagogue. For this reason his parents said, "He is of age; question him."

So a second time they called the man who had been blind and said to him, "Give God the praise! We know that this man is a sinner." He replied, "If he is a sinner, I do not know. One thing I do know is that I was blind and now I see." So they said to him, "What did he do to you? How did he open your eyes?" He answered them, "I told you already and you did not listen. Why do you want to hear it again? Do you want to become his disciples, too?" They ridiculed him and said, "You are that man's disciple; we are disciples of Moses! We know that God spoke to Moses, but we do not know where this one is from." The man answered and said to them, "This is what is so amazing, that you do not know where he is from, yet he opened my eyes. We know that God does not listen to sinners, but if one is devout and does his will, he listens to him. It is unheard of that anyone ever opened the eyes of a person born blind. If this man were not from God, he would not be able to do anything."] They answered and said to him, "You were born totally in sin, and are you trying to teach us?" Then they threw him out.

When Jesus heard that they had thrown him out, he found him and said, "Do you believe in the Son of Man?" He answered and said, "Who is he, sir, that I may believe in him?" Jesus said to him, "You have seen him, the one speaking with you is he." He said, "I do believe, Lord," and he worshiped him. [Then Jesus said, "I came into this world for judgment, so that those who do not see might see, and those who do see might become blind."

Some of the Pharisees who were with him heard this and said to him, "Surely we are not also blind, are we?" Jesus said to them, "If you were blind, you would have no sin; but now you are saying, 'We see,' so your sin remains."]

❖ *Understanding the Word*

Prior to our first reading, Saul had been anointed king at the behest of the people (1 Samuel 8:5), but he fails carry out God's commands (1 Samuel 15:11), and God rejects him as king (1 Samuel 16:1). Instead the prophet Samuel is sent to a family in Bethlehem to anoint a new king from among the sons of Jesse. The motif of younger son surpassing the elder (Genesis 4:2–5, 21:9–13; 27:28–40; 37:3–11; 49:3–4, 22–26) plays out in this narrative as well. The last and youngest son, who is not even named until the end, proves to be the chosen one of God. For not as humanity sees does God see, for God "looks into the heart" (1 Samuel 16:7).

The second reading from Ephesians uses the metaphor of light and darkness as a measurement of righteousness. Prior to their belief in Christ, the Ephesians dwelt in darkness (Ephesians 5:8), likely referring to their Gentile and polytheistic practices (Ephesians 5:12). But now they are to live as children of the light, producing goodness, righteousness, and truth (Ephesians 5:8–9). The passage concludes with a stanza from an early Christian hymn, "Awake, O sleeper, and arise from the dead, and Christ will give you light" (Ephesians 5:14).

The Gospel reading describes an encounter between Jesus, a blind man, and the Pharisees, which culminates in the answer to the disciples' question, "Who sinned?" In the ancient world, sickness was believed to be the manifestation of sin. In the case of the man born blind, the likely culprits would be the man's parents (John 9:2). But Jesus counters that not all sickness derives from sin, and in fact in this case, the man's blindness will lead not only to physical sight but spiritual vision as well (John 9:3). As the narrative continues, it becomes apparent that the man "sees" Jesus as a prophet (John 9:17) and recognizes him as a man from God (John 9:33), while the Pharisees remain blinded by their failure to recognize Jesus' true identity. "If you were blind, you would have no sin, but now you are saying, 'We see,' so your sin remains" (John 9:41). The disciples' question is answered. The sin of the Pharisees remains because they are confident in their own righteousness.

❖ Reflecting on the Word

How is your sight? As I get older, my eyesight depends upon the assistance of glasses. But my insight is clearer, more open to seeing beyond the surface in situations, events, or persons before making a judgment. Lent sharpens our vision by inviting us to look into the heart and see as God sees.

Jesus saw more than the surface in the man born blind. Jesus sees both a person and an opportunity to make the works of God visible through him. Ordinary clay, saliva, and washing heal the man's physical blindness. His openness frees him to do as Jesus asked and so he gains physical sight. As the story unfolds, he also gains insight into who Jesus is: naming him prophet, from God, and Son of Man. He also gains the courage to speak truth to the Pharisees, blinded by seeing only what they wanted to see. By their refusal to look into the heart and really see Jesus and the healed blind man, they choose sin. To sin one must know that something is wrong and choose to do it.

Our union with Christ gives us light to distinguish truth from falsehood, right from wrong, light from darkness. His light helps us see beyond mere appearance and preconceptions into the heart. Are we willing to see as God sees? Or does fear of rejection or change keep us blind, like the man's parents and the Pharisees? When we look into the heart, we see others and ourselves as God does, people of light and darkness, whose darkness, when named, can be healed. Turn to the light and ask the Divine Physician to open your eyes.

- When has blindness kept you in the dark and unable to see the works of God?
- When has bringing your sin or doubt to light freed you to experience God's incredible love?

❖❖ *Living and Praying with the Word*

Jesus, who heals all ills, open my eyes to see as you see. Fill me with your light so that I choose to see your goodness in others, the world, and myself. Heal the self-righteousness that keeps me blind.

April 2, 2017

FIFTH SUNDAY OF LENT

Today's Focus: That Stinks

Jesus is warned today that the tomb of Lazarus will have a stench. But Jesus has faced the stench of evil, sin, and death before—and has overcome it.

FIRST READING
Ezekiel 37: 12–14

Thus says the LORD GOD: O my people, I will open your graves and have you rise from them, and bring you back to the land of Israel. Then you shall know that I am the LORD, when I open your graves and have you rise from them, O my people! I will put my spirit in you that you may live, and I will settle you upon your land; thus you shall know that I am the LORD. I have promised, and I will do it, says the LORD.

PSALM RESPONSE
Psalm 130:7

With the Lord there is mercy and fullness of redemption.

SECOND READING
Romans 8:8–11

Brothers and sisters: Those who are in the flesh cannot please God. But you are not in the flesh; on the contrary, you are in the spirit, if only the Spirit of God dwells in you. Whoever does not have the Spirit of Christ does not belong to him. But if Christ is in you, although the body is dead because of sin, the spirit is alive because of righteousness. If the Spirit of the one who raised Jesus from the dead dwells in you, the one who raised Christ from the dead will give life to your mortal bodies also, through his Spirit dwelling in you.

GOSPEL
John 11:1–45 or 11: 3–7, 17, 20–27, 33b–45

In the shorter form of the reading, the passages in brackets are omitted.

[Now a man was ill, Lazarus from Bethany, the village of Mary and her sister Martha. Mary was the one who had anointed the Lord with perfumed oil and dried his feet with her hair; it was her brother Lazarus who was ill.] So the sisters sent word to Jesus saying, "Master, the one you love is ill." When Jesus heard this he said, "This illness is not to end in death, but is for the glory of God, that the Son of God may be glorified through it." Now Jesus loved Martha and her sister and Lazarus. So when he heard that he was ill, he remained for two days in the place where he was. Then after this he said to his disciples, "Let us go back to Judea." [The disciples said to him, "Rabbi, the Jews were just trying to stone you, and you want to go back there?" Jesus answered, "Are there not twelve hours in a day? If one walks during the day, he does not stumble, because he sees the light of this world. But if one walks at night, he stumbles, because the light is not in him." He said this, and then told them, "Our friend Lazarus is asleep, but I am going to awaken him." So the disciples said

82

to him, "Master, if he is asleep, he will be saved." But Jesus was talking about his death, while they thought that he meant ordinary sleep. So then Jesus said to them clearly, "Lazarus has died. And I am glad for you that I was not there, that you may believe. Let us go to him." So Thomas, called Didymus, said to his fellow disciples, "Let us also go to die with him."]

When Jesus arrived, he found that Lazarus had already been in the tomb for four days. [Now Bethany was near Jerusalem, only about two miles away. And many of the Jews had come to Martha and Mary to comfort them about their brother.] When Martha heard that Jesus was coming, she went to meet him; but Mary sat at home. Martha said to Jesus, "Lord, if you had been here, my brother would not have died. But even now I know that whatever you ask of God, God will give you." Jesus said to her, "Your brother will rise." Martha said to him, "I know he will rise, in the resurrection on the last day." Jesus told her, "I am the resurrection and the life; whoever believes in me, even if he dies, will live, and everyone who lives and believes in me will never die. Do you believe this?" She said to him, "Yes, Lord. I have come to believe that you are the Christ, the Son of God, the one who is coming into the world."

[When she had said this, she went and called her sister Mary secretly, saying, "The teacher is here and is asking for you." As soon as she heard this, she rose quickly and went to him. For Jesus had not yet come into the village, but was still where Martha had met him. So when the Jews who were with her in the house comforting her saw Mary get up quickly and go out, they followed her, presuming that she was going to the tomb to weep there. When Mary came to where Jesus was and saw him, she fell at his feet and said to him, "Lord, if you had been here, my brother would not have died." When Jesus saw her weeping and the Jews who had come with her weeping,] he became perturbed and deeply troubled, and said, "Where have you laid him?" They said to him, "Sir, come and see." And Jesus wept. So the Jews said, "See how he loved him." But some of them said, "Could not the one who opened the eyes of the blind man have done something so that this man would not have died?"

So Jesus, perturbed again, came to the tomb. It was a cave, and a stone lay across it. Jesus said, "Take away the stone." Martha, the dead man's sister, said to him, "Lord, by now there will be a stench; he has been dead for four days." Jesus said to her, "Did I not tell you that if you believe you will see the glory of God?" So they took away the stone. And Jesus raised his eyes and said, "Father, I thank you for hearing me. I know that you always hear me; but because of the crowd here I have said this, that they may believe that you sent me." And when he had said this, he cried out in a loud voice, "Lazarus, come out!" The dead man came out, tied hand and foot with burial bands, and his face was wrapped in a cloth. So Jesus said to them, "Untie him and let him go."

Now many of the Jews who had come to Mary and seen what he had done began to believe in him.

In a vision, Ezekiel is brought to a valley of dry bones (Ezekiel 37:1). He is told to prophesy over the bones and to announce that they will be revivified. God speaks through the prophet to the people in exile, promising to open their graves and bring them back to the land of Israel (Ezekiel 37:12). The graves are a metaphor for their state of exile. Their process of returning to the land will bring them new life, and thus they will know that God fulfills promises (Ezekiel 37:14).

Much of Paul's argument centers on dualities: flesh and spirit, law and Christ, sin and salvation. In the passage prior to today's reading, Paul had reminded the Roman believers that they had been freed from sin, becoming instead slaves of God. Through this new state, they received sanctification and eternal life (Romans 6:22). In Romans 8, the believers are cautioned, "Those who are in the flesh cannot please God" (Romans 8:8). Rather, they are to live as people imbued with the Spirit of God. The frequency of Paul's admonition to live in the spirit testifies to the ongoing struggle of the faithful to negotiate being in the world, but not of it (Romans 12:2). But the hardship is worth it, for "the one who raised Christ from the dead will give life to our mortal bodies also" (Romans 8:11).

The first eleven chapters of the Gospel of John are called the Book of Signs, because they describe seven miraculous events that point to the true identity of Jesus: first sign, John 2:1–11 (wine at Cana); second sign, John 4:46–53 (official's son restored to life); third sign, John 5:1–9 (healing of the crippled man); fourth sign, John 6:1–15 (feeding of the multitude); fifth sign, John 6:16–21 (Jesus walking on the water); sixth sign, John 9:1–12 (healing of the man born blind); and seventh sign, John 11:1–14 (Lazarus raised from death). In the final sign, Jesus reveals himself fully when he testifies to Martha, "I am the resurrection and the life, whoever believes in me, even if he dies, will live" (John 11:25). The raising of Lazarus from the dead also serves to foreshadow Jesus' own resurrection (John 20).

❖❖ *Reflecting on the Word*

My mother died when I was thirteen. I prayed for Jesus to come and raise her from the dead, like Lazarus. At the same time I believed that she was with him and free from the pain and suffering that she experienced before her death. Life and death are intimately connected. Often to find life we must name and face whatever is death-dealing in our lives.

"I will open your graves and have you rise from them" (Ezekiel 37:12). "I will put my spirit in you that you may live" (Ezekiel 37:14a). These words both comfort and challenge. To experience new life we have to do what Jesus did, go to the tomb and face the stench of whatever is deadly for us. By facing our darkness, sin, and death we can find light, forgiveness, and life. When we are willing to name and claim these realities, we invite Jesus to come and say, "Come out!" and go free. It takes a willingness to reorient our lives to the Spirit of God who dwells in us. The first step is honesty about our fears, frustrations, and faith like Mary and Martha, and a willingness to be misunderstood as Jesus was when he wept. When we can be vulnerable and honest about the darkness and sin in our lives, Jesus shows us a way to freedom and fullness of life. His Spirit works within us and in the community, who must be willing to see us differently, to untie us and let us become new.

We need not say, "Lord, if you had been here," like Mary and Martha. He is here. He comes to us in prayer, word, sacrament, and his living body. He says to us, "(Your name), come out and be free!"

✤ Consider/Discuss

- When has being brutally honest with God and another human being helped you find healing and forgiveness?
- What darkness or sin keeps you from the love and life God promises us?

✤ Living and Praying with the Word

With Jesus, we pray, "Father, I thank you for hearing me." Help us go to the tombs in our lives so your Spirit can open our graves and raise us from them.

It's Time to Order
Living the Word 2018: Year B

By now you have discovered what a prayerful and valuable scriptural resource *Living the Word* provides for you each Sunday of the year.

Don't miss a single week! Subscribe to *Living the Word 2018* today for yourself, your staff, parishioners, family, and friends, and share the gift of God's Word.

Order now to receive the same low price as 2017:

100 or more copies	$6.95 each
25–99 copies	$8.95 each
10–24 copies	$9.95 each
2–9 copies	$10.95 each
Single copies..	$14.95

MAKE A COPY OF THIS ORDER FORM AND FAX IT TODAY TO 888-957-3291 OR SCAN AND SEND TO WLPCS@JSPALUCH.COM.
(This will keep your current book intact!)

OR, CALL WLP CUSTOMER CARE AT 800-566-6150 TO PLACE YOUR ORDER.

[ ] Yes, I'd like to order *Living the Word 2018: Year B*. Please send me _____ copies at _____ each, plus shipping, handling and any applicable sales tax.

NAME _____ POSITION _____

PARISH/INSTITUTION_____

ADDRESS _____

CITY _____ STATE _____ ZIP _____

PHONE _____ FAX_____ E-MAIL_____

Please keep a copy of your order for reference.

Living the Word 2018 will be shipped and billed after October 1, 2017.

Add $7.95 for orders up to $20.00. Add 16% of total for orders over $20.00. Payment in U.S. currency only. No cash or stamps, please. Make checks payable to World Library Publications. Prices subject to change without notice.
Applicable sales tax will be added to orders based on individual state tax requirements.

World Library Publications
the music and liturgy division of J.S.Paluch Company, Inc.

3708 River Road, Suite 400 • Franklin Park, IL 60131-2158
800-566-6150 • wlpcs@jspaluch.com • wlpmusic.com

LTWB18

April 9, 2017

PALM SUNDAY OF THE PASSION OF THE LORD

Today's Focus: Emptied of Self, Filled with God

The death of Jesus on the cross was not merely a dutiful Son fulfilling his role. It was a total self-emptying, self-surrender, self-giving sacrifice that led him, and leads us, to resurrected life.

FIRST READING
Isaiah 50:4–7

The Lord God has given me
    a well-trained tongue,
that I might know how to speak to the weary
    a word that will rouse them.
Morning after morning
    he opens my ear that I may hear;
and I have not rebelled,
    have not turned back.
I gave my back to those who beat me,
    my cheeks to those who plucked my beard;
my face I did not shield
    from buffets and spitting.

The Lord God is my help,
    therefore I am not disgraced;
I have set my face like flint,
    knowing that I shall not be put to shame.

PSALM RESPONSE
Psalm 22:2a

My God, my God, why have you abandoned me?

SECOND READING
Philippians 2: 6–11

Christ Jesus, though he was in the form of God,
        did not regard equality with God
        something to be grasped.
Rather, he emptied himself,
        taking the form of a slave,
        coming in human likeness;
        and found human in appearance,
        he humbled himself,
        becoming obedient to the point of death,
        even death on a cross.
Because of this, God greatly exalted him
        and bestowed on him the name
        which is above every name,
        that at the name of Jesus
        every knee should bend,
        of those in heaven and on earth and under the earth,
        and every tongue confess that
        Jesus Christ is Lord,
        to the glory of God the Father.

87

In the shorter form of the Passion, the passages in brackets are omitted.

GOSPEL
Matthew
26:14 — 27:66
or 27:11–54

[One of the Twelve, who was called Judas Iscariot, went to the chief priests and said, "What are you willing to give me if I hand him over to you?" They paid him thirty pieces of silver, and from that time on he looked for an opportunity to hand him over.

On the first day of the Feast of Unleavened Bread, the disciples approached Jesus and said, "Where do you want us to prepare for you to eat the Passover?" He said, "Go into the city to a certain man and tell him, 'The teacher says, "My appointed time draws near; in your house I shall celebrate the Passover with my disciples." ' " The disciples then did as Jesus had ordered, and prepared the Passover.

When it was evening, he reclined at table with the Twelve. And while they were eating, he said, "Amen, I say to you, one of you will betray me." Deeply distressed at this, they began to say to him one after another, "Surely it is not I, Lord?" He said in reply, "He who has dipped his hand into the dish with me is the one who will betray me. The Son of Man indeed goes, as it is written of him, but woe to that man by whom the Son of Man is betrayed. It would be better for that man if he had never been born." Then Judas, his betrayer, said in reply, "Surely it is not I, Rabbi?" He answered, "You have said so."

While they were eating, Jesus took bread, said the blessing, broke it, and giving it to his disciples said, "Take and eat; this is my body." Then he took a cup, gave thanks, and gave it to them, saying, "Drink from it, all of you, for this is my blood of the covenant, which will be shed on behalf of many for the forgiveness of sins. I tell you, from now on I shall not drink this fruit of the vine until the day when I drink it with you new in the kingdom of my Father." Then, after singing a hymn, they went out to the Mount of Olives.

Then Jesus said to them, "This night all of you will have your faith in me shaken, for it is written:
  I will strike the shepherd,
    and the sheep of the flock will be dispersed;
but after I have been raised up, I shall go before you to Galilee." Peter said to him in reply, "Though all may have their faith in you shaken, mine will never be." Jesus said to him, "Amen, I say to you, this very night before the cock crows, you will deny me three times." Peter said to him, "Even though I should have to die with you, I will not deny you." And all the disciples spoke likewise.

Then Jesus came with them to a place called Gethsemane, and he said to his disciples, "Sit here while I go over there and pray." He took along Peter and the two sons of Zebedee, and began to feel sorrow and distress. Then he said to them, "My soul is sorrowful even to death. Remain here and keep watch with me." He advanced a little and fell prostrate in prayer, saying, "My Father, if it is possible, let this cup pass from me; yet, not as I will, but as you will." When he returned to his disciples he found them asleep. He said to Peter, "So you could not keep watch with me for one hour? Watch and pray that you may not undergo the test. The spirit is willing, but the flesh is weak." Withdrawing a second time, he prayed again, "My Father, if it is not possible that this cup pass without my drinking it, your will be done!" Then he returned once more and found them asleep, for they could not keep their eyes open. He left them and withdrew again and prayed a third time, saying the same thing again. Then he returned to his disciples and said to them, "Are you still sleeping and taking your rest? Behold, the hour is at hand when the Son of Man is to be handed over to sinners. Get up, let us go. Look, my betrayer is at hand."

While he was still speaking, Judas, one of the Twelve, arrived, accompanied by a large crowd, with swords and clubs, who had come from the chief priests and the elders of the people. His betrayer had arranged a sign with them, saying, "The man I shall kiss is the one; arrest him." Immediately he went over to Jesus and said, "Hail, Rabbi!" and he kissed him. Jesus answered him, "Friend, do what you have come for." Then stepping forward they laid hands on Jesus and arrested him. And behold, one of those who accompanied Jesus put his hand to his sword, drew it, and struck the high priest's servant, cutting off his ear. Then Jesus said to him, "Put your sword back into its sheath, for all who take the sword will perish by the sword. Do you think that I cannot call upon my Father and he will not provide me at this moment with more than twelve legions of angels? But then how would the Scriptures be fulfilled which say that it must come to pass in this way?" At that hour Jesus said to the crowds, "Have you come out as against a robber, with swords and clubs to seize me? Day after day I sat teaching in the temple area, yet you did not arrest me. But all this has come to pass that the writings of the prophets may be fulfilled." Then all the disciples left him and fled.

Those who had arrested Jesus led him away to Caiaphas the high priest, where the scribes and the elders were assembled. Peter was following him at a distance as far as the high priest's courtyard, and going inside he sat down with the servants to see the outcome. The chief priests and the entire Sanhedrin kept trying to obtain false testimony against Jesus in order to put him to death, but they found none, though many false witnesses came forward. Finally two came forward who stated, "This man said, 'I can destroy the temple of God and within three days rebuild it.'" The high priest rose and addressed him, "Have you no answer? What are these men testifying against you?" But Jesus was silent. Then the high priest said to him, "I order you to tell us under oath before the living God whether you are the Christ, the Son of God." Jesus said to him in reply, "You have said so. But I tell you:

From now on you will see 'the Son of Man
  seated at the right hand of the Power'
  and 'coming on the clouds of heaven.'"

Then the high priest tore his robes and said, "He has blasphemed! What further need have we of witnesses? You have now heard the blasphemy; what is your opinion?" They said in reply, "He deserves to die!" Then they spat in his face and struck him, while some slapped him, saying, "Prophesy for us, Christ: who is it that struck you?"

Now Peter was sitting outside in the courtyard. One of the maids came over to him and said, "You too were with Jesus the Galilean." But he denied it in front of everyone, saying, "I do not know what you are talking about!" As he went out to the gate, another girl saw him and said to those who were there, "This man was with Jesus the Nazarene." Again he denied it with an oath, "I do not know the man!" A little later the bystanders came over and said to Peter, "Surely you too are one of them; even your speech gives you away." At that he began to curse and to swear, "I do not know the man." And immediately a cock crowed. Then Peter remembered the word that Jesus had spoken: "Before the cock crows you will deny me three times." He went out and began to weep bitterly.

When it was morning, all the chief priests and the elders of the people took counsel against Jesus to put him to death. They bound him, led him away, and handed him over to Pilate, the governor.

Then Judas, his betrayer, seeing that Jesus had been condemned, deeply regretted what he had done. He returned the thirty pieces of silver to the chief priests and elders, saying, "I have sinned in betraying innocent blood." They said, "What is that to us? Look to it yourself." Flinging the money into the temple, he departed and went off and hanged himself. The chief priests gathered up the money, but said, "It is not lawful to deposit this in the temple treasury, for it is the price of blood." After consultation, they used it to buy the potter's field as a burial place for foreigners. That is why that field even today is called the Field of Blood. Then was fulfilled what had been said through Jeremiah the prophet,

And they took the thirty pieces of silver,
the value of a man with a price on his head,
a price set by some of the Israelites,
and they paid it out for the potter's field
just as the Lord had commanded me.

Now] Jesus stood before the governor, who questioned him, "Are you the king of the Jews?" Jesus said, "You say so." And when he was accused by the chief priests and elders, he made no answer. Then Pilate said to him, "Do you not hear how many things they are testifying against you?" But he did not answer him one word, so that the governor was greatly amazed.

Now on the occasion of the feast the governor was accustomed to release to the crowd one prisoner whom they wished. And at that time they had a notorious prisoner called Barabbas. So when they had assembled, Pilate said to them, "Which one do you want me to release to you, Barabbas, or Jesus called Christ?" For he knew that it was out of envy that they had handed him over. While he was still seated on the bench, his wife sent him a message, "Have nothing to do with that righteous man. I suffered much in a dream today because of him." The chief priests and the elders persuaded the crowds to ask for Barabbas but to destroy Jesus. The governor said to them in reply, "Which of the two do you want me to release to you?" They answered, "Barabbas!" Pilate said to them, "Then what shall I do with Jesus called Christ?" They all said, "Let him be crucified!" But he said, "Why? What evil has he done?" They only shouted the louder, "Let him be crucified!" When Pilate saw that he was not succeeding at all, but that a riot was breaking out instead, he took water and washed his hands in the sight of the crowd, saying, "I am innocent of this man's blood. Look to it yourselves." And the whole people said in reply, "His blood be upon us and upon our children." Then he released Barabbas to them, but after he had Jesus scourged, he handed him over to be crucified.

Then the soldiers of the governor took Jesus inside the praetorium and gathered the whole cohort around him. They stripped off his clothes and threw a scarlet military cloak about him. Weaving a crown out of thorns, they placed it on his head, and a reed in his right hand. And kneeling before him, they mocked him, saying, "Hail, King of the Jews!" They spat upon him and took the reed and kept striking him on the head. And when they had mocked him, they stripped him of the cloak, dressed him in his own clothes, and led him off to crucify him.

As they were going out, they met a Cyrenian named Simon; this man they pressed into service to carry his cross.

And when they came to a place called Golgotha—which means Place of the Skull , they gave Jesus wine to drink mixed with gall. But when he had tasted it, he refused to drink. After they had crucified him, they divided his garments by casting lots; then they sat down and kept watch over him there. And they placed over his head the written charge against him: This is Jesus, the King of the Jews. Two revolutionaries were crucified with him, one on his right and the other on his left. Those passing by reviled him, shaking their heads and saying, "You who would destroy the temple and rebuild it in three days, save yourself, if you are the Son of God, and come down from the cross!" Likewise the chief priests with the scribes and elders mocked him and said, "He saved others; he cannot save himself. So he is the king of Israel! Let him come down from the cross now, and we will believe in him. He trusted in God; let him deliver him now if he wants him. For he said, 'I am the Son of God.' " The revolutionaries who were crucified with him also kept abusing him in the same way.

From noon onward, darkness came over the whole land until three in the afternoon. And about three o'clock Jesus cried out in a loud voice, "Eli, Eli, *lema sabachthani*?" which means, "My God, my God, why have you forsaken me?" Some of the bystanders who heard it said, "This one is calling for Elijah." Immediately one of them ran to get a sponge; he soaked it in wine, and putting it on a reed, gave it to him to drink. But the rest said, "Wait, let us see if Elijah comes to save him." But Jesus cried out again in a loud voice, and gave up his spirit.

And behold, the veil of the sanctuary was torn in two from top to bottom. The earth quaked, rocks were split, tombs were opened, and the bodies of many saints who had fallen asleep were raised. And coming forth from their tombs after his resurrection, they entered the holy city and appeared to many. The centurion and the men with him who were keeping watch over Jesus feared greatly when they saw the earthquake and all that was happening, and they said, "Truly, this was the Son of God!" [There were many women there, looking on from a distance, who had followed Jesus from Galilee, ministering to him. Among them were Mary Magdalene and Mary the mother of James and Joseph, and the mother of the sons of Zebedee.

When it was evening, there came a rich man from Arimathea named Joseph, who was himself a disciple of Jesus. He went to Pilate and asked for the body of Jesus; then Pilate ordered it to be handed over. Taking the body, Joseph wrapped it in clean linen and laid it in his new tomb that he had hewn in the rock. Then he rolled a huge stone across the entrance to the tomb and departed. But Mary Magdalene and the other Mary remained sitting there, facing the tomb. The next day, the one following the day of preparation, the chief priests and the Pharisees gathered before Pilate and said, "Sir, we remember that this impostor while still alive said, 'After three days I will be raised up.' Give orders, then, that the grave be secured until the third day, lest his disciples come and steal him and say to the people, 'He has been raised from the dead.' This last imposture would be worse than the first." Pilate said to them, "The guard is yours; go, secure it as best you can." So they went and secured the tomb by fixing a seal to the stone and setting the guard.]

❖ Understanding the Word

Today's first reading is the third of four Servant of the Lord songs found in Isaiah. With each oracle, the personal costs increase until in Isaiah 52:13 — 53:12, the servant is killed and "a grave assigned him among the wicked" (Isaiah 53:9), a reading we hear on Good Friday. In this third song, the Servant speaks in the first person, accepting his vocation, even though he is abused and insulted. To pluck another's beard was a grave insult in the ancient world. Despite the abuse, the prophet is undeterred: "I have sent my face like flint, knowing that I shall not be put to shame" (Isaiah 50:7).

The hymn from Philippians, from which our second reading is taken, describes the humiliation and exaltation of Christ, reminiscent of the sufferings heaped upon the Servant of the Lord in Isaiah. The hymn acknowledges Christ's preexistence, which makes his willingness to take on the form a slave even more dramatic. His humiliation and obedience lead to his death, which is ultimately God's triumph, since Christ is then exalted. Paul prefaces the ancient hymn with verse 2 that centers on love: "Complete my joy by being of the same mind, with the same love, united in heart, thinking one thing." Christ's self-emptying becomes the ultimate example of that love.

The triumphal entry into Jerusalem that begins today's liturgy little prepares us for our Gospel, which is the Passion of Jesus according to Matthew. Throughout this Gospel, Jesus has lived under the threat of death. Joseph takes his family to safety, just as Herod unleashes his slaughter on the innocents (Matthew 2:13), and relocates to Nazareth to avoid Herod's son (Matthew 2:22). During Jesus' final days in Jerusalem, the chief priests and elders consult together in order to plan Jesus' death (Matthew 26:3–4). Matthew follows Mark's arrangement with some notable additions, including the regret of Judas (Matthew 27:3–10) and the prophetic dream of Pilate's wife (Matthew 27:19). At the Last Supper, Matthew inserts that the cup is the blood of the covenant, shed on behalf of many for the forgiveness of sins (Matthew 26:28). He also adds the earthquake, often a symbol of God's coming. The apocalyptic beginning of the final age is evidenced by the opening of tombs and the raising of the dead saints, who then enter into the holy city after Jesus' resurrection (Matthew 27:53).

❖ Reflecting on the Word

Every year the Passion account invites me to reflect on the words and what they reveal about the various characters. There are words of faith and surrender, "not as I will, but as you will;" remorse, "I have sinned in betraying innocent blood;" confidence, "Though all may have their faith in you shaken, mine will never be;" taunt and accusation, "Let him be crucified;" choice, "Let his blood be upon us and on our children;" seeming authority, "I order you;" fear, "Have nothing to do with that man;" denial, "I do not know him;" teaching, "all who take the sword will perish by the sword;" and love, "I shall not drink this fruit of the vine until the day when I drink it with you new."

Words can build up or tear down. They speak truth or falsehood. They reveal faith and fear. Words are powerful, which is why St. Francis de Sales cautions that they are to be used like the scalpel in the hands of a surgeon, cutting away only what is necessary and not so much as to result in unnecessary harm. He cautions us to speak little, well, gently, charitably, and amiably. Even when speaking a difficult truth, we can do so with love.

As we enter into Holy Week, we would do well to reflect on what our words say about us. Do they reveal love, life, truth, trust, and submission to the will of God, or hate, death, falsehood, fear, and submission to our will alone? Often mine reveal a mix of both. May we be like Jesus, who emptied himself and took on all our limitations with the exception of sin, even death, so that we can be servants with well-trained tongues that reveal our willingness to speak truth, wherever that might lead.

❖ Consider/Discuss

- How would you have responded in the various situations described in the Passion?
- What does your use of words reveal about your faith in Jesus and your willingness to do God's will?

❖ Living and Praying with the Word

Lord God, be my help. Remain close to me and fill me with your Spirit, so that all I say and do will confess that Jesus Christ is Lord, to your glory and praise.

During the Easter season, all our readings are taken from the New Testament. Rather than hearing of the promises of old, we learn how the promise has been fulfilled and the new community of believers is living in light of the Resurrection. Acts of the Apostles, from which our first readings are taken, is a narrative of the spread of the faith from Jerusalem to Judea and Samaria and finally toward the ends of the earth (Acts 1:8). The Easter Sunday reading from Acts 10 is part of a lengthy speech given by Peter in the house of the Gentile centurion Cornelius. Peter presents a summary of the gospel so that the Gentile audience might know more fully what Peter is preaching. Peter will also give a similar speech to a Jewish audience (Third Sunday). The portrait Luke paints of the early church is one of harmony in both prayer and communal life (Second Sunday). But as we quickly learn, not all was as rosy as first presented. The Greek-speaking Jews (Hellenists, from *hellas* or Greek) complained that the Jews of Palestine, who spoke Aramaic, were not caring for the Hellenist widows (Fifth Sunday). To answer the growing need, the apostles select assistants to serve the community. One such diaconal servant is Philip, who travels to Samaria to proclaim the Good News (Sixth Sunday). The following week, we are reminded of the apostles and disciples who accompanied Jesus in Galilee (Seventh Sunday). It is to these that Jesus sends his Spirit with gifts to empower the community of disciples to continue his mission (Pentecost).

Many of the readings for the second reading during the Easter season are taken from First Peter, a late first-century work written in the name of the Apostle Peter. Though utilizing a letter format, the work is likely a baptismal sermon. The language of new birth, infancy, and baptism is found throughout. For example, "new birth to a living hope" (1 Peter 1:3), being "born anew" (1 Peter 1:23), the description of newborn infants seeking spiritual milk (1 Peter 2:2), and "baptism" (1 Peter 3:21). The use of Peter's name may indicate that the letter originated in the Petrine circle of Rome and was meant to encourage the believers in Asia Minor, who seem to be undergoing suffering (1 Peter 1:6; 3:14; 4:1, 12; 5:8).

With the exception of the Third Sunday, the Gospel readings are taken from John, a late first-century text that uses a different framework and unique metaphors to describe the life of Jesus. The empty tomb is discovered not by a group of women, but by one woman, Mary of Magdala. Jesus himself is present in the upper room and breathes his Spirit upon all gathered (Second Sunday, Pentecost). The Johannine disciples are told that Jesus is both good shepherd and gate to the sheepfold (Fourth Sunday), and when he departs, he does so to prepare a dwelling place for his disciples (Fifth Sunday). Dwelling with Jesus requires that his disciples keep his commandments (Sixth Sunday), and in so doing they too will be one with the Father (Seventh Sunday).

April 16, 2017

EASTER SUNDAY

Today's Focus: Being an Easter Witness

The Easter scriptures give us many role models to be people who give witness to the Resurrection. We must overcome fear and boldly speak what we have come to know through faith.

FIRST READING
Acts 10:34a, 37–43

Peter proceeded to speak and said: "You know what has happened all over Judea, beginning in Galilee after the baptism that John preached, how God anointed Jesus of Nazareth with the Holy Spirit and power. He went about doing good and healing all those oppressed by the devil, for God was with him. We are witnesses of all that he did both in the country of the Jews and in Jerusalem. They put him to death by hanging him on a tree. This man God raised on the third day and granted that he be visible, not to all the people, but to us, the witnesses chosen by God in advance, who ate and drank with him after he rose from the dead. He commissioned us to preach to the people and testify that he is the one appointed by God as judge of the living and the dead. To him all the prophets bear witness, that everyone who believes in him will receive forgiveness of sins through his name.

PSALM RESPONSE
Psalm 118:24

This is the day the Lord has made; let us rejoice and be glad.

SECOND READING
Colossians 3: 1–4

Brothers and sisters: If then you were raised with Christ, seek what is above, where Christ is seated at the right hand of God. Think of what is above, not of what is on earth. For you have died, and your life is hidden with Christ in God. When Christ your life appears, then you too will appear with him in glory.

– or –

1 Corinthians 5: 6b–8

Brothers and sisters: Do you not know that a little yeast leavens all the dough? Clear out the old yeast, so that you may become a fresh batch of dough, inasmuch as you are unleavened. For our paschal lamb, Christ, has been sacrificed. Therefore, let us celebrate the feast, not with the old yeast, the yeast of malice and wickedness, but with the unleavened bread of sincerity and truth.

GOSPEL
John 20:1–9

On the first day of the week, Mary of Magdala came to the tomb early in the morning, while it was still dark, and saw the stone removed from the tomb. So she ran and went to Simon Peter and to the other disciple whom Jesus loved, and told them, "They have taken the Lord from the tomb, and we don't know where they put him." So Peter and the other disciple went out and came to the tomb. They both ran, but the other disciple ran faster than Peter and arrived at the tomb first; he bent down and saw the burial cloths there, but did not go in. When Simon Peter arrived after him, he went into the tomb and saw the burial cloths there, and the cloth that had covered his head, not with the burial cloths but rolled up in a separate place. Then the other disciple also went in, the one who had arrived at the tomb first, and he saw and believed. For they did not yet understand the Scripture that he had to rise from the dead.

✤ Understanding the Word

The first reading for Easter Sunday serves as a summary of the Gospel of Luke and a synopsis of the early Christian *kerygma* (proclamation about Jesus). Peter explains to the household of Cornelius the centurion that the faith began after Jesus' baptism by John, when God anointed Jesus of Nazareth with the Holy Spirit. Jesus was able to do good and to heal because of God's abiding presence. Peter and the others witnessed his ministry, his passion, and his resurrection. The resurrected Jesus commissioned Peter to preach, "that everyone who believes in him will receive forgiveness of sins through his name" (Acts 10:43).

Though there are two choices for today's second reading, both Colossians 3:1–4 and 1 Corinthians 5:6b–8 speak to the same theme: the newness that comes with being part of the body of Christ. In Colossians, we are reminded that our focus should be on the things of heaven, since our life is now in Christ and Christ is seated at God's right hand. In First Corinthians, we are to be fresh dough without old yeast. Christ is the Passover who was sacrificed and we are to respond with the bread of sincerity and truth. Both readings stress that new life in Christ requires a new set of behaviors. Malice and wickedness are to be replaced by sincerity and truth.

The Gospel reading describes John's version of the discovery of the empty tomb. Matthew, Mark, and Luke depict Mary of Magdala with several other women going to the tomb at dawn to anoint the body of Jesus. They enter the tomb and find the body missing. Angelic messengers declare that he is not there. But in John, there is no reason for the women to attend to the body after burial, since Nicodemus and Joseph of Arimathea had taken care of the burial customs prior to Jesus' placement in the tomb (John 19:40). Nonetheless, Mary of Magdala goes to the tomb while it is still dark and sees that the stone has been removed. She reports to Peter and the other disciple that Jesus' body is not there. They hasten to the scene and verify her discovery. Since in the Greco-Roman context, only male testimony was considered reliable, at least two male witnesses were needed to corroborate a fact. In our Gospel, the community—represented by Mary and Peter and the beloved disciple—are brought together in their grief and confusion. Very shortly, this same community will come to "understand the Scripture that [Jesus] had to rise from the dead" (John 20:9).

✦ Reflecting on the Word

In the Easter Sequence we sing, "Speak, Mary, declaring what you saw, wayfaring." Speaking what one sees, observes, and hears is a good definition for being a witness. Mary Magdalene was the first witness to the Resurrection, which is why she is called the "Apostle to the Apostles" and is patron of the Order of Preachers (Dominicans). She was the first to preach the Resurrection to the disciples, even though in their culture her witness and preaching needed the confirmation of two men, Peter and the disciple whom Jesus loved.

In the reading from Acts, Peter proclaims that the disciples are to be witnesses. They were "chosen by God in advance, who ate and drank with [Jesus] after he rose from the dead" (Acts 10:41). They were to declare what they saw, observed, and heard during Jesus' life, death, and resurrection appearances. Peter, who denied being part of Jesus' company, became a powerful witness to Jesus.

We are also called to witness our faith in Jesus Christ, since our lives have been hidden with Christ in God through baptism. Our words, deeds, and attitudes of sincerity and truth make Christ's presence known in our world today. Pope Francis said to those gathered at World Youth Day in 2013 that imposing beliefs isn't truly discussing God, but sharing the joy of faith is. When we speak and declare what we have seen, heard, known, and experienced of Jesus Christ, we share the joy of faith and the power of his life, death, and resurrection. Speak! Declare! Witness the power of the gospel!

✦ Consider/Discuss

- How do you witness your faith in Jesus Christ in ordinary ways?
- Whose witness has led you to deeper faith in the power of the Resurrection?

✦ Living and Praying with the Word

All-powerful God, we give thanks for the gift of your Son, Jesus, and the new life you give through his resurrection. Give us the courage of Mary, Peter, and all who have witnessed their faith throughout the ages, so that the world might believe in him.

April 23, 2017

SECOND SUNDAY OF EASTER

Today's Focus: A Matter of Life and Breath

Today the very breath of Jesus bestows the Holy Spirit on the disciples. Like our own breath, the breath of the Spirit is absolutely essential to our ongoing lives as followers of Jesus.

FIRST READING
Acts 2:42–47

They devoted themselves to the teaching of the apostles and to the communal life, to the breaking of bread and to the prayers. Awe came upon everyone, and many wonders and signs were done through the apostles. All who believed were together and had all things in common; they would sell their property and possessions and divide them among all according to each one's need. Every day they devoted themselves to meeting together in the temple area and to breaking bread in their homes. They ate their meals with exultation and sincerity of heart, praising God and enjoying favor with all the people. And every day the Lord added to their number those who were being saved.

PSALM RESPONSE
Psalm 118:1

Give thanks to the Lord for he is good, his love is everlasting.

SECOND READING
1 Peter 1:3–9

Blessed be the God and Father of our Lord Jesus Christ, who in his great mercy gave us a new birth to a living hope through the resurrection of Jesus Christ from the dead, to an inheritance that is imperishable, undefiled, and unfading, kept in heaven for you who by the power of God are safeguarded through faith, to a salvation that is ready to be revealed in the final time. In this you rejoice, although now for a little while you may have to suffer through various trials, so that the genuineness of your faith, more precious than gold that is perishable even though tested by fire, may prove to be for praise, glory, and honor at the revelation of Jesus Christ. Although you have not seen him you love him; even though you do not see him now yet believe in him, you rejoice with an indescribable and glorious joy, as you attain the goal of your faith, the salvation of your souls.

GOSPEL
John 20:19–31 On the evening of that first day of the week, when the doors were locked, where the disciples were, for fear of the Jews, Jesus came and stood in their midst and said to them, "Peace be with you." When he had said this, he showed them his hands and his side. The disciples rejoiced when they saw the Lord. Jesus said to them again, "Peace be with you. As the Father has sent me, so I send you." And when he had said this, he breathed on them and said to them, "Receive the Holy Spirit. Whose sins you forgive are forgiven them, and whose sins you retain are retained."

Thomas, called Didymus, one of the Twelve, was not with them when Jesus came. So the other disciples said to him, "We have seen the Lord." But he said to them, "Unless I see the mark of the nails in his hands and put my finger into the nailmarks and put my hand into his side, I will not believe."

Now a week later his disciples were again inside and Thomas was with them. Jesus came, although the doors were locked, and stood in their midst and said, "Peace be with you." Then he said to Thomas, "Put your finger here and see my hands, and bring your hand and put it into my side, and do not be unbelieving, but believe." Thomas answered and said to him, "My Lord and my God!" Jesus said to him, "Have you come to believe because you have seen me? Blessed are those who have not seen and have believed."

Now, Jesus did many other signs in the presence of his disciples that are not written in this book. But these are written that you may come to believe that Jesus is the Christ, the Son of God, and that through this belief you may have life in his name.

❖❖ Understanding the Word

In today's first reading, the author of Acts of the Apostles paints a utopian picture of the Resurrection community shortly after the experience of Pentecost. This "honeymoon" stage would not last long. In Chapter 5, Ananias and Sapphira skim profits from the sale of their property before giving it to the community, and in Chapter 6, the Greek-speaking Jews complain that the Palestinian Jews are ignoring their widows. Throughout Luke-Acts, the Word is readily accepted but enthusiasm often wanes. The cycle of acceptance and rejection is repeated until the final scene in which Paul is proclaiming in Rome, "Let it be known to you that this salvation of God has been sent to the Gentiles; they will listen" (Acts 28:28).

Writing in the name of the Apostle Peter, the author of today's second reading describes the benefits of belief in a series of metaphors. We have a "new birth" to "a living hope" through Jesus Christ's resurrection (1 Peter 1:3). We are given an imperishable inheritance, stored in heaven and awaiting us (1 Peter 1:4). Our faith is "more precious than gold" that is tested by fire (1 Peter 1:7). The use of concrete metaphors tied to everyday life reaches its pinnacle when First Peter describes believers as a "spiritual household" (1 Peter 2:5) and the "household of God" (4:17). Though utilizing a letter format, the work may actually have been a baptism sermon. The use of various metaphors would help the catechumen understand his or her new reality in Christ.

The Fourth Evangelist seems to have intentionally set up resonances with the creation stories of Genesis. Scholars have long noted the echo of Genesis 1:1 ("In the beginning, when God created the heavens and the earth") found in John 1:1 ("In the beginning was the Word, and the Word was with God"). In today's reading, we find yet another allusion. "The LORD God formed man out of the clay of the ground and blew into his nostrils the breath of life, and so man became a living being" (Genesis 2:7). The resurrected Jesus appears to the disciples, announcing peace and commissioning them. "He breathed on them and said to them, 'Receive the Holy Spirit' " (John 20:22). The divine breath brings forth the new life of creation in Genesis. In John, Jesus' divine breath shares his Spirit with the disciples, who are commissioned to continue Jesus' mission on earth.

✦ *Reflecting on the Word*

I often take the ability to breathe for granted. However, when a medical condition kept my lungs from filling and breathing was difficult, I understood what a gift breathing is. Jesus breathes on the disciples, saying, Receive the Holy Spirit. Forgive. To feel another's breath one must be near the other. Imagine how close Jesus was to the disciples that night. It was absent Thomas' doubt that invited Jesus to ask Thomas to come close enough to touch his hands and side. Like gasping for air gave me a deeper appreciation of the gift of breathing, Thomas' doubt led to a deep profession of faith: "My Lord and my God!"

We have not seen Jesus in the flesh, but we experience his presence at times, and without seeing him we love him and believe. Prayer deepens that love and can nurture and renew faith when we are in doubt. The earliest Christians devoted themselves to the breaking of the bread, prayer, and communal life. In prayer we aspire to God and God inspires or fills us with the breath of God. Celebrating Eucharist, we ask the Spirit to deepen our union with Jesus and each other. When belief or faith are difficult, the community can sustain us like an oxygen mask that helps someone breathe.

Take a deep breath and pray: Fill me with your breath, Lord. Exhale and give God whatever doubt, fear, or resistance lies within you. Breathe in the Spirit of God again. Let Jesus touch your hands, side, and heart to fill you with his everlasting love, even if this is a time of doubt, resistance, and fear for you. Give thanks to the Lord, who is good and who is as near as your very breath.

❖ Consider/Discuss

- When has doubt or resistance become the means through which you knew that Jesus was near?
- How do you pray when you need reassurance that God's presence and power are near?

❖ Living and Praying with the Word

Breathe on me, breath of God. Fill me with your life and your love, Jesus, that I might profess in word and deed that you are surely my Lord and my God!

April 30, 2017

THIRD SUNDAY OF EASTER

Today's Focus: Breaking Bread, Breaking Open Our Lives

The disciples knew Jesus in the breaking of the bread, but first they had to come to know how he had broken open his own life. As we still break bread in his name, so must we break open our lives.

FIRST READING
Acts 2:14, 22–23

Then Peter stood up with the Eleven, raised his voice, and proclaimed: "You who are Jews, indeed all of you staying in Jerusalem. Let this be known to you, and listen to my words. You who are Israelites, hear these words. Jesus the Nazarene was a man commended to you by God with mighty deeds, wonders, and signs, which God worked through him in your midst, as you yourselves know. This man, delivered up by the set plan and foreknowledge of God, you killed, using lawless men to crucify him. But God raised him up, releasing him from the throes of death, because it was impossible for him to be held by it. For David says of him:

I saw the Lord ever before me,
with him at my right hand I shall not be disturbed.
Therefore my heart has been glad and my tongue has exulted;
my flesh, too, will dwell in hope,
because you will not abandon my soul to the netherworld,
nor will you suffer your holy one to see corruption.
You have made known to me the paths of life;
you will fill me with joy in your presence.

"My brothers, one can confidently say to you about the patriarch David that he died and was buried, and his tomb is in our midst to this day. But since he was a prophet and knew that God had sworn an oath to him that he would set one of his descendants upon his throne, he foresaw and spoke of the resurrection of the Christ, that neither was he abandoned to the netherworld nor did his flesh see corruption. God raised this Jesus; of this we are all witnesses. Exalted at the right hand of God, he received the promise of the Holy Spirit from the Father and poured him forth, as you see and hear."

PSALM RESPONSE
Psalm 16:11a

Lord, you will show us the path of life.

Beloved: If you invoke as Father him who judges impartially according to each one's works, conduct yourselves with reverence during the time of your sojourning, realizing that you were ransomed from your futile conduct, handed on by your ancestors, not with perishable things like silver or gold but with the precious blood of Christ as of a spotless unblemished lamb.

He was known before the foundation of the world but revealed in the final time for you, who through him believe in God who raised him from the dead and gave him glory, so that your faith and hope are in God.

GOSPEL
Luke 24:13–35

That very day, the first day of the week, two of Jesus' disciples were going to a village seven miles from Jerusalem called Emmaus, and they were conversing about all the things that had occurred. And it happened that while they were conversing and debating, Jesus himself drew near and walked with them, but their eyes were prevented from recognizing him. He asked them, "What are you discussing as you walk along?" They stopped, looking downcast. One of them, named Cleopas, said to him in reply, "Are you the only visitor to Jerusalem who does not know of the things that have taken place there in these days?" And he replied to them, "What sort of things?" They said to him, "The things that happened to Jesus the Nazarene, who was a prophet mighty in deed and word before God and all the people, how our chief priests and rulers both handed him over to a sentence of death and crucified him. But we were hoping that he would be the one to redeem Israel; and besides all this, it is now the third day since this took place. Some women from our group, however, have astounded us: they were at the tomb early in the morning and did not find his body; they came back and reported that they had indeed seen a vision of angels who announced that he was alive. Then some of those with us went to the tomb and found things just as the women had described, but him they did not see." And he said to them, "Oh, how foolish you are! How slow of heart to believe all that the prophets spoke! Was it not necessary that the Christ should suffer these things and enter into his glory?" Then beginning with Moses and all the prophets, he interpreted to them what referred to him in all the Scriptures. As they approached the village to which they were going, he gave the impression that he was going on farther. But they urged him, "Stay with us, for it is nearly evening and the day is almost over." So he went in to stay with them. And it happened that, while he was with them at table, he took bread, said the blessing, broke it, and gave it to them. With that their eyes were opened and they recognized him, but he vanished from their sight. Then they said to each other, "Were not our hearts burning within us while he spoke to us on the way and opened the Scriptures to us?" So they set out at once and returned to Jerusalem where they found gathered together the eleven and those with them who were saying, "The Lord has truly been raised and has appeared to Simon!" Then the two recounted what had taken place on the way and how he was made known to them in the breaking of bread.

Today's readers need to attend carefully to what our scriptures actually say, for quick and uncritical reading has led to dangerous assumptions. In our first reading, we hear Peter address the gathering of curious Jews who have heard the noise of the Spirit and seen the disciples' behavior. After explaining that Jesus was commended by God, Peter announces, "This man, delivered up by the set plan and foreknowledge of God, you killed, using lawless men to crucify him" (Acts 2:23). Peter isn't accusing his fellow Jews, but narrating the steps of salvation. The death of Jesus was not a random act, but part of the mystery of God's plan that allows for Jesus' resurrection and his now exalted place at God's right hand.

As part of a baptismal sermon, our reading from First Peter addresses the newly baptized, who now "invoke as Father him who judges impartially" (1 Peter 1:17). Though their baptism has initiated them into a new relationship with God, they are now in an estranged relationship with the world. Their "sojourning" indicates that they must conduct themselves by a different standard, since they are called to "be holy because I am holy" (1 Peter 1:16). The perishable treasures of silver and gold did not ransom them into this new life, but "the precious blood of Christ" (1 Peter 1:19).

In order to stress particular themes and to remind his audience of what has transpired, Luke inserts summaries into his two-volume work of Luke-Acts (Luke 4:14–15; 6:17–19; Acts 2:42–47; 4:32–35; 5:12–14). Today's Gospel reading includes one such summary. Two disillusioned disciples leave the city of Jerusalem, presumably traveling home to Emmaus. When they encounter a curious stranger, Cleopas presents a quick summary of not only what happened in Jerusalem but also what led up to those tragic events. "Jesus the Nazarene, who was a prophet mighty in deed and word," was handed over to death and crucified, and now his tomb is empty. The stranger, whom the reader knows is the resurrected Jesus, will now interpret those events as the fulfillment of scripture.

❖ *Reflecting on the Word*

A theology professor noted that today's Gospel about the disciples on the road to Emmaus is one of the best summaries we have about celebrating Eucharist. We bring all that we have and are with us when we come to Mass: the disciples "were conversing about all the things that had occurred." The story of faith is proclaimed in the Liturgy of the Word: they told the "stranger" what had occurred in Jerusalem. The homily interprets life in light of the Word of God, "he interpreted to them what referred to him in all the Scriptures." We become aware of Christ's presence in our midst, "Stay with us." And in the Liturgy of the Eucharist we recognize him in the breaking of bread, sent forth to share our faith, "They set out at once . . . [and] recounted what had taken place." Celebrating word and sacrament transforms us to take Christ to the world and see with new eyes.

In Acts, Peter tells the story of Jesus, the *kerygma*, and connects it with all the scriptures to help his hearers see who Jesus was and to invite their faith in him. In the second reading Peter exhorts his hearers to live differently because of their faith: put your faith and hope in God who judges impartially.

Today we are invited to reflect on our lives in the light of the life, death, and resurrection of Jesus Christ. Where does what we hear and celebrate make our hearts burn? How does celebrating the liturgy help us know Christ's presence as clearly as those disciples did on the road? How do you proclaim the good news of the Gospel in ways that invite others to live differently and come to know Christ in the breaking of our lives?

❖ Consider/Discuss

- When has your celebration of the Eucharist transformed you, as the disciples were on the road to Emmaus?
- Give concrete examples about how you have been a living gospel of Jesus Christ.

❖ Living and Praying with the Word

Walk with us along the journey of life, Lord, not as a stranger but as the one who makes our hearts burn with love for you and a desire to be your messengers to all the world.

May 7, 2017

FOURTH SUNDAY OF EASTER

Today's Focus: Recognizing the Shepherd

Jesus, the Good Shepherd, is always with us and tends us. But the members of his flock still fail to hear or know his voice, and scatter off in many directions without knowing their shepherd is near.

FIRST READING
Acts 2:14a, 36–41

Then Peter stood up with the Eleven, raised his voice, and proclaimed: "Let the whole house of Israel know for certain that God has made both Lord and Christ, this Jesus whom you crucified."

Now when they heard this, they were cut to the heart, and they asked Peter and the other apostles, "What are we to do, my brothers?" Peter said to them, "Repent and be baptized, every one of you, in the name of Jesus Christ for the forgiveness of your sins; and you will receive the gift of the Holy Spirit. For the promise is made to you and to your children and to all those far off, whomever the Lord our God will call." He testified with many other arguments, and was exhorting them, "Save yourselves from this corrupt generation." Those who accepted his message were baptized, and about three thousand persons were added that day.

PSALM RESPONSE
Psalm 23:1

The Lord is my shepherd; there is nothing I shall want.

SECOND READING
1 Peter 2:20b–25

Beloved: If you are patient when you suffer for doing what is good, this is a grace before God. For to this you have been called, because Christ also suffered for you, leaving you an example that you should follow in his footsteps.
He committed no sin, and no deceit was found in his mouth.

When he was insulted, he returned no insult; when he suffered, he did not threaten; instead, he handed himself over to the one who judges justly. He himself bore our sins in his body upon the cross, so that, free from sin, we might live for righteousness. By his wounds you have been healed. For you had gone astray like sheep, but you have now returned to the shepherd and guardian of your souls.

GOSPEL
John 10:1–10

Jesus said: "Amen, amen, I say to you, whoever does not enter a sheepfold through the gate but climbs over elsewhere is a thief and a robber. But whoever enters through the gate is the shepherd of the sheep. The gatekeeper opens it for him, and the sheep hear his voice, as the shepherd calls his own sheep by name and leads them out. When he has driven out all his own, he walks ahead of them, and the sheep follow him, because they recognize his voice. But they will not follow a stranger; they will run away from him, because they do not recognize the voice of strangers." Although Jesus used this figure of speech, the Pharisees did not realize what he was trying to tell them.

So Jesus said again, "Amen, amen, I say to you, I am the gate for the sheep. All who came before me are thieves and robbers, but the sheep did not listen to them. I am the gate. Whoever enters through me will be saved, and will come in and go out and find pasture. A thief comes only to steal and slaughter and destroy; I came so that they might have life and have it more abundantly."

❖ *Understanding the Word*

The audience of Jews who overheard the commotion of Pentecost is now invited to receive the Holy Spirit themselves in today's first reading. For Peter explained, "the promise is made to you and to your children and to all those far off" (Acts 2:39). Baptism in the name of Jesus Christ for the forgiveness of sin opens the new members to the gifts of the Holy Spirit. But as Peter noted, the gift is not only a promise fulfilled for the Jews, but is also for those "far off," indicating that shortly the Good News will be preached to the Gentiles.

One of the more difficult things to explain to the newly baptized is why suffering would accompany their new life. This is even more true for the slaves who joined the community. In the passage prior to today's second reading, the author directs slaves to bear the pain of unjust suffering. Quoting the Suffering Servant song of Isaiah 53:4–12, the author of First Peter notes that Christ's own suffering serves as an example. First Peter 2:11 — 3:12 has been described as similar to ancient "household codes" that outlined the appropriate behavior for various types of people (husbands, wives, slaves, children).

The good shepherd discourse from which our Gospel reading is taken continues Jesus' confrontation with the Pharisees (John 9: 41). The allegory is meant to label the Pharisees as thieves and robbers who sneak into the sheepfold. They are the strangers whose voice the sheep do not recognize, and flee from in fear (John 10:5). The stark condemnation must be read in response to the Pharisees' excommunication of the man born blind (John 9:34). Confirming Jesus' remark about their own blindness, "the Pharisees did not realize what he was trying to tell them" (John 10:6). The ongoing conflict in John's Gospel is not between Jesus and the religious authorities, but between those who recognize Jesus and those who fail to do so.

In 2013, at the Chrism Mass for the Diocese of Rome, Pope Francis asked bishops and priests to "be shepherds with the smell of the sheep." Smelling like the sheep requires getting close to them. Shepherds got close: they slept at the entry to the pen to protect the sheep and keep them from wandering off. Sheep recognized the shepherd's voice and followed; the shepherd held a wandering sheep around his neck to reinforce his smell and remind the sheep not to wander again.

Jesus got close to the people. The Pharisees set themselves apart. He still comes close, taking on human flesh. He healed by giving himself to us and to God on the cross. He took the high road: not returning insult, not threatening, but submitting to those who judged unjustly. To be close to him, we need to follow his example by reorienting our lives to live his unconditional, merciful love. Submission does not mean becoming doormats. Instead, we find strength in suffering and the power that comes from the work of dying to self. Filled with the Holy Spirit we can forgive, speak truth in love, avoid becoming defensive or going on the attack, and live like Christ, the servant of God, our shepherd.

The pope, bishops, priests, or religious are not the only ones to smell like the sheep. All of us are sheep and shepherds, called to care for one another in the name of Jesus Christ. By getting close to one another, we can help others hear the shepherd's voice, feel the shepherd's love, and experience the shepherd's forgiveness. Just as the sheep gate is the doorway to the sheep pen, so are our lives doors through which Jesus Christ, the Good Shepherd, dwells in our midst and is made known.

❖ Consider/Discuss

- When have you been a sheep gate that has opened the way to Christ for someone else?
- Who has been a sheep gate for you?

❖ Living and Praying with the Word

You, Lord, are my shepherd. Thank you for coming so close that I know your love in my life. Help me get close enough to my sisters and brothers that I smell like them, because I live with them as lovingly as you have chosen to live with us.

May 14, 2017

FIFTH SUNDAY OF EASTER

Today's Focus: Growing Pains

Like every other aspect of our lives, our spiritual lives go through times of growth and change, times that are not always easy. As the church did from the beginning, we need to keep the Lord near.

FIRST READING
Acts 6:1–7

As the number of disciples continued to grow, the Hellenists complained against the Hebrews because their widows were being neglected in the daily distribution. So the Twelve called together the community of the disciples and said, "It is not right for us to neglect the word of God to serve at table. Brothers, select from among you seven reputable men, filled with the Spirit and wisdom, whom we shall appoint to this task, whereas we shall devote ourselves to prayer and to the ministry of the word." The proposal was acceptable to the whole community, so they chose Stephen, a man filled with faith and the Holy Spirit, also Philip, Prochorus, Nicanor, Timon, Parmenas, and Nicholas of Antioch, a convert to Judaism. They presented these men to the apostles who prayed and laid hands on them. The word of God continued to spread, and the number of the disciples in Jerusalem increased greatly; even a large group of priests were becoming obedient to the faith.

PSALM RESPONSE
Psalm 33:22

Lord, let your mercy be on us, as we place our trust in you.

SECOND READING
1 Peter 2:4–9

Beloved: Come to him, a living stone, rejected by human beings but chosen and precious in the sight of God, and, like living stones, let yourselves be built into a spiritual house to be a holy priesthood to offer spiritual sacrifices acceptable to God through Jesus Christ. For it says in Scripture:

Behold, I am laying a stone in Zion,
a cornerstone, chosen and precious,
and whoever believes in it shall not be put to shame.

Therefore, its value is for you who have faith, but for those without faith:

The stone that the builders rejected
has become the cornerstone,

and

A stone that will make people stumble,
and a rock that will make them fall.

They stumble by disobeying the word, as is their destiny.

You are "a chosen race, a royal priesthood, a holy nation, a people of his own, so that you may announce the praises" of him who called you out of darkness into his wonderful light.

Jesus said to his disciples: "Do not let your hearts be troubled. You have faith in God; have faith also in me. In my Father's house there are many dwelling places. If there were not, would I have told you that I am going to prepare a place for you? And if I go and prepare a place for you, I will come back again and take you to myself, so that where I am you also may be. Where I am going you know the way." Thomas said to him, "Master, we do not know where you are going; how can we know the way?" Jesus said to him, "I am the way and the truth and the life. No one comes to the Father except through me. If you know me, then you will also know my Father. From now on you do know him and have seen him." Philip said to him, "Master, show us the Father, and that will be enough for us." Jesus said to him, "Have I been with you for so long a time and you still do not know me, Philip? Whoever has seen me has seen the Father. How can you say, 'Show us the Father'? Do you not believe that I am in the Father and the Father is in me? The words that I speak to you I do not speak on my own. The Father who dwells in me is doing his works. Believe me that I am in the Father and the Father is in me, or else, believe because of the works themselves. Amen, amen, I say to you, whoever believes in me will do the works that I do, and will do greater ones than these, because I am going to the Father."

✛ Understanding the Word

Though Luke presents an idyllic picture of the early church gathered in prayer and sharing all things in common, very shortly the community experienced growing pains. In today's first reading, we hear about a conflict brewing between the Palestinian Aramaic-speaking Jewish Christians and the Hellenistic Greek-speaking Jewish Christians. While the stated problem concerns the widows, likely they are only an example of the various difficulties that arose as the gospel was proclaimed in different cultures. As Acts explains, the answer to the problem was to appoint more servants to assist the Twelve in their ministry. Two of those chosen—Stephen and Philip—will be instrumental in the gospel's spread outside of Jerusalem.

The author of First Peter uses metaphors and images common to the experience of his readers, who are "newborn infants" (1 Peter 2:2) in the faith. Christ is the cornerstone of their faith and is foundational to their spiritual life. By virtue of his resurrection, he is a "living stone, rejected by human beings but chosen and precious in the sight of God" (1 Peter 2:4). Believers are themselves to become like living stones and serve as a holy priesthood. The titles once reserved for Israel are now granted to the faithful in Christ who are "a chosen race, a royal priesthood, a holy nation, a people of his own" (1 Peter 2:9).

In today's Gospel reading from John, Jesus assures his disciples that in his Father's house, there are many dwelling places. Here John is combining two important themes found throughout his Gospel: that of "house" (John 14:2) and "to dwell" (John 14:10) "House" is a frequent word in the Gospel (John 2:16–17; 7:53; 11:31; 12:3). In today's reading, the image of a house with plenty of space for resting resembles a typical Roman atrium house with many cubicles. The front door opened to the street and allowed visible access to the interior. A householder wanted his or her status visible to those who passed by. Clients came and went. Only the family members remained. The Greek word for "to dwell" (also "abide," "stay," "remain") is *menō* and becomes the designation and destination for a true disciple. The disciple is called to dwell in Jesus (John 15:4).

❖ Reflecting on the Word

Have you experienced life's growing pains? As a young parish musician, it wasn't until the priest/choir director was transferred and I became the director that I wondered if I had what I needed to take on that role. Friends, colleagues, and choir members assured me that I did. They'd show me the way. They did and I became a director. Growing pains!

Jesus prepares the disciples for his return to the Father. They experience growing pains and need his reassurance. Jesus tells them they know the way. He had shown it to them. They continue to show it to each other by living what Jesus taught them. The early church experienced growing pains when Gentile and Jewish Christians were treated differently. The community prayed, asked the Spirit's guidance, and seven were called forth. Through the laying on of hands in the power of the Holy Spirit a new ministry, that of deacon, developed. Peter reminded the community that they are, "a chosen race, a royal priesthood, a holy nation, a people of his own." They announce the praises of the One who called them out of darkness into a wonderful life (1 Peter 2:9). Growing pains.

We experience growing pains in our lives of faith. Certainty can be followed by wonderment. We ask, "Is God near? Does our faith make any difference at all?" We need to remember that Jesus is our cornerstone. We've seen him in those who make his presence known. He has chosen us as his own people and made us a holy priesthood to give God praise and worship. When in doubt, turn to God in prayer. Call on the Holy Spirit and let Jesus, our way, our truth, and our life, be your guide.

❖ Consider/Discuss

- How have you responded to life's growing pains?
- How do you recharge your identity as Christ's chosen, holy people when that is needed?

❖ Living and Praying with the Word

Jesus, the stone rejected by the builders, you are our foundation. Refresh your life within us each day, so that we might give you flesh, and others may see you and know your way today.

May 21, 2017

SIXTH SUNDAY OF EASTER

Today's Focus: Dwelling With and Within

Jesus uses his own intimate relationship with the Father to assure his followers that he—and the Father—are equally close to them and dwell with them through the power of the Spirit.

FIRST READING
Acts 8:5–8, 14–17

Philip went down to the city of Samaria and proclaimed the Christ to them. With one accord, the crowds paid attention to what was said by Philip when they heard it and saw the signs he was doing. For unclean spirits, crying out in a loud voice, came out of many possessed people, and many paralyzed or crippled people were cured. There was great joy in that city.

Now when the apostles in Jerusalem heard that Samaria had accepted the word of God, they sent them Peter and John, who went down and prayed for them, that they might receive the Holy Spirit, for it had not yet fallen upon any of them; they had only been baptized in the name of the Lord Jesus. Then they laid hands on them and they received the Holy Spirit.

PSALM RESPONSE
Psalm 66:1

Let all the earth cry out to God with joy.

SECOND READING
1 Peter 3:15–18

Beloved: Sanctify Christ as Lord in your hearts. Always be ready to give an explanation to anyone who asks you for a reason for your hope, but do it with gentleness and reverence, keeping your conscience clear, so that, when you are maligned, those who defame your good conduct in Christ may themselves be put to shame. For it is better to suffer for doing good, if that be the will of God, than for doing evil. For Christ also suffered for sins once, the righteous for the sake of the unrighteous, that he might lead you to God. Put to death in the flesh, he was brought to life in the Spirit.

GOSPEL
John 14:15–21

Jesus said to his disciples: "If you love me, you will keep my commandments. And I will ask the Father, and he will give you another Advocate to be with you always, the Spirit of truth, whom the world cannot accept, because it neither sees nor knows him. But you know him, because he remains with you, and will be in you. I will not leave you orphans; I will come to you. In a little while the world will no longer see me, but you will see me, because I live and you will live. On that day you will realize that I am in my Father and you are in me and I in you. Whoever has my commandments and observes them is the one who loves me. And whoever loves me will be loved by my Father, and I will love him and reveal myself to him."

❖ Understanding the Word

The theme of Acts of the Apostles is the spread of the faith from Jerusalem to the ends of the earth (Acts 1:8). In today's first reading, we hear of the first steps to realize that vision. Philip, who was among the seven reputable men chosen to meet the needs of the growing community, traveled to Samaria "and proclaimed the Christ to them" (Acts 8:5). While the selection of the seven was to free up the Twelve for the ministry of proclamation (Acts 6: 4), both Stephen and Philip prove to be effective evangelizers. But as our reading details, Philip's efforts must be confirmed by apostolic representatives, Peter and John (Acts 8:14). Throughout Acts, the author is keen to demonstrate the continuity of the mission. The ministry of the word is rooted first in the Twelve and then extends to those whom they have appointed.

Scholars are at pains to find historical evidence of any government-sanctioned persecution of Christians during the time that First Peter is likely to have been written. The suffering alluded to may be rooted in societal misunderstandings and the ostracism of believers. "Always be ready to give an explanation to anyone who asks you for a reason for your hope" (1 Peter 3:15). The reminder to live exemplary lives "with gentleness and reverence" suggests that Christian believers are to uphold proper societal expectations, thus lessening the suspicion of their non-believing neighbors. The codes of proper behavior enumerated in 1 Peter 2:11 — 3:12 seem to confirm this strategy.

In the Gospel reading, Jesus makes an extraordinary statement, "I am in my Father and you are in me and I in you" (John 14:20). This total integration with the Father has been the hallmark of Jesus' self-identity, but now that union is extended to the disciples. But there's a catch. The disciples are to keep Jesus' commandments as a visible testament of their love for him (John 14:21). Because of the disciples' love, Jesus asks the Father to give them another Advocate. This Spirit of truth will remain with the disciples as Jesus' abiding presence, thus sealing his promise, "I will not leave you orphans" (John 14:18).

Jesus is in the Father, the disciples are in him, and he is in them. Sounds like a puzzle. We put it together by keeping his commandments. To keep is to act. We often say, "Actions speak louder than words." When we live the commandments, our actions make that known. The same Spirit that connects Jesus with the Father is the promised Advocate who connects God with us and us with one another. That same Spirit was given to those in Samaria when the apostles laid hands on them. That same Spirit helped Peter's audience keep their consciences clear because of their good conduct in Christ. That same Spirit helps our actions speak louder than words.

We were baptized in the name of the Father and of the Son and of the Holy Spirit. The gift of the Spirit was deepened within us in confirmation. How do people know that the Spirit is within us? We manifest the gifts of the Holy Spirit: wisdom, understanding, counsel, fortitude, knowledge, piety, and fear of the Lord. When our actions make clear that the Spirit of God guides us, people see that we remain in Jesus Christ and he remains in us.

St. Francis de Sales taught that human beings love by doing good. The wisdom, counsel, understanding, and knowledge of the Holy Spirit give us courage to do good and live Jesus' command to love. Withdraw into your heart this week. Turn to our Advocate, the Holy Spirit. Reflect on the gifts of the Spirit and ask for the courage to act on them. Then love as Jesus loved. Your actions will show that he remains in you and you remain in him. Actions speak louder than words.

✢ *Consider/Discuss*

- When have people told you that they see your faith in your words, deeds, or attitudes?
- Which gift of the Holy Spirit most helps you keep Jesus' commands?

✢ *Living and Praying with the Word*

Come, Holy Spirit, fill my heart this day. Guide my mind to know how I can do the good that will make your presence known in my actions, so people see that you remain in me and I remain in you.

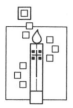

May 25 or 28, 2017

ASCENSION OF THE LORD

Many dioceses in the United States celebrate the Ascension on May 28, replacing the Seventh Sunday of Easter.

Today's Focus: Neck Strain

Just like sitting in the front row at the movie theater, standing in place and looking heavenward does nothing to help bring about the reign of God. It only gives us stiff necks.

FIRST READING
Acts 1:1–11

In the first book, Theophilus, I dealt with all that Jesus did and taught until the day he was taken up, after giving instructions through the Holy Spirit to the apostles whom he had chosen. He presented himself alive to them by many proofs after he had suffered, appearing to them during forty days and speaking about the kingdom of God. While meeting with them, he enjoined them not to depart from Jerusalem, but to wait for "the promise of the Father about which you have heard me speak; for John baptized with water, but in a few days you will be baptized with the Holy Spirit."

When they had gathered together they asked him, "Lord, are you at this time going to restore the kingdom to Israel?" He answered them, "It is not for you to know the times or seasons that the Father has established by his own authority. But you will receive power when the Holy Spirit comes upon you, and you will be my witnesses in Jerusalem, throughout Judea and Samaria, and to the ends of the earth." When he had said this, as they were looking on, he was lifted up, and a cloud took him from their sight. While they were looking intently at the sky as he was going, suddenly two men dressed in white garments stood beside them. They said, "Men of Galilee, why are you standing there looking at the sky? This Jesus who has been taken up from you into heaven will return in the same way as you have seen him going into heaven."

PSALM RESPONSE
Psalm 47:6

God mounts his throne to shouts of joy: a blare of trumpets for the Lord.

SECOND READING
Ephesians 1:17–23

Brothers and sisters: May the God of our Lord Jesus Christ, the Father of glory, give you a Spirit of wisdom and revelation resulting in knowledge of him. May the eyes of your hearts be enlightened, that you may know what is the hope that belongs to his call, what are the riches of glory in his inheritance among the holy ones, and what is the surpassing greatness of his power for us who believe, in accord with the exercise of his great might, which he worked in Christ, raising him from the dead and seating him at his right hand in the heavens, far above every principality, authority, power, and dominion, and every name that is named not only in this age but also in the one to come. And he put all things beneath his feet and gave him as head over all things to the church, which is his body, the fullness of the one who fills all things in every way.

GOSPEL
Matthew 28:16–20

The eleven disciples went to Galilee, to the mountain to which Jesus had ordered them. When they saw him, they worshiped, but they doubted. Then Jesus approached and said to them, "All power in heaven and on earth has been given to me. Go, therefore, and make disciples of all nations, baptizing them in the name of the Father, and of the Son, and of the Holy Spirit, teaching them to observe all that I have commanded you. And behold, I am with you always, until the end of the age."

✥ Understanding the Word

Jerusalem has pride of place in Luke-Acts. The Gospel opens with Zachariah offering incense in the temple and concludes with Jesus' appearance to the disciples in Jerusalem. Jesus sets his face resolutely toward Jerusalem (Luke 9:51), the city that kills the prophets (Luke 13:34). In today's first reading, Jesus tells the disciples not to depart from Jerusalem. Instead they are "to wait for 'the promise of the Father' " (Acts 1:4)—their baptism with the Holy Spirit. After Pentecost, the disciples will then become "witnesses in Jerusalem, throughout Judea and Samaria and to the ends of the earth" (Acts 1:8). Jesus' ascension signals the movement of the word now beyond Jerusalem.

Ephesians is a sermon in letter format that purports to be from the apostle Paul, but is likely written long after his death. Today's second reading is part of a thanksgiving section in which the author blesses God (Ephesians 1:17), Christ (Ephesians 1:20–221), the Ephesians themselves (Ephesians 1:17–10), and finally the church (Ephesians 1:22–23). Whereas in genuine Pauline letters, Christ is the body (1 Corinthians 12; Romans 12:4–8), here in Ephesians (and Colossians 1:18), Christ is the head of the body, and the body itself is the church. The more developed ecclesiology evidences a date later than Paul's genuine letters.

Matthew's depiction of the Ascension differs markedly from Luke's. First, Matthew places Jesus back in Galilee. The Eleven have been ordered to return to a particular mountain. The mountain imagery in Matthew (Matthew 4:8; 5:1; 17:1) is meant to remind Matthew's Jewish Christian readers of the parallel between Moses and Jesus. As Moses brought forth the Law from Mount Sinai, Jesus becomes the new law. Jesus has been vested with authority: "All power in heaven and on earth has been given to me." He then directs the disciples to make disciples of all nations (Matthew 28:19). These disciples are to observe the new commandments of Jesus, which supersede the commandments of Moses.

❖ *Reflecting on the* Word

How do you know who you are and what you are to do with your life? For me it was the love of my mother and grandfather, who raised me and rooted me in faith. Teachers affirmed my gifts for music and working with people. Friends taught me how to love and how not to love. Prayer and reflecting upon my heart's desires in light of my faith, gifts, successes, and failures deepened my identity and gave me life direction.

In both Ascension accounts Jesus invites the disciples to reflect on who they are and to act accordingly. On the Ascension mount Jesus gives them a pep talk and command: You are my disciples. All power has been given me. Know that I am with you always so trust yourselves. Make disciples of others as I made disciples of you. On Mt. Olivet Jesus invites trust and makes a promise. Wait. Pray for the gift of the Holy Spirit. You will receive power to be my witnesses to the ends of the earth. They need time in prayer to become confident of their discipleship through the power of the Holy Spirit.

At baptism we joined the Church, the body of which Christ is head. We belong to him. May the power of the Spirit enlighten our hearts to believe we are Christ's and give us strengthen to act on that belief. The Ascension invites us to take time for prayer so that we can deepen our awareness that the Holy Spirit is within us. Rooted in this knowledge, believe more deeply. Then act on that faith. Live Jesus clearly to make disciples of those we meet. Sr. Caroleen taught me that Christ is with us always in all ways. Look for and be that presence always in all ways, too.

❖ *Consider/Discuss*

- Do you simply stand around looking up to heaven or do you act on your faith? How?
- When have you been aware of the presence and power of the Holy Spirit in your life?

❖ *Living and Praying with the* Word

Jesus, you promise to be with us always, in all ways, even to the ends of the earth. Thank you for your trust in us. Help me to trust in you more fully so that the power of the Holy Spirit can help me witness your presence in my life.

May 28, 2017

SEVENTH SUNDAY OF EASTER

Today's Focus: Praying with Christ

The Gospels give us several portraits of Jesus at prayer. If he, who was one with the Father and the Spirit, needed to pray, how much more do we need to do the same?

FIRST READING
Acts 1:12–14

After Jesus had been taken up to heaven the apostles returned to Jerusalem from the mount called Olivet, which is near Jerusalem, a sabbath day's journey away.

When they entered the city they went to the upper room where they were staying, Peter and John and James and Andrew, Philip and Thomas, Bartholomew and Matthew, James son of Alphaeus, Simon the Zealot, and Judas son of James. All these devoted themselves with one accord to prayer, together with some women, and Mary the mother of Jesus, and his brothers.

PSALM RESPONSE
Psalm 27:13

I believe that I shall see the good things of the Lord in the land of the living.

SECOND READING
1 Peter 4:13–16

Beloved: Rejoice to the extent that you share in the sufferings of Christ, so that when his glory is revealed you may also rejoice exultantly. If you are insulted for the name of Christ, blessed are you, for the Spirit of glory and of God rests upon you. But let no one among you be made to suffer as a murderer, a thief, an evildoer, or as an intriguer. But whoever is made to suffer as a Christian should not be ashamed but glorify God because of the name.

GOSPEL
John 17:1–11a

Jesus raised his eyes to heaven and said, "Father, the hour has come. Give glory to your son, so that your son may glorify you, just as you gave him authority over all people, so that your son may give eternal life to all you gave him. Now this is eternal life, that they should know you, the only true God, and the one whom you sent, Jesus Christ. I glorified you on earth by accomplishing the work that you gave me to do. Now glorify me, Father, with you, with the glory that I had with you before the world began.

"I revealed your name to those whom you gave me out of the world. They belonged to you, and you gave them to me, and they have kept your word. Now they know that everything you gave me is from you, because the words you gave to me I have given to them, and they accepted them and truly understood that I came from you, and they have believed that you sent me. I pray for them. I do not pray for the world but for the ones you have given me, because they are yours, and everything of mine is yours and everything of yours is mine, and I have been glorified in them. And now I will no longer be in the world, but they are in the world, while I am coming to you."

In the Gospel of Luke, after Jesus spent a night in prayer on the mount, he summoned the twelve disciples whom he called apostles (Luke 6:14–16). These same twelve are given power and authority over all demons and the ability to cure diseases. They are to proclaim the kingdom of God (Luke 9:1–2). In today's reading from Acts, these apostles are reintroduced. Now missing Judas Iscariot, the Eleven return to the upper room from the Mount of Olives (Luke calls it "Olivet"). Along with some women and Jesus' mother and brothers, they devote themselves to prayer. Luke means to stress that those who were called and empowered by Jesus during his ministry in Galilee are the very same apostles who form the foundation of this new community.

In the reading from First Peter, we find evidence of why members of the community may have been persecuted. It is not for the crime of murder, theft, or any evil doing (1 Peter 4:15) that the faithful are sharing in the sufferings of Christ. But rather, it is for the crime of being called a "Christian." "If you are insulted for the name of Christ, blessed are you" (1 Peter 4:14). In the early second century, the Roman governor of Pontus and Bithynia, Pliny the Younger, wrote to the Emperor Trajan to ask for a ruling on how to deal with "Christians." Pliny wondered "whether the name itself, even without offenses, or only the offenses associated with the name are to be punished" (Pliny, *Letters*, 10.96).

Only three times in the Gospel of John is Jesus portrayed at prayer: at the tomb of Lazarus (John 11:41), prior to the Last Supper (John 12:27–28), and in today's Gospel reading (John 17). Since the Johannine Jesus is one with the Father, he is always in communion with God and outward prayer is done for the sake of those present (John 11:42). Chapter 17 is an extended prayer in the presence of the disciples. Jesus' prayer for glorification begins by confirming that he has completed his work, that of revealing God's name and words to the disciples (John 17:1–5). The prayer consists of three requests: to keep disciples in God's name (John 17:11), to consecrate the disciples in truth (John 17:17), and that the disciples remain as one (John 17:21).

❖❖ *Reflecting on the Word*

As the saying goes, we cannot change anyone else, we can only change ourselves. My religious community's founder, Blessed Louis Brisson, OSFS, says that our individual strength lies with each of us, called upon to make full use of what God has given us. By doing all we can to deepen and live our relationship with God, in Christ, through the Spirit, others are attracted to what we have and often change their lives accordingly.

Jesus prays for his disciples, asking God to keep them rooted in what they've come to believe. He also seems to ask that they know God's presence with them while they continue living in the world after he goes to the Father. Eternal life will be to "know you, the only true God, and the one whom you sent, Jesus Christ" (John 17:3). These tender words express a very deep bond. The gathering of the apostles, Mary, and the other women in the upper room expresses their bond, and their prayer changed them as prayer changes us.

Jesus' prayer is also meant for us. We are his disciples. No one else can live discipleship for us. Rejoice in the gift of faith that empowers us to respond. In times of suffering and hardship, turn to Christ for guidance and support to respond. When we suffer because we are Christians, as Peter's community did, we respond. Return to this prayer often and hear Jesus' voice praying on your behalf. Let these tender words touch your hearts in ways that deepen faith and create trust in God's abiding presence. Then make full use of the gifts that God has given you.

❖ Consider/Discuss

- Do you make full use of the gifts that God has given you? How?
- How does thinking about eternal life as something already begun by knowing God through Jesus make a difference to you?

❖ Living and Praying with the Word

Almighty God, you sent your Son, Jesus Christ, to make your presence known in human flesh and blood. May his prayer for us deepen our discipleship in ways that help him remain in our flesh and blood and help us remain rooted in you.

June 4, 2017

PENTECOST SUNDAY: MASS DURING THE DAY

Today's Focus: Gifts of the Spirit, Gifts from the Spirit

Like the gifts we receive for birthdays or on Christmas, the best way to show that we truly appreciate the gifts of the Spirit is to use them—and make them Spirit-gifts for others.

FIRST READING
Acts 2:1–11

When the time for Pentecost was fulfilled, they were all in one place together. And suddenly there came from the sky a noise like a strong driving wind, and it filled the entire house in which they were. Then there appeared to them tongues as of fire, which parted and came to rest on each one of them. And they were all filled with the Holy Spirit and began to speak in different tongues, as the Spirit enabled them to proclaim.

Now there were devout Jews from every nation under heaven staying in Jerusalem. At this sound, they gathered in a large crowd, but they were confused because each one heard them speaking in his own language. They were astounded, and in amazement they asked, "Are not all these people who are speaking Galileans? Then how does each of us hear them in his native language? We are Parthians, Medes, and Elamites, inhabitants of Mesopotamia, Judea and Cappadocia, Pontus and Asia, Phrygia and Pamphylia, Egypt and the districts of Libya near Cyrene, as well as travelers from Rome, both Jews and converts to Judaism, Cretans and Arabs, yet we hear them speaking in our own tongues of the mighty acts of God."

PSALM RESPONSE
Psalm 104:30

Lord, send out your Spirit, and renew the face of the earth.

SECOND READING
1 Corinthians 12:3b–7, 12–13

Brothers and sisters: No one can say, "Jesus is Lord," except by the Holy Spirit. There are different kinds of spiritual gifts but the same Spirit; there are different forms of service but the same Lord; there are different workings but the same God who produces all of them in everyone. To each individual the manifestation of the Spirit is given for some benefit.

As a body is one though it has many parts, and all the parts of the body, though many, are one body, so also Christ. For in one Spirit we were all baptized into one body, whether Jews or Greeks, slaves or free persons, and we were all given to drink of one Spirit.

On the evening of that first day of the week, when the doors were locked, where the disciples were, for fear of the Jews, Jesus came and stood in their midst and said to them, "Peace be with you." When he had said this, he showed them his hands and his side. The disciples rejoiced when they saw the Lord. Jesus said to them again, "Peace be with you. As the Father has sent me, so I send you." And when he had said this, he breathed on them and said to them, "Receive the Holy Spirit. Whose sins you forgive are forgiven them, and whose sins you retain are retained."

❖ *Understanding the Word*

The coming of the Holy Spirit in Acts is depicted as both a visual and sonic event. Tongues of flames separate and come to rest on everyone gathered in the upper room, who are immediately filled with the Holy Spirit. The first tangible gift of the Spirit is the ability of the disciples to speak in different tongues (Acts 2:4). The sound of the "strong driving wind" attracts the attention of passersby, but it is the speech of the disciples that confounds them (Acts 2:6). Those gathered outside had come from various parts of the empire and beyond. They spoke a multiplicity of languages, and yet "each one heard them speaking in his own language" (Acts 2:6). Jesus had told the disciples that the Spirit would teach them what to say (Luke 12:12), and in today's reading, those disciples are not only given the words to speak but the ability to communicate in every language. This reversal of the Tower of Babel (Genesis 11:1–9) testifies to the nearness of the reign of God (Luke 21:15).

Paul's beautiful description of the workings of the Spirit and the metaphor of the body as a unity of many parts provides a vivid image of new life in Christ. But his words were not meant as poetic utterances. Rather, Paul is attempting to counter the schisms arising within the Corinthian community (1 Corinthians 1:10). The community seems to have misinterpreted Paul's theology of the Spirit. They now argue over who has the greatest spiritual gift. So Paul answers, "There are different kinds of spiritual gifts but the same Spirit" (1 Corinthians 12:4), and each gift is given for the benefit of the community.

When Mary Magdalene found the empty tomb, Peter and John were needed as official witnesses (John 20:3). Now in today's Gospel reading, Jesus' physical body testifies that he is truly Jesus and is indeed resurrected (John 20:20). The importance of the body as proof is made explicit in the encounter with Thomas (John 20:27). Because Jesus is resurrected and therefore fully glorified, he is able to impart his Spirit, the Advocate whom he promised (John 14:25). With Jesus' Spirit, the disciples now share fully in his mission: "As the Father has sent me, so I send you" (John 20:21).

When I was in novitiate, our novice master once told us that he had been given the gift of a candle. The person who gave it to him noticed that it remained unlit on his table and asked, "Is something wrong with the candle that I gave you or don't you like it?" He answered, "Nothing is wrong with it, I like it very much. Why do you ask?" "Well," said his friend, "you haven't lit it and candles are meant to be lit." The point of the story was that gifts are given to be used and shared, not simply admired and hoarded. It is a lesson that I've not forgotten in over forty years.

Jesus enters the upper room, breathes on those gathered, and gives them peace and the Holy Spirit. He tells them to use those gifts to forgive or retain sins. The gifts were given to be shared. Even when given as mighty wind and tongues of flame, the gift of the Spirit was given to be shared: "The Spirit enabled them to proclaim" (Acts 2: 4). And people understood in their own languages! Paul tells us that "the manifestation of the Spirit is given for some benefit" (1 Corinthians 12:7).

There are many gifts from the same Spirit. They are given to us to be shared and not kept to ourselves. The best way that we can affirm our own gifts and admire those of others is to use the gifts that God has given us. We pray in today's Sequence, "Come, source of all our store! Come, within our bosoms shine." What gift or gifts has God given you in the power of the Spirit? How do you use them for the good of others, the Church, and the world?

❖ Consider/Discuss

- Reflect on and name the gifts that you've been given to do good in the name of the Holy Spirit.
- What helps you use your gifts and what holds you back?

❖ Living and Praying with the Word

Come, Holy Spirit. Fill the hearts of your faithful. Kindle in us the fire of your love. Fire us up to share our gifts whether through tongues of fire, mighty wind, or gentle breath.

Introduction to Ordinary Time II

The second segment of Ordinary Time opens with two solemnities, the Most Holy Trinity and the Most Holy Body and Blood of Christ. The feast of the Transfiguration of the Lord will also be celebrated on a Sunday. On Trinity Sunday, we are reminded that "God so loved the world" (John 3:16), and thus, as Paul admonishes, we are to live in that love (2 Corinthians 13:11). The readings for the Most Holy Body and Blood of Christ remind us that Jesus is the "living bread" (John 6:51), and Paul tells the Corinthians that at the Lord's Supper, we participate in the body of Christ (1 Corinthians 10:16).

The first readings for this season are taken from each of the sections of the Old Testament: the Pentateuch (Holy Trinity and Body and Blood of Christ, Thirtieth Sunday in Ordinary Time), the historical books (Thirteenth, Seventeenth, Nineteenth Sundays in Ordinary Time), wisdom literature (Sixteenth, Twenty-fourth, Thirty-second, Thirty-third Sundays), and the Prophets (Twelfth, Fourteenth, Fifteenth, Twentieth, Twenty-first, Twenty-second, Twenty-third, Twenty-fifth through Twenty-ninth and Thirty-first Sundays).

Nearly all of Chapters 5–11 of Paul's Letter to the Romans is read during these weeks. Passages from Paul's Letter to the Philippians are read on the Twenty-fifth through Twenty-eighth Sundays, and First Thessalonians on the Twenty-ninth through Thirty-third Sundays.

The Gospel continues Matthew's presentation of the story of Jesus, focusing on courage under persecution and the costs of discipleship (Twelfth, Thirteenth, and Twenty-second Sundays). In the midst of his Galilean teaching, Jesus utters a spontaneous prayer to the Father, sharing similar themes with John's Gospel (Fourteenth Sunday). Parables are the focus for the Fourteenth through Seventeenth, Twenty-fourth and Twenty-fifth, Twenty-seventh and Twenty-eighth, and Thirty-second and Thirty-third Sundays. The miracle of walking on the water is read for the Nineteenth Sunday. The theme of inclusion of the Gentiles is found in all readings for the Twentieth Sunday. Matthew's Gospel places particular emphasis on Peter, as seen in the Gospel reading for the Twenty-first Sunday, in which Jesus gives Peter the keys to the kingdom. Matthew has a strong ethical tone, as evidenced in the reading for the Twenty-third Sunday, in which Jesus describes right behavior among church members. It is not the empty promises but actual response that will gain one entrance into the kingdom of heaven (Twenty-sixth Sunday). The animosity among religious leaders against Jesus continues to grow (Twenty-ninth and Thirtieth Sundays), until finally Jesus utters a series of "woes" against them (Thirty-first Sunday).

June 11, 2017

THE MOST HOLY TRINITY

Today's Focus: Grace Times Three

When we know the Father's grace, sharing that grace as members of the Body of Christ, we are living in the grace of the Holy Spirit.

FIRST READING
Exodus 34:4b–6, 8–9

Early in the morning Moses went up Mount Sinai as the LORD had commanded him, taking along the two stone tablets.

Having come down in a cloud, the LORD stood with Moses there and proclaimed his name, "LORD." Thus the LORD passed before him and cried out, "The LORD, the LORD, a merciful and gracious God, slow to anger and rich in kindness and fidelity." Moses at once bowed down to the ground in worship. Then he said, "If I find favor with you, O LORD, do come along in our company. This is indeed a stiff-necked people; yet pardon our wickedness and sins, and receive us as your own."

PSALM RESPONSE
Daniel 3:52b

Glory and praise for ever!

SECOND READING
2 Corinthians 13:11–13

Brothers and sisters, rejoice. Mend your ways, encourage one another, agree with one another, live in peace, and the God of love and peace will be with you. Greet one another with a holy kiss. All the holy ones greet you.

The grace of the Lord Jesus Christ and the love of God and the fellowship of the Holy Spirit be with all of you.

GOSPEL
John 3:16–18

God so loved the world that he gave his only Son, so that everyone who believes in him might not perish but might have eternal life. For God did not send his Son into the world to condemn the world, but that the world might be saved through him. Whoever believes in him will not be condemned, but whoever does not believe has already been condemned, because he has not believed in the name of the only Son of God.

How far the relationship between God and Moses has come since their first encounter in the third chapter of Exodus! Then a skeptical and distrusting Moses asked for God's name (Exodus 3:13–14). In the ancient Near East, to know the name of someone was to have power over them. God offers a rather enigmatic "I am who I am." After the plagues, the Passover, the Exodus, and now in the midst of the wanderings, their relationship has become one of divine intimacy. God not only offers God's name, Lord (in the English and Greek the term signifies the Hebrew *Yahweh*), but God self-discloses God's qualities: merciful, gracious, slow to anger, and rich in kindness and fidelity. Moses' only response is one of reverence and honesty: "this is indeed a stiff-necked people; yet pardon our wickedness" (Exodus 34:9).

In the second reading, the behavior of a different group of "stiff-necked people" is front and center. In 2 Corinthians 10–13, from which our reading is taken, Paul has harangued the Corinthians for their disobedience and distrust of him. If the Corinthians would only behave rightly—mend their ways, encourage one another, agree with one another—then they will receive God's peace. Thus a threefold blessing will be theirs: grace of the Lord Jesus Christ, the love of God, and the fellowship of the Holy Spirit.

In the Gospel reading, we learn how God's love is made explicit: in the sacrifice of God's only Son for those who believe. It is not for judgment but for salvation that the Son is sent into the world. Throughout John's Gospel, Jesus utters numerous "I AM" statements (see, for example, John 4:26; 6:20; 8:24, 28, 58; 13:19; 18; 5, 6, 8), directly meant to parallel God's self-revelation in Exodus 3:14. The divine intimacy God offered Moses is innate for the Johannine Jesus, who says, "The Father and I are one" (John 10:30). Later in John, Jesus will promise the coming of the Advocate, who will be his Spirit abiding in and directing the community (John 14:16). In the Johannine portrait of Jesus, we see the presence of the Trinity in action.

✢✢ *Reflecting on the Word*

"The grace of our Lord Jesus Christ and the love of God and the fellowship of (communion with) the Holy Spirit be with all of you."

"And with your spirit."

In this dialogue we call each other to live the image and likeness of our Triune God. We wish each other God's grace, participation in the life of God. Grace is a gift given to us by Jesus Christ, God made visible. By being merciful, slow to anger, and rich in kindness and fidelity, God's self-description to Moses, we manifest grace. The Holy Spirit, the life force within God and between God and us, unites us with God and each other. This communion through the Holy Spirit is a great gift and a real challenge.

Being conscious of God's merciful, gracious, kind, and faithful nature calls me to gratitude. I give thanks by showing mercy to another who wrongs me, or being kind to someone who hurts me, or gracious when someone ignores me or takes me for granted. Gratitude is also expressed by being slow to anger rather than quick-tempered. Living this gratitude can be challenging, can it not? Yet, when I don't mend my ways and live in gratitude, I can inhibit communion with God and with others. The solemnity of the Most Holy Trinity reminds us that our one God is a community of three persons. Being created in that image and likeness calls us to build community, too.

Give glory to the Father, Son, and Holy Spirit by becoming more aware of God's grace within you. Manifest that grace by becoming more merciful, gracious, kind, and faithful. By so doing the communion of the Holy Spirit will be made known.

❖ Consider/Discuss

- How have you experienced communion with God through Christ, in the Holy Spirit? What are some concrete examples from your life?
- What gets in the way of being merciful, slow to anger, and rich in kindness and fidelity?

❖ Living and Praying with the Word

O Most Holy Trinity, thank you for dwelling within me through the gift of the Holy Spirit. Fill me with your grace so that I can be more merciful, kind, and gracious each day, and so express my fidelity to you.

June 18, 2017

THE MOST HOLY
BODY AND BLOOD OF CHRIST

Today's Focus: Guiding, Feeding, Drinking

In the Eucharistic elements, Christ feeds us with spiritual food and quenches our thirst with the cup of salvation. Thus, he continues to guide the Church.

FIRST READING
Deuteronomy 8:2–3, 14b–16a

Moses said to the people: "Remember how for forty years now the LORD, your God, has directed all your journeying in the desert, so as to test you by affliction and find out whether or not it was your intention to keep his commandments. He therefore let you be afflicted with hunger, and then fed you with manna, a food unknown to you and your fathers, in order to show you that not by bread alone does one live, but by every word that comes forth from the mouth of the LORD.

"Do not forget the LORD, your God, who brought you out of the land of Egypt, that place of slavery; who guided you through the vast and terrible desert with its saraph serpents and scorpions, its parched and waterless ground; who brought forth water for you from the flinty rock and fed you in the desert with manna, a food unknown to your fathers."

PSALM RESPONSE
Psalm 147:12

Praise the Lord, Jerusalem.

SECOND READING
1 Corinthians 10:16–17

Brothers and sisters: The cup of blessing that we bless, is it not a participation in the blood of Christ? The bread that we break, is it not a participation in the body of Christ? Because the loaf of bread is one, we, though many, are one body, for we all partake of the one loaf.

GOSPEL
John 6:51–58

Jesus said to the Jewish crowds: "I am the living bread that came down from heaven; whoever eats this bread will live forever; and the bread that I will give is my flesh for the life of the world."

The Jews quarreled among themselves, saying, "How can this man give us his flesh to eat?" Jesus said to them, "Amen, amen, I say to you, unless you eat the flesh of the Son of Man and drink his blood, you do not have life within you. Whoever eats my flesh and drinks my blood has eternal life, and I will raise him on the last day. For my flesh is true food, and my blood is true drink. Whoever eats my flesh and drinks my blood remains in me and I in him. Just as the living Father sent me and I have life because of the Father, so also the one who feeds on me will have life because of me. This is the bread that came down from heaven. Unlike your ancestors who ate and still died, whoever eats this bread will live forever."

In today's first reading, the Israelites are reminded that God first afflicted them with hunger and then sated their hunger with manna, a strange substance they had never seen. (The word in Hebrew may be translated "What is it?") This test was meant to teach the people of God that they were to live not by bread alone "but by every word that comes forth from the mouth of the LORD" (Deuteronomy 8:3). Jesus will cite this verse when tempted by the devil to use his powers for his own benefit (Matthew 4:4; Luke 4:4).

The Corinthian community struggled mightily to live their new life in Christ surrounded by their Gentile culture and former religious practices. The second reading is taken from First Corinthians, Chapter 10, in which Paul addresses idolatry in terms of sacrifices and their effect (1 Corinthians 10:7, 14). The Christian sacrifice of Eucharist (1 Corinthians 10:16–17) binds them to Christ; therefore, they cannot participate in Jewish (1 Corinthians 10:18) or pagan (1 Corinthians 10:20) practices. "You cannot drink the cup of the Lord and also the cup of demons" (1 Corinthians 10:21). Participation in Christian Eucharist is exclusive and incompatible with the sacrificial practices of other religions, because the believer is part of the body of Christ (1 Corinthians 10:16).

The Gospel reading is taken from the longer "Bread of Life" discourse in John's Gospel and is best understood within its larger context. In John 6:22–34, Jesus chides the crowd for seeking after him only because they have been fed (v. 26). They ask for a sign, like the manna given to their ancestors (v. 31). Jesus corrects their misunderstanding. It was not Moses but God who gave the bread from heaven, bread that gives life to the world (v. 33). Jesus then describes himself as this bread of life (vv. 34, 48) and God's revelation (v. 38). The tone changes in verses 51–58, from which our reading is taken. Jesus expands on his self-declaration, adding, "I am the living bread that came down from heaven" (v. 51). Two different verbs are used to describe eating in verses 54–58. When Jesus references himself, the word is *trōgō*, a term used of animals that gnaw their food (vv. 54, 56, 58), but when the reference is to manna the term is *esthiō*, which more often refers to human consumption. No wonder many of his disciples react and depart from him (vv. 60–71)

❖❖ *Reflecting on the Word*

Today we celebrate our belief that under the appearance of bread and wine, we see, eat, and drink the real presence of Christ as true food and true drink. We adore the Body and Blood of Christ with processions, exposition of the Blessed Sacrament, and Benediction as extensions of what we celebrate in the Eucharist.

There we take bread and wine, bless and thank God for them, break the bread and share the cup, to eat and drink the Body and Blood of Christ they have become. But we don't stop there. We are sent into the world to be Christ's body broken in service and his blood poured out in love for our sisters and brothers. We become what we eat and drink, as St. Augustine commanded: "Be who you are, the Body of Christ." And then we live what we have become.

Our celebration of the Eucharist and of this solemnity calls us to be for our world what God was for our ancestors in the desert: a guide through the deserts of human lives, water of life for places that are parched and dry, and the loving food of hope, healing, mercy, and light that Jesus was in his day and time. Become what we eat, the Body of Christ. Become what we drink, the Blood of Christ. Celebrate the Eucharist and befriend one another with Jesus' love that refreshes, offers eternal goodness, and satisfies the hungry heart. Eat. Drink. Become the light and food that dispel the gloom of night.

❖ Consider/Discuss

- How do you become the body and blood of Christ to feed others with his presence?
- How does belief in Christ's presence in the Eucharist guide you as a person in the deserts of life, quenching your deepest thirsts or feeding you with hope?

❖ Living and Praying with the Word

Generous God, how holy is this feast, when Christ becomes our food. By eating and drinking the Body and Blood of Christ and knowing Christ present in the Eucharist, help me to feed the world with your loving and merciful presence today.

June 25, 2017

TWELFTH SUNDAY IN ORDINARY TIME

Today's Focus: The Fearless Flock

Frequently the scriptures tell us not to be afraid, for we have God with us; as members of Christ's flock, we are called to live this fearlessness.

FIRST READING
Jeremiah 20:10–13

Jeremiah said:
   "I hear the whisperings of many:
      'Terror on every side!
      Denounce! let us denounce him!'
   All those who were my friends
      are on the watch for any misstep of mine.
   'Perhaps he will be trapped; then we can prevail,
      and take our vengeance on him.'
   But the LORD is with me, like a mighty champion:
      my persecutors will stumble, they will not triumph.
   In their failure they will be put to utter shame,
      to lasting, unforgettable confusion.
   O LORD of hosts, you who test the just,
      who probe mind and heart,
   let me witness the vengeance you take on them,
      for to you I have entrusted my cause.
   Sing to the LORD,
      praise the LORD,
   for he has rescued the life of the poor
      from the power of the wicked!"

PSALM RESPONSE
Psalm 69:14c

Lord, in your great love, answer me.

SECOND READING
Romans 5: 12–15

Brothers and sisters: Through one man sin entered the world, and through sin, death, and thus death came to all men, inasmuch as all sinned—for up to the time of the law, sin was in the world, though sin is not accounted when there is no law. But death reigned from Adam to Moses, even over those who did not sin after the pattern of the trespass of Adam, who is the type of the one who was to come.

But the gift is not like the transgression. For if by the transgression of the one the many died, how much more did the grace of God and the gracious gift of the one man Jesus Christ overflow for the many.

Jesus said to the Twelve: "Fear no one. Nothing is concealed that will not be revealed, nor secret that will not be known. What I say to you in the darkness, speak in the light; what you hear whispered, proclaim on the housetops. And do not be afraid of those who kill the body but cannot kill the soul; rather, be afraid of the one who can destroy both soul and body in Gehenna. Are not two sparrows sold for a small coin? Yet not one of them falls to the ground without your Father's knowledge. Even all the hairs of your head are counted. So do not be afraid; you are worth more than many sparrows. Everyone who acknowledges me before others I will acknowledge before my heavenly Father. But whoever denies me before others, I will deny before my heavenly Father."

❖ Understanding the Word

The reading from Jeremiah is part of his longer sixth lament (Jeremiah 20:7–18), in which the prophet first accuses God of seducing him and making him a laughingstock (v. 7). Jeremiah vows not to speak in God's name. But God's word rages as fire in his heart, and Jeremiah cannot hold it in (v. 9). Our reading opens with "terror on every side," as those who were Jeremiah's friends now seek to attack him (v. 10). Despite his fear, Jeremiah is confident of God's presence and God's vengeance (vv. 11–12). The reading concludes with Jeremiah's song of praise, reminiscent of the Song of the Sea (Exodus 15:21).

For Paul, Adam signifies the origin of sin in the world, while Christ, as the new Adam, is the antidote (1 Corinthians 15:45; Romans 5:17). Paul understands sin in the singular. It is the pervasive malevolent power that causes humanity to revolt against God. The consequence of sin is death. "But the gift is not like the transgression" (Romans 5:15). Where Adam's disobedience led to death, Christ's complete obedience—even unto death—leads to life. The Letter to the Romans likely was addressed to a primarily Gentile audience, who though not under "the Law" (Romans 5:12), were also subject to Adam's sin (Romans 2:14–15).

Matthew Chapter 10 opens with the selection of the Twelve (vv. 1–4) and their commission to proclaim to Israel that the kingdom of heaven is at hand. Only here are the Twelve called "apostles" in the Gospel of Matthew (v. 2). But the mission comes with a caveat. Jesus announces the coming persecutions (vv. 16–23). Then, as our reading opens, Jesus consoles his disciples: "Fear no one" (Matthew 10:26). What is secret (the coming reign of God) and given to them in darkness, the disciples are charged to proclaim and "speak in the light" (Matthew 10:27). In a series of sayings (likely from the Q source shared with Luke), Jesus exhorts his disciples and assures them of God's protection. "Do not be afraid; you are worth more than many sparrows" (v. 31).

✤ Reflecting on the Word

When I was a choir director, my choir sang a song based on Luke 12:32: "Do not be afraid any longer, little flock, for your Father is pleased to give you the kingdom." While we learned the piece I asked people to share their fears. Some answers were the future, change, a past secret being made public, rejection, being alone, and death. We discussed whether or not we could control or alter any of those fears and realized that we had little or no control over any of them. So what could we do to "have no fear"? Trust God's promise to be with us to find a way to face whatever comes.

That reflects Jeremiah's wisdom: "The LORD is with me, like a mighty champion: my persecutors . . . will not prevail" (Jeremiah 20:11a). Being aware of God's presence, God's grace, makes all the difference. We know the overflowing gift of God's grace through Jesus Christ, as our second reading proclaims. St. Francis de Sales notes that when we realize God's all-encompassing presence, we experience a safety that grows in us day by day in proportion as God's grace grows in us, for grace brings forth confidence and confidence is never confounded.

Have no fear, little flock—which is easier said than done, but is not impossible. Try this exercise. Recall that you are always in God's presence. With that awareness name your fears. Take a deep breath and give those fears to God as you release that breath. Then breathe deeply into your entire being the all-encompassing presence of God. Have no fear.

✤ Consider/Discuss

- Whom or what do you fear?
- What has calmed your fears in the past?

✤ Living and Praying with the Word

Loving God, you promise to remain with us always. Fill me with the breath of your Holy Spirit, and make me aware of your promise so that I can trust your promise more and more.

July 2, 2017

THIRTEENTH SUNDAY IN ORDINARY TIME

Today's Focus: The First Relationship

Our lives are networks of relationships, which can change over the course of time. We are challenged in the changes to keep Christ as our primary relationship.

FIRST READING
2 Kings 4:8–11, 14–16a

One day Elisha came to Shunem, where there was a woman of influence, who urged him to dine with her. Afterward, whenever he passed by, he used to stop there to dine. So she said to her husband, "I know that Elisha is a holy man of God. Since he visits us often, let us arrange a little room on the roof and furnish it for him with a bed, table, chair, and lamp, so that when he comes to us he can stay there." Sometime later Elisha arrived and stayed in the room overnight.

Later Elisha asked, "Can something be done for her?" His servant Gehazi answered, "Yes! She has no son, and her husband is getting on in years." Elisha said, "Call her." When the woman had been called and stood at the door, Elisha promised, "This time next year you will be fondling a baby son."

PSALM RESPONSE
Psalm 89:2a

For ever I will sing the goodness of the Lord.

SECOND READING
Romans 6:3–4, 8–11

Brothers and sisters: Are you unaware that we who were baptized into Christ Jesus were baptized into his death? We were indeed buried with him through baptism into death, so that, just as Christ was raised from the dead by the glory of the Father, we too might live in newness of life.

If, then, we have died with Christ, we believe that we shall also live with him. We know that Christ, raised from the dead, dies no more; death no longer has power over him. As to his death, he died to sin once and for all; as to his life, he lives for God. Consequently, you too must think of yourselves as dead to sin and living for God in Christ Jesus.

GOSPEL
Matthew 10:37–42

Jesus said to his apostles: "Whoever loves father or mother more than me is not worthy of me, and whoever loves son or daughter more than me is not worthy of me; and whoever does not take up his cross and follow after me is not worthy of me. Whoever finds his life will lose it, and whoever loses his life for my sake will find it. Whoever receives you receives me, and whoever receives me receives the one who sent me. Whoever receives a prophet because he is a prophet will receive a prophet's reward, and whoever receives a righteous man because he is a righteous man will receive a righteous man's reward. And whoever gives only a cup of cold water to one of these little ones to drink because the little one is a disciple—amen, I say to you, he will surely not lose his reward."

❖ Understanding the Word

The stories of the prophets Elijah and Elisha form a cycle of stories incorporated within First and Second Kings. As Elijah's protégé, Elisha accomplishes similar miracles. But today's first reading does not focus on Elisha's prophetic abilities ("This time next year you will be cradling a baby son," v. 16) as much as it portrays the receptivity and hospitality of the Gentile Shunammite woman and her husband ("Let us arrange a little room on the roof," v. 10). The woman's kindness to Elisha is repaid when she bears a son (v. 17), and later Elisha raises the child from the dead (vv. 32–35).

The belief that God granted salvation despite our "wickedness" may have led some Roman Christians to continue in sinful behavior (Romans 3:5–8). In two verses preceding today's second reading, Paul poses a question, "Shall we persist in sin that grace may abound?" (Romans 6:1). This confrontational question sets up Paul's answer. Those who have been baptized into Christ's death have died to sin. If the wages of sin are death, and Christ has been raised from the dead, then all who have been baptized in Christ will also be raised to new life with God. The new life precludes sin.

The Gospel reading continues the missionary discourse (Matthew 10:5–42) addressed to Jesus' disciples—and indirectly to Matthew's church community. Total renunciation of familial responsibilities and a willingness to take up the cross and follow Jesus are expectations of a true disciple. But Jesus also states expectations and promises rewards for those who receive the disciples. Scholars suggest that in these verses Matthew is directing his own community to respond with hospitality and receptivity to God's disciples, prophets, holy people, and "little ones" who come in the name of the Lord. Similarly the *Didache*, an early Christian manual (late first century to early second century), described the expectations and limits of hospitality for wandering prophets.

What is your most important relationship? How does it impact your values and the decisions you make? As seminarians, our community practice was to stay together to celebrate Christmas Day before going on home visit. Some brothers wanted to change this and go home in time for Christmas. However, we decided not to make that change since our future ministries would often keep us from being with our families of origin on Christmas Day. Our vows meant that our primary relationship was with our religious community. Of course family is still important, but relationships change when we make other commitments. Couples have similar struggles about how to divide time with each spouse's family on holidays. Those decisions change as children are born. Primary relationships color our values and choices.

Today's readings are an example of that. The couple that welcomes Elisha develops a relationship with him, even providing him with a furnished room. He seeks a way to thank them and learns that the woman is without a child. He promises that will change. Jesus instructs his followers that their relationship with him must take precedence over all others. And being in relationship with him includes welcoming others who have a relationship with God: prophets, righteous people, and disciples. Baptism asks the same of us. We are now dead to sin and alive for God and all who belong to God in Christ Jesus.

Making our relationship with Jesus Christ primary helps us to take up our cross: the afflictions, mortifications, troubles, and contradictions that come our way in life. How can we live in ways that make clear that our relationship with Jesus Christ is our primary commitment, whatever our way or state in life?

❖ Consider/Discuss

- How does your baptism, your belonging to Jesus Christ, affect your other relationships?
- When has welcoming someone—because that person is a child of God—changed your life?

❖ Living and Praying with the Word

Gracious God, by our baptism we have become your daughters and sons. Open our eyes to welcome all people in your name, and help us to make clear that belonging to your Son, Jesus, makes a real difference in our lives.

July 9, 2017

FOURTEENTH SUNDAY IN ORDINARY TIME

Today's Focus: Not Knowing It All

Jesus continually surprised people with unexpected wisdom from unexpected sources. We still must be open to new knowledge coming to us from places we don't expect.

FIRST READING
Zechariah 9:9–10

Thus says the Lord:
  Rejoice heartily, O daughter Zion,
    shout for joy, O daughter Jerusalem!
See, your king shall come to you;
  a just savior is he,
meek, and riding on an ass,
  on a colt, the foal of an ass.
He shall banish the chariot from Ephraim,
  and the horse from Jerusalem;
the warrior's bow shall be banished,
  and he shall proclaim peace to the nations.
His dominion shall be from sea to sea,
  and from the River to the ends of the earth.

PSALM RESPONSE
Psalm 145:1

I will praise your name for ever, my king and my God.

SECOND READING
Romans 8:9, 11–13

Brothers and sisters: You are not in the flesh; on the contrary, you are in the spirit, if only the Spirit of God dwells in you. Whoever does not have the Spirit of Christ does not belong to him. If the Spirit of the one who raised Jesus from the dead dwells in you, the one who raised Christ from the dead will give life to your mortal bodies also, through his Spirit that dwells in you. Consequently, brothers and sisters, we are not debtors to the flesh, to live according to the flesh. For if you live according to the flesh, you will die, but if by the Spirit you put to death the deeds of the body, you will live.

GOSPEL
Matthew
11:25–30

At that time Jesus exclaimed: "I give praise to you, Father, Lord of heaven and earth, for although you have hidden these things from the wise and the learned you have revealed them to little ones. Yes, Father, such has been your gracious will. All things have been handed over to me by my Father. No one knows the Son except the Father, and no one knows the Father except the Son and anyone to whom the Son wishes to reveal him.

"Come to me, all you who labor and are burdened, and I will give you rest. Take my yoke upon you and learn from me, for I am meek and humble of heart; and you will find rest for yourselves. For my yoke is easy, and my burden light."

❖❖ *Understanding the Word*

In the reading from the book of Zechariah, the prophet offers words of comfort and encouragement. A century after the return of the exiles and the rebuilding of the temple, the people still have national aspirations. Zechariah's oracles announce the coming of an eschatological king who will return to Jerusalem and so end war and division and proclaim peace to the nations. The symbolic ride on a donkey demonstrates the humility of the coming king (Genesis 49:11; Judges 5:10; 10:4), and counters the image of a warrior king on horseback. Thus Jesus' entrance into Jerusalem on a donkey is a prophetic act announcing the type of kingdom he will usher in (Matthew 21:5 even quotes Zechariah).

In the reading from Romans last week, Paul used the image of baptism to instill in the Christian community the knowledge that they were dead to sin and therefore should forsake immoral behavior. In this week's reading, Paul turns to the image of the Spirit to strengthen his argument. The believers at Rome are not in the flesh (*sarx*) but of the Spirit (*pneuma*). He's not suggesting that they cease to be corporal beings but rather that the limitations and enticements of the flesh are no longer their concern. If the Spirit of God dwells in them, they too will live, even if their mortal bodies die. The struggle for Christian believers was that the fullness of God's salvation was still to come. In the meantime, they had to live in hope of the promise's fulfillment, surrounded by enticement.

Throughout Matthew's Gospel, the evangelist sets up a dichotomy between the so-called "religious professionals" and the "little ones" (Jesus' disciples and/or Matthew's community). In today's reading, Jesus praises God for having revealed mysteries to the "little ones" that are hidden from the "wise." In Chapter 5, Jesus had directed his disciples not to pray like the hypocrites do (Matthew 5:5). In Chapter 23, Jesus will denounce the scribes and the Pharisees as hypocrites. These and other passage suggest that the "wise" from whom the Father has hidden understanding are those who fancy themselves "experts." The burden that Jesus lifts likely refers to the overly scrupulous interpretation of the Law by the scribes and Pharisees. In contrast, the yoke of obedience to Jesus' word brings rest from one's labors.

Have you ever worked with a "know-it-all?" You know, people who seem to have all the answers and the one correct way to do something. Could that be you? As a novice my ministry was to make sandwiches for a parish food line. While I was cutting bologna with a meat slicer, a coworker said, "Paul, divide the meat in thirds. Then remove the skin and it will be easier to slice that bologna." My way was working just fine, so I responded, "Brother, there is more than one way to slice bologna." Which of us was the know-it-all? Maybe both of us were.

Jesus invites the wise and learned know-it-alls of his day to change their hearts. He affirms the little, less learned, and maybe wiser ones. They seem more willing to learn from him. They are open to the discipline, the yoke he offers, that is easier and less burdensome than the scrupulosity of their religious leaders. By so doing they grow in the Spirit of the God Jesus makes known. Jesus is the ruler foretold by Zechariah, who banishes the warrior's bow and proclaims peace.

Warrior language is often used to describe following this Prince of Peace, expressions like *prayer warriors, fighting the battle* of faith, and *taking up arms* against Satan. While Jesus' yoke is easy, we still struggle. I wonder what images might better reflect following the One who proclaimed peace as we take on his yoke to find rest? St. Francis de Sales used gentle strength as one image, and called us to face difficulties by bending them over the course of time rather than breaking them. Admit that there is more than one way to slice bologna, that I don't know it all. That's when I'm most open to taking on a new way of living.

✢ Consider/Discuss

- When has thinking that you had to know it all gotten in the way of learning and growing for you?
- What weaknesses and burdens have become means for finding gentle strength in your life?

✢ Living and Praying with the Word

Praise to you Father, Lord of heaven and earth, for the gift of your light and your truth. Help us accept weakness and burdens in ways that teach us your wisdom, give us strength, and plant the seed of your peace in our hearts.

July 16, 2017

FIFTEENTH SUNDAY IN ORDINARY TIME

Today's Focus: Imagine That!

Jesus taught in parables, often from the natural world. Our sacraments use things that come to us from the natural realm, too. All can lead us to imagine God's reign among us.

FIRST READING
Isaiah 55:10–11

Thus says the LORD:
Just as from the heavens
    the rain and snow come down
and do not return there
    till they have watered the earth,
    making it fertile and fruitful,
giving seed to the one who sows
    and bread to the one who eats,
so shall my word be
    that goes forth from my mouth;
my word shall not return to me void,
    but shall do my will,
    achieving the end for which I sent it.

PSALM RESPONSE
Luke 8:8

The seed that falls on good ground will yield a fruitful harvest.

SECOND READING
Romans 8:18–23

Brothers and sisters: I consider that the sufferings of this present time are as nothing compared with the glory to be revealed for us. For creation awaits with eager expectation the revelation of the children of God; for creation was made subject to futility, not of its own accord but because of the one who subjected it, in hope that creation itself would be set free from slavery to corruption and share in the glorious freedom of the children of God. We know that all creation is groaning in labor pains even until now; and not only that, but we ourselves, who have the firstfruits of the Spirit, we also groan within ourselves as we wait for adoption, the redemption of our bodies.

In the shorter form of the reading, the passages in brackets are omitted.

GOSPEL
Matthew
13:1–23
or 13:1–9

On that day, Jesus went out of the house and sat down by the sea. Such large crowds gathered around him that he got into a boat and sat down, and the whole crowd stood along the shore. And he spoke to them at length in parables, saying: "A sower went out to sow. And as he sowed, some seed fell on the path, and birds came and ate it up. Some fell on rocky ground, where it had little soil. It sprang up at once because the soil was not deep, and when the sun rose it was scorched, and it withered for lack of roots. Some seed fell among thorns, and the thorns grew up and choked it. But some seed fell on rich soil, and produced fruit, a hundred or sixty or thirtyfold. Whoever has ears ought to hear."

[The disciples approached him and said, "Why do you speak to them in parables?" He said to them in reply, "Because knowledge of the mysteries of the kingdom of heaven has been granted to you, but to them it has not been granted. To anyone who has, more will be given and he will grow rich; from anyone who has not, even what he has will be taken away. This is why I speak to them in parables, because

they look but do not see and hear but do not listen or understand.

Isaiah's prophecy is fulfilled in them, which says:

You shall indeed hear but not understand,
   you shall indeed look but never see.
Gross is the heart of this people,
   they will hardly hear with their ears,
   they have closed their eyes,
   lest they see with their eyes
   and hear with their ears
and understand with their hearts and be converted,
   and I heal them.

"But blessed are your eyes, because they see, and your ears, because they hear. Amen, I say to you, many prophets and right-eous people longed to see what you see but did not see it, and to hear what you hear but did not hear it.

"Hear then the parable of the sower. The seed sown on the path is the one who hears the word of the kingdom without understand-ing it, and the evil one comes and steals away what was sown in his heart. The seed sown on rocky ground is the one who hears the word and receives it at once with joy. But he has no root and lasts only for a time. When some tribulation or persecution comes because of the word, he immediately falls away. The seed sown among thorns is the one who hears the word, but then worldly anxiety and the lure of riches choke the word and it bears no fruit. But the seed sown on rich soil is the one who hears the word and understands it, who indeed bears fruit and yields a hundred or sixty or thirtyfold."]

Writing to the people in exile, the prophet known as Second Isaiah encourages hopefulness, using nature as his inspiration. Just as rain and snow fulfill their goal—that of making the earth fertile—so too will God's word be fulfilled. Set within an invitation to a banquet (Isaiah 55:1), Second Isaiah charges the people to "seek the LORD" by forsaking wickedness and turning to God, who is merciful (Isaiah 55:6–7). The prophet attempts to explain the mysterious nature of God (Isaiah 55:8) by appealing to the efficacy of natural phenomena. In our Gospel, Jesus will also appeal to nature to explain the kingdom of heaven.

The wages of sin are death (Romans 6:23), so Paul can rightly acknowledge that "creation awaits with eager expectation the revelation of the children of God" (Romans 8:19), because creation also experiences death. Paul does not accuse creation of sin. Rather, he recognizes that the cosmic dimensions of salvation are meant not only for humanity, "who are led by the Spirit" (Romans 8:14), but also for all of creation. However, this redemption is yet to be complete, so "all creation is groaning in labor pains even until now" (Romans 8:22). Charged with hope, we are to "wait with endurance" (Romans 8:25) the fullness of redemption.

The thread of nature is woven throughout our three readings. In the first, nature is a metaphor for God's faithfulness. In Romans, creation shares in the same hope of redemption with humanity. And in today's Gospel, Jesus tells the parable of the sower and the seed to describe receptivity to his word. While the explanation of the parable (vv. 18–23) likely belongs to the early church and not Jesus, both parable and explanation focus on who can or cannot receive understanding. When asked why he speaks in parables to those gathered, Jesus answers, "Because knowledge of the mysteries of the kingdom of heaven has been granted to you" (v. 11). The quote from Isaiah (vv. 14–15) is used to explain why some accept Jesus' proclamation and others do not. "They have closed their eyes" (v. 15). Like the seed that fell on unfavorable places and could not grow, so also some people were destined not to accept Jesus. The explanation of the parable (vv. 18–23) addresses the question of the early church: Why have so many not believed?

❖❖ *Reflecting on the Word*

St. Thomas Aquinas taught that grace builds on nature. To understand God more fully, look at and try to discover what nature teaches us. Discover what a sign or symbol's use in everyday life can reveal about its use in sacramental life. Jesus did that. He tried to open eyes and ears by using parables, everyday realities that could shed light on who God is and how God's Spirit works among us. The Gospel uses the parable of the sower. St. Paul uses the image of labor and childbirth. Isaiah uses rain and snow.

Are we open to hear what God is saying to us in the events of life and how we respond to them, or have we become as hard as the ground that cannot receive the seed? Do we labor to understand God when we are asked to change familiar attitudes or ways of living? Do we allow the rain of God's reign to fall upon us in ways that soften us so that the seed of God's will can sow mercy, biblical justice, and reconciliation in us and our world?

Take time to reflect on the kind of soil that you are. What will it take for God's word to take root in you so that you remain as faithful in difficult times as in easy ones? What thorns of anxiety choke you and keep you from trusting God's promise to be with you at all times? What will it take to make the soil of your life rich and pliable rather than hard and unyielding? Open your eyes and ears to the world around and within you. Invite God's grace to build on nature by raining into the soil that you are and letting God's presence bear fruit beyond imagining.

❖ Consider/Discuss

- How do I till the soil of my heart to let God's seed grow within me?
- What keeps my heart hardened to the ways in which God invites growth and life?

❖ Living and Praying with the Word

Open my ears to hear your word, O God. Open my eyes to see your presence at all times. May your Spirit cultivate my heart so that it can be fertile ground that bears the fruit of the love you made visible in Jesus Christ.

July 23, 2017

SIXTEENTH SUNDAY IN ORDINARY TIME

Today's Focus: Re-focus

It can be easy to focus on what's wrong in life and in the world. Some time spent focused on grace and goodness can lead us to a brighter day.

FIRST READING
Wisdom 12:13, 16–19

There is no god besides you who have the care of all,
    that you need show you have not unjustly condemned.
For your might is the source of justice;
    your mastery over all things makes you lenient to all.
For you show your might when the perfection
        of your power is disbelieved;
    and in those who know you, you rebuke temerity.
But though you are master of might,
        you judge with clemency,
    and with much lenience you govern us;
    for power, whenever you will, attends you.
And you taught your people, by these deeds,
    that those who are just must be kind;
and you gave your children good ground for hope
    that you would permit repentance for their sins.

PSALM RESPONSE
Psalm 86:5a

Lord, you are good and forgiving.

SECOND READING
Romans 8:26–27

Brothers and sisters: The Spirit comes to the aid of our weakness; for we do not know how to pray as we ought, but the Spirit himself intercedes with inexpressible groanings. And the one who searches hearts knows what is the intention of the Spirit, because he intercedes for the holy ones according to God's will.

In the shorter form of the reading, the passages in brackets are omitted.

GOSPEL
Matthew
13:24–43
or 13:24–30

Jesus proposed another parable to the crowds, saying: "The kingdom of heaven may be likened to a man who sowed good seed in his field. While everyone was asleep his enemy came and sowed weeds all through the wheat, and then went off. When the crop grew and bore fruit, the weeds appeared as well. The slaves of the householder came to him and said, 'Master, did you not sow good seed in your field? Where have the weeds come from?' He answered, 'An enemy has done this.' His slaves said to him, 'Do you want us to go and pull them up?' He replied, 'No, if you pull up the weeds you might uproot the wheat along with them. Let them grow together until harvest; then at harvest time I will say to the harvesters, "First collect the weeds and tie them in bundles for burning; but gather the wheat into my barn." ' "

[He proposed another parable to them. "The kingdom of heaven is like a mustard seed that a person took and sowed in a field. It is the smallest of all the seeds, yet when full-grown it is the largest of plants. It becomes a large bush, and the 'birds of the sky come and dwell in its branches.' "

He spoke to them another parable. "The kingdom of heaven is like yeast that a woman took and mixed with three measures of wheat flour until the whole batch was leavened."

All these things Jesus spoke to the crowds in parables. He spoke to them only in parables, to fulfill what had been said through the prophet:

I will open my mouth in parables,
I will announce what has lain hidden from the foundation of the world.

Then, dismissing the crowds, he went into the house. His disciples approached him and said, "Explain to us the parable of the weeds in the field." He said in reply, "He who sows good seed is the Son of Man, the field is the world, the good seed the children of the kingdom. The weeds are the children of the evil one, and the enemy who sows them is the devil. The harvest is the end of the age, and the harvesters are angels. Just as weeds are collected and burned up with fire, so will it be at the end of the age. The Son of Man will send his angels, and they will collect out of his kingdom all who cause others to sin and all evildoers. They will throw them into the fiery furnace, where there will be wailing and grinding of teeth. Then the righteous will shine like the sun in the kingdom of their Father. Whoever has ears ought to hear."]

✤ Understanding the Word

The verses that comprise today's first reading are taken from a section of the book of Wisdom in which the author deviates from the topic of God's providence during the Exodus (Wisdom 11:2 — 19:22) to address the topic of God's mercy (Wisdom 11:17 — 12:22). The reading begins with an echo of the *Shema* (Deuteronomy 6:4–9) that acknowledges "there is no god besides you" (Wisdom 12:13). The very power and might of God lead to God's justice and leniency. God's examples should teach the people "that those who are just must be kind" (Wisdom 12:19).

The second reading continues the theme from the previous week, in which Paul acknowledges that "the sufferings of this present time are as nothing compared with the glory to be revealed to us" (Romans 8:18). Baptism into Christ has brought believers into a new relationship with God, so that they can rightly claim to be "children of God" (Romans 8:14). Until the fullness of that relationship is revealed, the Spirit is given to the community so as to strengthen the weak and to intercede on their behalf.

The Gospel reading presents three parables on the nature of the kingdom of heaven. The source of the parable of the mustard seed is Mark 4:30–32, while the source of the parable of the yeast is "Q" (a collection of sayings used by Matthew and Luke in addition to their material borrowed from Mark). But the parable of the weeds and wheat is unique to Matthew, and in fact frames this lection. The explanation found vv. 36–43 demonstrates that if this parable originated with Jesus, it has been thoroughly reworked by Matthew. Several sayings unique to Matthew stress the presence of good and bad within the Matthean community (13:47–50; 25:1–13; 31–46). That the weeds and wheat grow together until the "harvest" suggests that the ultimate decision about who is "weed" and who is "wheat" will be the prerogative of Jesus at the final judgment (25:31).

✤ Reflecting on the Word

A few years ago I asked my dentist about a small growth on my gum. He examined it and asked if it hurt when pushed. I answered "No." He wondered if it got in the way of normal functioning. I answered "No." He continues to monitor it and will only remove it if it changes shape or becomes problematic. It took me a while to accept this foreign growth. Now it makes sense to avoid unnecessary surgery.

Weeds and wheat, bad and good, sin and grace coexist in life. News reports tend to highlight the former over the latter. People ask, "Why does God allow this?" Great minds have addressed this question. The most common answer: Without choice there is no real love. Life is what it is with both good and bad. We can choose to accept that both the weeds and wheat, the bad and good, are part of life and choose the good as much as possible. Or we can spend so much energy on the "why" that we miss the good before us. Like the growth on my gum, the less we focus on it, the less power evil has. The more we feed the good, the more we rob evil of its power and grow in trust that God's merciful love will reign in the end.

The Letter to the Romans assures us, "The Spirit comes to the aid of our weakness" (Romans 8:26). If we turn to God in truth, even when we have a growth that might need removing, we can discover what we need to accept, what we can change, and the wisdom needed to know the difference.

✤ Consider/Discuss

- What are the weeds and wheat that invite you to discern God's will in your life?
- How do you know the difference between what you need to accept and what you can change in life?

✤ Living and Praying with the Word

Come, Holy Spirit; come to the aid of my weakness and open my eyes to your grace. Give me your wisdom to know what to keep and what to release in my life.

July 30, 2017

SEVENTEENTH SUNDAY IN ORDINARY TIME

Today's Focus: The Promise of Love

Our covenant of love with God is our security and strength. May it also be the song that fills our hearts and lives each day.

FIRST READING
1 Kings 3:5, 7–12

The LORD appeared to Solomon in a dream at night. God said, "Ask something of me and I will give it to you." Solomon answered: "O LORD, my God, you have made me, your servant, king to succeed my father David; but I am a mere youth, not knowing at all how to act. I serve you in the midst of the people whom you have chosen, a people so vast that it cannot be numbered or counted. Give your servant, therefore, an understanding heart to judge your people and to distinguish right from wrong. For who is able to govern this vast people of yours?"

The LORD was pleased that Solomon made this request. So God said to him: "Because you have asked for this—not for a long life for yourself, nor for riches, nor for the life of your enemies, but for understanding so that you may know what is right—I do as you requested. I give you a heart so wise and understanding that there has never been anyone like you up to now, and after you there will come no one to equal you."

PSALM RESPONSE
Psalm 119:97a

Lord, I love your commands.

SECOND READING
Romans 8:28–30

Brothers and sisters: We know that all things work for good for those who love God, who are called according to his purpose. For those he foreknew he also predestined to be conformed to the image of his Son, so that he might be the firstborn among many brothers and sisters. And those he predestined he also called; and those he called he also justified; and those he justified he also glorified.

GOSPEL
Matthew
13:44–52
or 13:44–46

Jesus said to his disciples: "The kingdom of heaven is like a treasure buried in a field, which a person finds and hides again, and out of joy goes and sells all that he has and buys that field. Again, the kingdom of heaven is like a merchant searching for fine pearls. When he finds a pearl of great price, he goes and sells all that he has and buys it. [Again, the kingdom of heaven is like a net thrown into the sea, which collects fish of every kind. When it is full they haul it ashore and sit down to put what is good into buckets. What is bad they throw away. Thus it will be at the end of the age. The angels will go out and separate the wicked from the righteous and throw them into the fiery furnace, where there will be wailing and grinding of teeth.

"Do you understand all these things?" They answered, "Yes." And he replied, "Then every scribe who has been instructed in the kingdom of heaven is like the head of a household who brings from his storeroom both the new and the old."]

❖❖ *Understanding the Word*

The books of First and Second Samuel and First and Second Kings were edited by the hand of a historian, who stressed that Israel's exile had resulted from the poor religious and political leadership of its kings and the failure of the people to uphold the covenant. Very few kings stand as righteous under the critical eye of this writer. Solomon is an exception. In today's reading, Solomon acknowledges his limitations and asks God for help. And because Solomon asked not for the temporal trappings of power but for wisdom to rule God's people, God grants his request. "I give you a heart so wise and understanding that there has never been anyone like you up to now" (1 Kings 3:12).

Paul is writing to a community he has not met, but hopes will receive him well and financially support his ministry to Spain (Romans 15:24). He has carefully outlined his "gospel" as the fulfillment of scripture (Romans 1:1), and assured the Roman believers that their baptism into Christ is a baptism into his death and resurrection (Romans 6:3). In today's reading, Paul assures us that the purpose of God is being accomplished (Romans 8:28). Step by step, salvation is being worked out. First we are predestined, then called, then justified, and finally glorified.

The series of three parables and concluding saying read in today's Gospel are unique to Matthew and shed light on the evangelist's understanding of discipleship. The first two (the parable of the buried treasure and the parable of the pearl of great price) make the same point. The discovery of something of unparalleled value requires the relinquishment of all one's possessions. In Matthew 19:21, this point is stated directly in relation to discipleship. Here it clearly refers to those who have "found" Jesus. The parable of the net thrown into the sea picks up the same theme as the parable of the weeds and wheat (Matthew 13:24–30). At the end of the age, the angels will "separate the wicked from the righteous" (Matthew 13:49). The concluding saying about the scribe instructed in the kingdom of heaven is often thought to be an autobiographical comment about the evangelist, who may have been a scribe himself.

❖ Reflecting on the Word

I recently spoke with a woman about why she went to visit her husband in an assisted living facility every day, even though Alzheimer's disease kept him from recognizing her as his wife of sixty-plus years. Without missing a beat she said, "Because I love him and he would do the same for me." She added, "And as much as I love him, I know that after he's gone only my faith will support me and keep us connected until we are in heaven, where he'll recognize me again." Their marital love is a great a treasure to her. Her faith is her pearl of great price and the net in which they will be collected together again. What wisdom!

The things of this world pass away, even those we love. Only our faith in God is with us at all times, through thick and thin, sickness and health, from death to eternal life. Solomon asks God for the wisdom of faith: "Give [me] an understanding heart to judge your people and to distinguish right from wrong" (1 Kings 3:9). Our psalm echoes these words "The revelation of your words sheds light, giving understanding to the simple" (Psalm 119:130). Faith in God is the only treasure that remains with us when all else is gone and all other paths fail.

St. Francis de Sales offered a prayer for wisdom that went something like this: "Lord Jesus, I surrender to you. Make me a lute that you play. Touch any string and allow me to make music in harmony with you." Faith gives us the wisdom to love as Christ loved, live as he lived, and surrender all for that greatest treasure. Therein lies wisdom at all times!

❖ Consider/Discuss

- Who or what is my pearl of great price?
- What role does my faith play in the decisions I make, whether big or small?

❖ Living and Praying with the Word

Give me your wisdom, O God, to know right from wrong and to discover and live your will. Make me an instrument through whom the world hears and sings the music of your compassionate, merciful love.

August 6, 2017

THE TRANSFIGURATION OF THE LORD

Today's Focus: The Transfiguring Voice

We hear God's affirming voice from heaven as Jesus is gloriously transfigured. Our own words and voices have the power to transform—for good or ill—those around us.

FIRST READING
Daniel 7:9–10, 13–14

As I watched:
Thrones were set up
    and the Ancient One took his throne.
His clothing was snow bright,
    and the hair on his head as white as wool;
his throne was flames of fire,
    with wheels of burning fire.
A surging stream of fire
    flowed out from where he sat;
Thousands upon thousands were ministering to him,
    and myriads upon myriads attended him.
The court was convened and the books were opened.

As the visions during the night continued, I saw
    One like a Son of man coming,
        on the clouds of heaven;
    When he reached the Ancient One
        and was presented before him,
    The one like a Son of man received dominion, glory, and kingship;
        all peoples, nations, and languages serve him.
    His dominion is an everlasting dominion
        that shall not be taken away,
        his kingship shall not be destroyed.

PSALM RESPONSE
Psalm 97:1a, 9a

The Lord is king, the most high over all the earth.

SECOND READING
2 Peter 1:16–19

Beloved: We did not follow cleverly devised myths when we made known to you the power and coming of our Lord Jesus Christ, but we had been eyewitnesses of his majesty. For he received honor and glory from God the Father when that unique declaration came to him from the majestic glory, "This is my Son, my beloved, with whom I am well pleased." We ourselves heard this voice come from heaven while we were with him on the holy mountain. Moreover, we possess the prophetic message that is altogether reliable. You will do well to be attentive to it, as to a lamp shining in a dark place, until day dawns and the morning start rises in your hearts.

GOSPEL

Matthew 17:1–9

Jesus took Peter, James, and his brother, John, and led them up a high mountain by themselves. And he was transfigured before them; his face shone like the sun and his clothes became white as light. And behold, Moses and Elijah appeared to them, conversing with him. Then Peter said to Jesus in reply, "Lord, it is good that we are here. If you wish, I will make three tents here, one for you, one for Moses, and one for Elijah." While he was still speaking, behold, a bright cloud cast a shadow over them, then from the cloud came a voice that said, "This is my beloved Son, with whom I am well pleased; listen to him." When the disciples heard this they fell prostrate and were very much afraid. But Jesus came and touched them, saying, "Rise, and do not be afraid." And when the disciples raised their eyes, they saw no one else but Jesus alone.

As they were coming down from the mountain, Jesus charged them, "Do not tell the vision to anyone until the Son of Man has been raised from the dead."

❖❖ *Understanding the Word*

Underlying all three of today's readings is a first-century theological understanding about the end-times. Eschatology—the Bible's understandings about the end-times—holds that in some future time God will intervene to judge the world and to set in motion a new reality. Apocalypticism is a form of eschatology that sees a catastrophic end to history in a cosmic battle between good and evil. Apocalpytic eschatology emerged out of the suffering of the religious Jews under the Seleucid kings. Humanity is also divided between good and bad, and while this evil age holds sway now, God's justice will rule in the time to come. In apocalyptic understanding, the Son of Man would usher in the cosmic beginning of the Reign of God, but would then depart. After a period of time, the Messiah would come, and the New Age would be complete.

Using apocalyptic imagery, Daniel's visions in chapters 7–12 anticipate the raising of the dead to judgment, the triumph of the Kingdom of God, and the coming of the "one like a Son of Man" (Daniel 7:13). This Son of Man would receive dominion, glory, and kingship (Daniel 7:14). Elsewhere in Daniel the worldly kingdoms are represented by fantastic and terrifying animals, but the kingdom of God is presented as a human figure.

The reading from Second Peter refers to the story of Jesus' transfiguration to assure the community that their faith is not based on "cleverly devised myths," (2 Peter 1:16), but eyewitness accounts (2 Peter 1:18). "This is my Son, my beloved, with whom I am well pleased" (2 Peter 1:17) parallels the version found in Matthew, suggesting that the author of the pseudepigraphical (written by someone else) work had access to the Gospel of Matthew.

All three Synoptic Gospels (Matthew, Mark, Luke) include the event of the Transfiguration, which served to foreshadow Jesus' glorification after his death. But Matthew's description more fully draws on apocalyptic imagery from Daniel. Jesus' face "shone like the sun" (Matthew 17:2), echoing Daniel 10:6. Only Matthew includes the disciples' response to the heavenly voice ("they fell prostrate and were very much afraid" [Matthew 17:6]), and Jesus' touching them and telling them, "rise and do not be afraid" (Matthew 17:7), similar to Daniel 10:9–10, 18–19.

❖ Reflecting on the Word

Only Matthew's account of the Transfiguration has the voice proclaiming Jesus as the one "with whom I am well pleased." Peter's eyewitness account in Acts repeats these words. Jesus is the Son of Man, transformed in looks and clothing, and the One with whom God is well pleased, the beloved to whom we are to listen. No wonder his face shone like the sun.

Our words can transform people for good and for ill. I have seen someone's face, posture, and entire being changed when praised and when ridiculed. While affirming a young woman in recovery last week, her face lit up and she beamed. The face of a young man who shared that he and his wife were pregnant gleamed and he glowed. Similarly, when speaking with someone who was abused, I have seen a face drain while the person shared his or her story and their appearance become listless and lifeless.

We put on Christ in baptism. We became adopted daughters and sons of God, called to be God's beloved and give dominion, glory, and power to the Transfigured Christ. We promised to listen to him and rise up out of any fear that our own sin makes us inadequate to the task of living Jesus and shining with the light of God. We can live in ways that are pleasing to God or that are not because they reveal our preference for darkness to the light of the Transfigured One. Like Peter, James, and John, we are witnesses to Jesus' transforming power. While challenging, that good news can make our faces shine like the sun and fill the world with the light of the Son.

❖ Consider/Discuss

- What helps you see yourself as God's beloved child? What gets in the way?
- When have you beamed because of your faith? Describe the experience you had.

❖ Living and Praying with the Word

Life-giving God, in baptism you have made us your daughters and sons and filled us with the light of your beloved, Jesus Christ. Help us shine like the sun because we choose what is pleasing to you. Through us, fill the world with the light of your beloved Son.

August 13, 2017

NINETEENTH SUNDAY IN ORDINARY TIME

Today's Focus: Our Daily Prayer

We ask God to give us our daily bread, but prayer is another kind of nourishment also necessary for our spiritual life.

FIRST READING
1 Kings 19:9a, 11–13a

At the mountain of God, Horeb, Elijah came to a cave where he took shelter. Then the LORD said to him, "Go outside and stand on the mountain before the LORD; the LORD will be passing by." A strong and heavy wind was rending the mountains and crushing rocks before the LORD—but the LORD was not in the wind. After the wind there was an earthquake—but the LORD was not in the earthquake. After the earthquake there was fire—but the LORD was not in the fire. After the fire there was a tiny whispering sound. When he heard this, Elijah hid his face in his cloak and went and stood at the entrance of the cave.

PSALM RESPONSE
Psalm 85:8

Lord, let us see your kindness, and grant us your salvation.

SECOND READING
Romans 9:1–5

Brothers and sisters: I speak the truth in Christ, I do not lie; my conscience joins with the Holy Spirit in bearing me witness that I have great sorrow and constant anguish in my heart. For I could wish that I myself were accursed and cut off from Christ for the sake of my own people, my kindred according to the flesh. They are Israelites; theirs the adoption, the glory, the covenants, the giving of the law, the worship, and the promises; theirs the patriarchs, and from them, according to the flesh, is the Christ, who is over all, God blessed forever. Amen.

GOSPEL
Matthew
14:22–33
After he had fed the people, Jesus made the disciples get into a boat and precede him to the other side, while he dismissed the crowds. After doing so, he went up on the mountain by himself to pray. When it was evening he was there alone. Meanwhile the boat, already a few miles offshore, was being tossed about by the waves, for the wind was against it. During the fourth watch of the night, he came toward them walking on the sea. When the disciples saw him walking on the sea they were terrified. "It is a ghost," they said, and they cried out in fear. At once Jesus spoke to them, "Take courage, it is I; do not be afraid." Peter said to him in reply, "Lord, if it is you, command me to come to you on the water." He said, "Come." Peter got out of the boat and began to walk on the water toward Jesus. But when he saw how strong the wind was he became frightened; and, beginning to sink, he cried out, "Lord, save me!" Immediately Jesus stretched out his hand and caught Peter, and said to him, "O you of little faith, why did you doubt?" After they got into the boat, the wind died down. Those who were in the boat did him homage, saying, "Truly, you are the Son of God."

❖ Understanding the Word

The cycle of stories about Elijah and Elisha reflects the struggle between prophet and king during the period of the divided monarchy. In today's first reading, Elijah has taken refuge on the mountain of God, Horeb, after narrowly escaping the wrath of Jezebel, the wife of King Ahab (1 Kings 19:2), and nearly dying in the wilderness (1 Kings 19:4). Like Moses before him on the same mountain (Exodus 19:16–19; 33:18–23; 34:5–6), Elijah encounters manifestations of the divine in natural phenomena. But the actual divine presence is found in the whispering sound (1 Kings 19:12).

A continual source of anguish for the Apostle Paul was the lack of belief in Christ by the majority of Israel. So strong was his heartbreak that in today's reading he would suffer separation from Christ if it would bring Israel to true righteousness (Romans 9:3). The question of Israel's rejection of Jesus was a serious concern for early believers, since the divine plan was rooted in God's election of Israel. In Romans 9 — 11, Paul attempts to answer those concerns by assuring the Roman community that God has not rejected them (Romans 11:2).

In today's Gospel, Jesus is able to find time for prayer, which had been interrupted by the crowds (Matthew 14:14). Jesus sends the disciples off in the boat without him. When he sees the boat being tossed by the sea, he walks toward it on the water. Into Mark's version, Matthew inserts the story of Peter's attempt to walk on the water. Jesus' question to Peter, "Why did you doubt?" may have brought solace to the community of Matthew, which saw Peter as its founding leader. The community could take heart that though Peter struggled, he could respond with the others in the boat, "Truly, you are the Son of God" (Matthew 14:33). So too could they surmount their own doubt, hearing Jesus' words to the disciples as if addressed to them: "Take courage, it is I; do not be afraid" (Matthew 14:27).

Peter gives me hope and strength. He was the leader of the apostles, the rock, but that rock was cracked by doubt, fear, and misunderstanding. One moment he got it and the next Jesus rebuked him. That reflects my faith journey. When I take time to pray I keep my eyes on Jesus and the God he came to reveal. The Spirit lessens my fears and doubts and helps me trust in God's constant presence in my life, even when I feel most alone and unworthy. When I do not take that time I focus only on me. I feel alone, inadequate, and I begin to fall and sink.

St. Francis de Sales tells us that we ought to make time to pray each day. When we feel that we don't have enough time for prayer, we should take even more time. Why? Because in prayer we aspire to God, that is, we seek to do God's will and breathe as one with God. In prayer God also inspires us and breathes as one with us. Daily prayer is a compass that helps to keep our focus on God, through Christ, in the Spirit. In prayer we become so one with God that our breath and God's breath are in sync. Then, whether the waters of life are treacherous or smooth, we can see Jesus coming to us, walking with us, and guiding our way. Then we are quiet enough to hear God's voice in the tiny whispering sound. By taking time to pray, we invite Jesus to come to us, we can better hear his invitation to come to him, and we can see the face that lessens our doubts and calms our spirits. Breathe deeply. Be one with Jesus, the Son of God, who is always with us.

❖ *Consider/Discuss*

- When have you experienced Jesus' presence in ways that helped you walk across life's rough waters?
- What helps you to breathe as one with God in prayer?

❖ *Living and Praying with the Word*

Ever-present God, you are with us always and in all ways. Help me take time to focus on your Son, Jesus, each day, so that I can walk on the waters of life guided by your Holy Spirit.

August 15, 2017

THE ASSUMPTION OF
THE BLESSED VIRGIN MARY

Today's Focus: Loving Completely

In Mary we see a child of God and follower of Christ, filled with the Holy Spirit. She gave herself completely to God's will; in this she is our supreme example.

FIRST READING
Revelation 11:19a; 12:1–6a; 10ab

God's temple in heaven was opened, and the ark of his covenant could be seen in the temple.

A great sign appeared in the sky, a woman clothed with the sun, with the moon beneath her feet, and on her head a crown of twelve stars. She was with child and wailed aloud in pain as she labored to give birth. Then another sign appeared in the sky; it was a huge red dragon, with seven heads and ten horns, and on its heads were seven diadems. Its tail swept away a third of the stars in the sky and hurled them down to the earth. Then the dragon stood before the woman about to give birth, to devour her child when she gave birth. She gave birth to a son, a male child, destined to rule all the nations with an iron rod. Her child was caught up to God and his throne. The woman herself fled into the desert where she had a place prepared by God.

Then I heard a loud voice in heaven say:
"Now have salvation and power come,
    and the Kingdom of our God
    and the authority of his Anointed One."

PSALM RESPONSE
Psalm 45: 10 bc

The queen stands at your right hand, arrayed in gold.

SECOND READING
1 Corinthians 15:20–27

Brothers and sisters: Christ has been raised from the dead, the firstfruits of those who have fallen asleep. For since death came through man, the resurrection of the dead came also through man. For just as in Adam all die, so too in Christ shall all be brought to life, but each one in proper order: Christ the firstfruits; then, at his coming, those who belong to Christ; then comes the end, when he hands over the kingdom to his God and Father, when he has destroyed every sovereignty and every authority and power. For he must reign until he has put all his enemies under his feet. The last enemy to be destroyed is death, for "he subjected everything under his feet."

GOSPEL
Luke 1:39–56

Mary set out and traveled to the hill country in haste to a town of Judah, where she entered the house of Zechariah and greeted Elizabeth. When Elizabeth heard Mary's greeting, the infant leaped in her womb, and Elizabeth, filled with the Holy Spirit, cried out in a loud voice and said, "Blessed are you among women, and blessed is the fruit of your womb. And how does this happen to me, that the mother of my Lord should come to me? For at the moment the sound of your greeting reached my ears, the infant in my womb leaped for joy. Blessed are you who believed that what was spoken to you by the Lord would be fulfilled."

And Mary said:
"My soul proclaims the greatness of the Lord;
    my spirit rejoices in God my Savior
    for he has looked upon his lowly servant.
From this day all generations will call me blessed:
    the Almighty has done great things for me
    and holy is his Name.
    He has mercy on those who fear him
    in every generation.
He has shown the strength of his arm,
    and has scattered the proud in their conceit.
He has cast down the mighty from their thrones,
    and has lifted up the lowly.
He has filled the hungry with good things,
    and the rich he has sent away empty.
He has come to the help of his servant Israel
    for he has remembered his promise of mercy,
    the promise he made to our fathers,
    to Abraham and his children for ever."

Mary remained with her about three months and then returned to her home.

✢ Understanding the Word

The book of Revelation, from which our first reading is taken, is the only complete apocalyptic work in the New Testament. Apocalypticism anticipated the end of the current age, which was under the dominion of evil, and the emergence of a new age of God's reign. The orderly consummation of history would conclude with God's triumph and the last enemy to be destroyed would be death. Typical of apocalyptic works, the book of Revelation is filled with symbols and images that serve as coded language. Today's reading speaks of God's appearance (theophany) as symbolized by the visible Ark of the Covenant. The dramatic imagery of a woman giving birth has often been thought to symbolize Mary the mother of Jesus. However, as scholars note, the woman is likely an image of the church in travail, caught between the end of the evil age and God's reign. The twelve stars are reminiscent of the Twelve Tribes so that this church is the heir to the Old Testament covenant. The dragon in ancient myths represents the powers against God, and red indicates death. In Revelation, the seven-headed dragon is also the symbol of the satanic empire (17:3). After giving birth, the woman flees into the desert, a place where God's people have traditionally been cared for.

Paul shares a similar apocalyptic world-view with the author of Revelation. The resurrection of Jesus demonstrated that this new age had dawned and was in the process of fulfillment. According to Paul, Adam represents humanity enslaved by sin, and Christ is the firstfruits who will redeem humanity.

The Gospel reading presents the story of the Visitation of Mary and Elizabeth, which also serves to foreshadow the encounter between John the Baptist and Jesus at his baptism. With Mary's greeting, Elizabeth's child leaps in her womb and she is filled with the Holy Spirit. Elizabeth calls Mary "the mother of my Lord" showing her recognition of Jesus' destiny. John will evidence similar respect when he points out that one mightier than himself will come, baptizing with the Holy Spirit and fire (Luke 3:16).

✢ Reflecting on the Word

The assumption of Mary into heavenly glory is in one sense the most recent doctrine of the Catholic Church, defined by Pope Pius XII in 1950. But that is only the date of its official declaration. There is evidence of Christians believing this as early as the fifth century, and it is noteworthy that, to our knowledge, no one has ever claimed to have a relic of Mary's body, implying that Mary's body was presumed to be gone. But whether this belief is recent or ancient, we might still ask *why* Christians came to believe this about Mary. There is no scriptural account of this event. Why, then, have Christians believed that Mary is, body and soul, with her Son Jesus in heavenly glory?

We do know from the scriptures that Mary made herself available to God's plan of salvation in both body and soul. Indeed, Mary had the unique role in the history of salvation of giving birth to Emmanuel: God-with-us. One might say that because of the Incarnation, Mary's physical existence had a role in salvation surpassed only by that of Jesus. Opening her soul to God would not have been enough to fulfill God's purposes. She had to be open to God with the totality of her being.

St. Augustine wrote: "My weight is my love. Wherever I am carried, my love is carrying me. By your gift we are set on fire and carried upwards; we grow red hot and ascend" (*Confessions*, 8.9.10). Mary loved God with her whole self, body and soul. Our belief in her assumption grows from our belief that the love kindled in her by God's grace has carried her, body and soul, into heavenly glory. And we further believe that what has come to pass in Mary is the destiny of all lovers of God, whose bodies will be raised at Christ's second coming.

❖ Consider/Discuss

- How do I imagine the "heavenly glory" in which Mary now dwells? What images come to my mind?
- Do I make myself available to God in both my soul and my body, but living out my faith on a daily basis?

❖ Praying with the Word

Holy Spirit, enkindle us with the fire of the same love that burned within the Virgin Mary, so that we might rise up to God in prayer. Amen.

August 20, 2017

TWENTIETH SUNDAY IN ORDINARY TIME

Today's Focus: Finished Feuds

When we open our hearts to let in the reconciling power of God, we can discover how petty and useless many of our squabbles can be.

FIRST READING
Isaiah 56:1, 6–7

Thus says the LORD:
Observe what is right, do what is just;
    for my salvation is about to come,
    my justice, about to be revealed.

The foreigners who join themselves to the LORD,
    ministering to him,
loving the name of the LORD,
    and becoming his servants—
all who keep the sabbath free from profanation
    and hold to my covenant,
them I will bring to my holy mountain
    and make joyful in my house of prayer;
their burnt offerings and sacrifices
    will be acceptable on my altar,
for my house shall be called
    a house of prayer for all peoples.

PSALM RESPONSE
Psalm 67:4

O God, let all the nations praise you!

SECOND READING
Romans 11: 13–15, 29–32

Brothers and sisters: I am speaking to you Gentiles. Inasmuch as I am the apostle to the Gentiles, I glory in my ministry in order to make my race jealous and thus save some of them. For if their rejection is the reconciliation of the world, what will their acceptance be but life from the dead?

For the gifts and the call of God are irrevocable. Just as you once disobeyed God but have now received mercy because of their disobedience, so they have now disobeyed in order that, by virtue of the mercy shown to you, they too may now receive mercy. For God delivered all to disobedience, that he might have mercy upon all.

At that time, Jesus withdrew to the region of Tyre and Sidon. And behold, a Canaanite woman of that district came and called out, "Have pity on me, Lord, Son of David! My daughter is tormented by a demon." But Jesus did not say a word in answer to her. Jesus' disciples came and asked him, "Send her away, for she keeps calling out after us." He said in reply, "I was sent only to the lost sheep of the house of Israel." But the woman came and did Jesus homage, saying, "Lord, help me." He said in reply, "It is not right to take the food of the children and throw it to the dogs." She said, "Please, Lord, for even the dogs eat the scraps that fall from the table of their masters." Then Jesus said to her in reply, "O woman, great is your faith! Let it be done for you as you wish." And the woman's daughter was healed from that hour.

❖ Understanding the Word

The themes of justice, righteousness, and salvation sound throughout the entire book of Isaiah, and serve to open the third section of the book (Isaiah 56:1), written by an unknown prophet referred to as Third Isaiah. The universalism indicated in Isaiah 49:6 ("I will make you a light to the nations") is further developed here. Foreigners who desire to join themselves to the LORD, love the name of the LORD, keep the Sabbath, and hold to the covenant will be brought to God's holy mountain.

It is not foreigners who are Paul's concern in the second reading, but his own people. Israel's rejection allowed for the mission to the Gentiles. Paul glories in this mission, hoping to stir jealousy among his own people and thus draw them into the faith (Romans 11:13). But he warns the Gentile believers not to be "wise in their estimation" (Romans 11:25). Israel remains beloved of God, "for the gifts and call of God are irrevocable" (Romans 11:29).

The Gospel reading presents an interesting narrative about a "foreigner" who does not wish to join herself to the Lord but nonetheless seeks out Jesus. Matthew edits Mark's original story about a Syro-Phoenician mother so that the woman is now a Canaanite, Israel's dreaded enemy. Matthew has the Canaanite woman come out to meet Jesus, presumably on the road in Gentile territory. She acknowledges Jesus' Jewish identity by calling him "Son of David" (Matthew 15:22). When Jesus announces, "I was sent only to the lost sheep of the house of Israel . . . It is not right to take the food of children and throw it to the dogs" (Matthew 15:24–26), the woman's clever response wins Jesus over. "Even the dogs eat the scraps" (Matthew 15:27). In the two encounters with Gentiles in Matthew's Gospel, Jesus has commended their great faith (Matthew 8:10; 15:28), foreshadowing that Gentiles would later join the Christian community.

I remember what "breaking news" it was when the Hatfields and McCoys, long-time bitter enemies, reconciled. It was also "breaking news" when we learned that Pope Francis would meet with Patriarch Kirill of the Russian Orthodox Church after a thousand-year split. Who are the bitter and age-old enemies that would surprise you if they finally met and began a journey to reconciliation? That is the power of the meeting between the Canaanite woman and Jesus. We hear his resistance: "I was sent only to the lost sheep of the house of Israel . . . It is not right to take the food of the children and throw it to the dogs." How would you respond if you were called a dog, whether directly or indirectly? But the woman's faith leads her to persist respectfully "Please, Lord, for even the dogs eat the scraps that fall from the table of their masters." Jesus is moved by her great faith and her daughter is healed.

Isaiah tells us that God's holy mountain is a house of prayer for all people. That includes even that "so-and-so who done me dirt," as my Aunt Sophia would say. God cannot be hemmed in by our littleness and our limitations. We pray in Eucharistic Prayer for Reconciliation II: "By your Spirit you move human hearts that enemies may speak to each other again, adversaries join hands, and peoples seek to meet together." Just as it took a while for Jesus to be moved by the Canaanite woman, meeting and reconciling take time. But the "breaking news" is that such meeting and reconciliation is possible, for "God delivered all to disobedience, that he might have mercy upon all" (Romans 11:32).

✦ *Consider/Discuss*

- Who is the Hatfield to your McCoy or the enemy with whom you can't imagine reconciling?
- Where has God surprised you and brought healing where you least expected?

✦ *Living and Praying with the Word*

Almighty God, creator of all, too often we divide what you unite and are blind to the breadth of your merciful love. Open the eyes of our hearts that we might see you in those we least expect. Please give us the persistent, respectful, and powerful faith of the Canaanite woman.

August 27, 2017

TWENTY-FIRST SUNDAY IN ORDINARY TIME

Today's Focus: Open Up!

We live in a world filled with locks and keys, with all kinds of devices meant to keep others out. But prayer is a key we are given to open up our lives to God and to others.

FIRST READING
Isaiah 22:19–23

Thus says the LORD to Shebna, master of the palace:
"I will thrust you from your office
    and pull you down from your station.
On that day I will summon my servant
    Eliakim, son of Hilkiah;
I will clothe him with your robe,
    and gird him with your sash,
    and give over to him your authority.
He shall be a father to the inhabitants of Jerusalem,
    and to the house of Judah.
I will place the key of the House of David on Eliakim's shoulder;
    when he opens, no one shall shut
    when he shuts, no one shall open.
I will fix him like a peg in a sure spot,
    to be a place of honor for his family."

PSALM RESPONSE
Psalm 138:8bc

Lord, your love is eternal; do not forsake the work of your hands.

SECOND READING
Romans 11:33–36

Oh, the depth of the riches and wisdom and knowledge of God!
How inscrutable are his judgments and how unsearchable his ways!
    For who has known the mind of the Lord
        or who has been his counselor?
    Or who has given the Lord anything
        that he may be repaid?
For from him and through him and for him are all things. To him be glory forever. Amen.

GOSPEL
Matthew
16:13–20

Jesus went into the region of Caesarea Philippi and he asked his disciples, "Who do people say that the Son of Man is?" They replied, "Some say John the Baptist, others Elijah, still others Jeremiah or one of the prophets." He said to them, "But who do you say that I am?" Simon Peter said in reply, "You are the Christ, the Son of the living God." Jesus said to him in reply, "Blessed are you, Simon son of Jonah. For flesh and blood has not revealed this to you, but my heavenly Father. And so I say to you, you are Peter, and upon this rock I will build my church, and the gates of the netherworld shall not prevail against it. I will give you the keys to the kingdom of heaven. Whatever you bind on earth shall be bound in heaven; and whatever you loose on earth shall be loosed in heaven." Then he strictly ordered his disciples to tell no one that he was the Christ.

❖ Understanding the Word

We are used to hearing the grand visions and oracles of the prophet Isaiah, so today's condemnation of Shebna, a mere palace official, seems a bit beneath him. Scholars propose that Isaiah may have objected to Shebna's luxurious lifestyle, including the construction of a tomb (Isaiah 22:16) and his fondness for chariots (Isaiah 22:18). In his place God directs Isaiah to install Eliakim, upon whom God will place "the key of the House of David" (Isaiah 22:22). Later, Eliakim will prove to be a disappointing replacement (Isaiah 22:24–25).

The reading from Paul's Letter to the Romans serves as the conclusion of his section addressing the rejection and role of Israel in God's salvific plan. Both Jew and Gentile were given over to sin, and both received God's mercy (Romans 11:30–31). The profound plan of God is beyond comprehension. Echoing Isaiah 40:13 and Wisdom 9:13, Paul asks, "For who has known the mind of the Lord or who has been his counselor?" (Romans 11:34). In the concluding doxology, Paul appears to have integrated Stoic ideas of God as the creator, sustainer, and goal of the universe (Romans 11:36).

As the first reading recorded, God vests with power and authority only those worthy of the task. Simon Peter answers Jesus' query with profound insight, "You are the Christ, the Son of the living God" (Matthew 16:16). Like Eliakim in the reading from Isaiah, Jesus gives the symbol of authority, the keys of the kingdom of heaven, to Simon (Matthew 16:19), who becomes the rock upon which Jesus will build the church (Matthew 16:18). The term translated as "church," comes from the Greek *ekklesia*, which means an assembly, and is a synonym for synagogue. Matthew's community may have been excluded from worship in the synagogue because of their declaration of Jesus as the Messiah. Thus, the Jewish Christians gather in a new synagogue, which they call "church." Peter stands as the foundation of this new assembly, "and the gates of the netherworld shall not prevail against it" (Matthew 16:18).

Who do you say that Jesus is? Peter's response came not from mere flesh and blood but from "my heavenly Father" (Matthew 16:17). Peter's rock was a reliance on God that comes from prayer. Peter became the rock of the church, the assembly of God's people in Christ, and the keys of the kingdom were given to him and the early church. Similarly, Eliakim was given the keys to the House of David.

Keys lock and unlock, open and close. When someone has an insight into someone or something, that insight is called key because it unlocks the mind and offers understanding. When someone has a necessary role in a family or organization, one is often referred to as key to that family or organization. Key to our faith is whether or not we are willing to submit ourselves to God, through Christ, in the Spirit. Eliakim was chosen because Shebna thought himself more essential than the king and God he served and was unwilling to serve them. Peter was chosen because he relied on God and returned to God, submitting his will to God, when he got it wrong or denied knowing Jesus because of fear. Prayer is key to submitting our lives to reliance on God's will in order to live our faith. In prayer we speak to God, yes; but we must also listen for God's voice. In prayer we can learn the mind of God, who alone opens our minds and hearts to the wisdom that proclaims Jesus as the Christ, the Son of God. Take time to pray. Ask yourself, "Who do I say that Jesus is?" May your words, deeds, and attitudes proclaim that Jesus Christ is the Son of God, our rock, to whom we give glory now and forever. Amen.

✣ Consider/Discuss

- How do you answer Jesus' question, "Who do you say that I am?"
- What difference does your answer make in how you live each day?

✣ Living and Praying with the Word

Bind me to yourself, O God, and open the eyes of my mind to your Word, that I might know your will and have the courage to live it. Heal the cracks in the rock of my faith, and help all that I say, do, and am proclaim my belief in your Son, Jesus Christ.

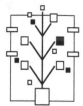

September 3, 2017

TWENTY-SECOND SUNDAY IN ORDINARY TIME

Today's Focus: Tough Questions, Tough Times

Though we'd prefer an always-easy life, life isn't that way. A deepened relationship with God is the ultimate place to turn.

FIRST READING
Jeremiah 20:7–9

You duped me, O Lord, and I let myself be duped;
  you were too strong for me, and you triumphed.
All the day I am an object of laughter;
  everyone mocks me.

Whenever I speak, I must cry out,
  violence and outrage is my message;
the word of the Lord has brought me
  derision and reproach all the day.

I say to myself, I will not mention him,
  I will speak in his name no more.
But then it becomes like fire burning in my heart,
  imprisoned in my bones;
I grow weary holding it in, I cannot endure it.

PSALM RESPONSE
Psalm 63:2b

My soul is thirsting for you, O Lord my God.

SECOND READING
Romans 12:1–2

I urge you, brothers and sisters, by the mercies of God, to offer your bodies as a living sacrifice, holy and pleasing to God, your spiritual worship. Do not conform yourselves to this age but be transformed by the renewal of your mind, that you may discern what is the will of God, what is good and pleasing and perfect.

GOSPEL
Matthew 16:21–27

Jesus began to show his disciples that he must go to Jerusalem and suffer greatly from the elders, the chief priests, and the scribes, and be killed and on the third day be raised. Then Peter took Jesus aside and began to rebuke him, "God forbid, Lord! No such thing shall ever happen to you." He turned and said to Peter, "Get behind me, Satan! You are an obstacle to me. You are thinking not as God does, but as human beings do."

Then Jesus said to his disciples, "Whoever wishes to come after me must deny himself, take up his cross, and follow me. For whoever wishes to save his life will lose it, but whoever loses his life for my sake will find it. What profit would there be for one to gain the whole world and forfeit his life? Or what can one give in exchange for his life? For the Son of Man will come with his angels in his Father's glory, and then he will repay all according to his conduct."

Jeremiah's lament in today's first reading is a poignant first-person account of the costs of prophecy. The book of Jeremiah itself is a compilation of narratives, oracles, and first-person laments in a seemingly random arrangement. Scholars conclude that the editing of the Jeremiah materials occurred over time and may reflect the theological interests of the Deuteronomistic circle, who were probably of a priestly caste and concerned with giving Israel a consistent historical viewpoint. The complex literary history makes the overall authenticity of the work suspect. However, with the vivid personal laments (12:1–16; 15:15–21; 17:14–18; 18:19–23; 20:7–18) we may actually catch a glimpse of the historical prophet who struggled mightily under the yoke of God's word, but nonetheless, yielded. "It becomes like a fire burning in my heart . . . I grow weary holding it in" (Jeremiah 20:9).

Paul's Letter to the Romans is chiefly concerned with providing the largely Gentile community with ethical direction. Previously the Law of Moses had provided a guide for righteous behavior (Romans 7:6), but by virtue of their incorporation into Christ's body they share in his death, which is death to the Law (Romans 7:4). Without the Law as moral guide, Paul directs the believers to "offer your bodies as a living sacrifice" (Romans 12:1). No longer are they to follow the dictates of either the Law or "this age, " but rather, believers are to discern God's will by means of the graces given to them (Romans 12:6).

We hear in today's Gospel reading the first prediction of Jesus' passion in Matthew. Earlier Peter had been praised for his seemingly perceptive recognition that Jesus was "the Christ, the Son of the living God" (Matthew 16:16). But in today's reading, Peter is called an "obstacle." The Greek word—*scandalon*—refers to a trap set by one's enemies and later came to mean a "stumbling block." Jesus is accusing Peter of attempting to prevent his mission. Likely Peter's understanding of the role and work of the Messiah was decidedly different than Jesus'. While many first-century Palestinian Jews awaited the coming of the Messiah, the concept of messiah varied. Many longed for a descendant of David who would reclaim the throne and overthrow the Romans. Others, like those who wrote the Dead Sea Scrolls, expected an eschatological priest to reform the temple and its priesthood. Likely no one anticipated a messiah who would suffer greatly and be killed. Peter's reaction reflects his shock.

❖ Reflecting on the Word

"Why do bad things happen . . . to me, to those I love, to good people, in the world?" How often I've asked and heard others ask this question. We prefer life without suffering, sadness, or hardship, an ultra-gentle baby-shampoo, a no-tears life. However, life does include hardship. "It is what it is," as some say. I ask, "What really is?" Jesus proclaims that suffering, pain, evil, and death do not have the last word; the Son of Man will come with his angels in his Father's glory and repay all according to their conduct.

How do we conduct ourselves to share in this promise? We take up our cross. We accept life's mortifications, afflictions, contradictions, and troubles and find God right there. To find life we need to be willing to lose it as we know it. There is no way around that reality. Jeremiah knew this all too well. His message was not popular. People opposed him, yet he could not stop speaking God's word. It was a fire burning in his heart, a fire of love. He fell in love with God and could do none other than be God's prophet, even in the face of opposition and hardship. Had God's love not duped him, he'd probably have given up. So would we.

Paul's advice to the Romans applies to us: Be transformed by deepening your relationship with God every day and conform your ways to God's ways. Then "discern what is the will of God, what is good and pleasing and perfect" (Romans 12:2). There we discover God's presence even in difficulty, the courage to take up our cross, and are washed in a love that brings life through the tears that are part of what is on life's journey.

✤ Consider/Discuss

- What cross or crosses have you taken up in your life?
- How have you found God to be present by embracing them?

✤ Living and Praying with the Word

O God, the God whom I seek, thank you for your faithful love. Help me to remember your love when the hardships and difficulties of life overwhelm me, so I might continue to seek you, have the courage to be faithful to you, and always find joy in the shadow of your wings.

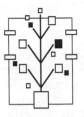

September 10, 2017

TWENTY-THIRD SUNDAY IN ORDINARY TIME

Today's Focus: Responsible Relationships

When there is discord in any relationship or group, it is difficult—and necessary, because it is difficult—to recall that we must still treat everyone respectfully, as an image of a loving God.

FIRST READING
Ezekiel 33:7–9

Thus says the LORD: You, son of man, I have appointed watchman for the house of Israel; when you hear me say anything, you shall warn them for me. If I tell the wicked, "O wicked one, you shall surely die," and you do not speak out to dissuade the wicked from his way, the wicked shall die for his guilt, but I will hold you responsible for his death. But if you warn the wicked, trying to turn him from his way, and he refuses to turn from his way, he shall die for his guilt, but you shall save yourself.

PSALM RESPONSE
Psalm 95:8

If today you hear his voice, harden not your hearts.

SECOND READING
Romans 13:8–10

Brothers and sisters: Owe nothing to anyone, except to love one another; for the one who loves another has fulfilled the law. The commandments, "You shall not commit adultery; you shall not kill; you shall not steal; you shall not covet," and whatever other commandment there may be, are summed up in this saying, namely, "You shall love your neighbor as yourself." Love does no evil to the neighbor; hence, love is the fulfillment of the law.

GOSPEL
Matthew 18:15–20

Jesus said to his disciples: "If your brother sins against you, go and tell him his fault between you and him alone. If he listens to you, you have won over your brother. If he does not listen, take one or two others along with you, so that 'every fact may be established on the testimony of two or three witnesses.' If he refuses to listen to them, tell the church. If he refuses to listen even to the church, then treat him as you would a Gentile or a tax collector. Amen, I say to you, whatever you bind on earth shall be bound in heaven, and whatever you loose on earth shall be loosed in heaven. Again, amen, I say to you, if two of you agree on earth about anything for which they are to pray, it shall be granted to them by my heavenly Father. For where two or three are gathered together in my name, there am I in the midst of them."

All of today's readings speak of the importance of right relationship and personal responsibility. The prophet Ezekiel is unique in that his call came when he was in Babylon (Ezekiel 1:1). His prophetic ministry is to a people already separated from their home and experiencing the devastation of exile. In today's reading, Ezekiel has been appointed as a watchman for these exiled people. He must warn them of danger. In this scenario, the danger is their own guilt before God. Ezekiel is not responsible for their behavior. His responsibility is to carry out the word of God. In Chapters 3–24, the prophet was charged with proclaiming judgment. The revelation in today's reading opens a new section, in which the prophet is called to announce salvation (Chapters 33–48).

Both the evangelist Matthew and the apostle Paul describe how a believer is to interpret the dictates of the Law (Matthew 5:17–48). In Matthew, Jesus notes that not the smallest letter of the Law will go unfulfilled. In today's second reading, Paul echoes that statement by noting that "love is the fulfillment of the law" (Romans 13:10). The motivation for such love is the recognition that "our salvation is nearer now than when we first believed" (Romans 13:11). Thus believers must conduct themselves properly in anticipation of the final judgment.

The third reading is taken from the fourth teaching section in Matthew's Gospel. Scholars propose that these five sections (Sermon on the Mount, 4:23 — 7:29; missionary discourse, 10:1–11; parables, speech to Israel and disciples, 13:1–58; community order and discipline, 18:1–35; millennial discourse, 24:1 — 25:46) are meant to parallel the five books of Moses, or Pentateuch. In today's reading, Jesus directs his disciples (and Matthew speaks to his "church" community) about standards of communal behavior. A procedure is outlined in which a "brother" or sister who has strayed must be confronted and either welcomed back into the church or ostracized.

✣ *Reflecting on the Word*

Are you familiar with the principle of subsidiarity? First go to the lowest level needed to settle a conflict. Go first to your brother or sister. If that settles it, all is well. If not, move up to the next level of authority. If that does not settle the situation, take witnesses to ensure fairness to you and your opponent. If that does not bring resolution, invoke the entire community. If that doesn't work, treat the person like an outsider. Treating someone like a Gentile or tax collector can mean ignoring and mistreating the person. Faithful Jews thought of Gentiles and sinners as unworthy of respect. Others apply Jesus' teaching about loving one's neighbor, even one's enemy, love to the outsider: "You shall love your neighbor as yourself." In other words, even tough love includes basic respect.

Tough love sets boundaries that can separate someone from the community until the person chooses to change. It's their choice. That's Ezekiel's message: Tell the wicked one what needs to change. They must make the choice. If we speak, we have done our part. If we do not speak out, then we will be held responsible for the actions of the wicked.

St. Catherine of Siena said, "Speak the truth in love." That's how God treats us, even when we turn away from God. Speak from the desire that the other will change, not to destroy them. This requires inner subsidiarity to God's spirit within us. It also requires being caring rather than judgmental—again, like God treats us. Speak in the way that you would want someone to speak to you. Love your neighbor as yourself. Seek not to do evil to your neighbor and thus fulfill the law.

❖ Consider/Discuss

- When has speaking the truth in love led to change or healing?
- How can you apply the principle of subsidiarity to your everyday life?

❖ Living and Praying with the Word

Holy God, you call us to love our sisters and brothers as ourselves. That can be difficult in the face of conflict or rejection. Keep me from being judgmental. Help me find ways to say difficult things to others in the way that I would like to hear them said to me.

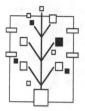

September 17, 2017

TWENTY-FOURTH SUNDAY IN ORDINARY TIME

Today's Focus: Self-gift

We think of extending forgiveness is an act of giving a gift to another person. But we also receive a gift when we forgive others.

FIRST READING
Sirach 27:30 — 28:7

Wrath and anger are hateful things,
    yet the sinner hugs them tight.
The vengeful will suffer the Lord's vengeance,
    for he remembers their sins in detail.
Forgive your neighbor's injustice;
    then when you pray, your own sins will be forgiven.
Could anyone nourish anger against another
    and expect healing from the Lord?
Could anyone refuse mercy to another like himself,
    can he seek pardon for his own sins?
If one who is but flesh cherishes wrath,
    who will forgive his sins?
Remember your last days, set enmity aside;
    remember death and decay, and cease from sin!
Think of the commandments, hate not your neighbor;
    remember the Most High's covenant, and overlook faults.

PSALM RESPONSE
Psalm 103:8

The Lord is kind and merciful, slow to anger, and rich in compassion.

SECOND READING
Romans 14:7–9

Brothers and sisters: None of us lives for oneself, and no one dies for oneself. For if we live, we live for the Lord, and if we die, we die for the Lord; so then, whether we live or die, we are the Lord's. For this is why Christ died and came to life, that he might be Lord of both the dead and the living.

GOSPEL
Matthew
18:21–35

Peter approached Jesus and asked him, "Lord, if my brother sins against me, how often must I forgive? As many as seven times?" Jesus answered, "I say to you, not seven times but seventy-seven times. That is why the kingdom of heaven may be likened to a king who decided to settle accounts with his servants. When he began the accounting, a debtor was brought before him who owed him a huge amount. Since he had no way of paying it back, his master ordered him to be sold, along with his wife, his children, and all his property, in payment of the debt. At that, the servant fell down, did him homage, and said, 'Be patient with me, and I will pay you back in full.' Moved with compassion the master of that servant let him go and forgave him the loan. When that servant had left, he found one of his fellow servants who owed him a much smaller amount. He seized him and started to choke him, demanding, 'Pay back what you owe.' Falling to his knees, his fellow servant begged him, 'Be patient with me, and I will pay you back.' But he refused. Instead, he had the fellow servant put in prison until he paid back the debt. Now when his fellow servants saw what had happened, they were deeply disturbed, and went to their master and reported the whole affair. His master summoned him and said to him, 'You wicked servant! I forgave you your entire debt because you begged me to. Should you not have had pity on your fellow servant, as I had pity on you?' Then in anger his master handed him over to the torturers until he should pay back the whole debt. So will my heavenly Father do to you, unless each of you forgives your brother from your heart."

❖ Understanding the Word

The book of Sirach, also known as the Wisdom of Ben Sira (Ecclesiasticus) is a collection of sayings from a sage living in Jerusalem in the second century B.C. Originally written in Hebrew, the text was translated by his grandson. Wisdom in the ancient world resulted from reflection on human experience, which revealed the underlying world order and resulted in appropriate social and personal order in life. In today's reading Ben Sira offers his critical assessment of the costs of wrath and anger. In addition to the havoc it causes on human relations, it has devastating consequences on one's relationship with God: "The vengeful will suffer the LORD's vengeance" (Sirach 28:1).

Today's brief second reading is taken from a longer section of Romans Chapter 14 in which Paul recommends compassion toward those of weaker conscience. Having explained how the reality of Christ has ended the subjugation to the Law, Paul must now help the community negotiate life without the guide of the Law. Under that Law certain days were held as festivals (Romans 14:5), and particular dietary customs directed one's eating habits (Romans 14:3). Paul offers that whoever eats or abstains from eating does so for the Lord, because "none of us lives for oneself . . . we live for the Lord" (Romans 14:8).

175

The Gospel reading is a continuation from the section known as the sermon on community order and discipline (Matthew 18:1–35). Throughout the Gospel, Jesus has presented a new interpretation of the Law (Matthew 5:21–22; 27–28; 33–34; 38–39; 43–44). Peter presents Jesus with a question about limited forgiveness. The seven and seventy-seven times may be allusions to Genesis 4:24, but in the Old Testament reading, Cain is avenged seven times and his son Lamech's vengeance is symbolically limitless (seventy-seven). As unbounded as Lamech's vengeance, so unbounded are the disciples to be in their forgiveness. Jesus then uses a parable to illustrate the answer to Peter's question and thereby expound on "how much" forgiveness is required.

❖ Reflecting on the Word

I agree with the saying "Reconciliation is a gift we give to someone else, but forgiveness is a gift we give ourselves." It takes more energy to hold on to hurt than it does to try and be free of it. Try this. Make as a tight a fist as you can. Feel how much energy that takes, and if your nails need trimming, how they cut into your palms. Now open your hands. Energy is released and you make room for new possibilities. Hugging wrath and anger, holding hurt and pain are like holding our fists tight. They take a lot of energy and often only hurt us. Releasing these feelings can open us to experience the forgiveness and peace that God has already offered us and opens the door to future reconciliation, if that becomes possible.

Holding on to anger dissipates any forgiveness given to us, as it did for the forgiven servant who refused to forgive the servant who owed a lesser debt. The first servant's refusal to forgive was viewed by his peers as a great injustice and so he lost everything, including respectability. That servant lived only for himself. Our call is to live for the Lord by loving one another as God loves and forgives us, not seven or seventy-seven times, but infinitely. The way we do or do not forgive is the measure for how we experience God's presence in our lives. Vengeance can seem sweet at the time, but it only opens the door to the Lord's vengeance, as Sirach notes. Not because God is vengeful, but because our hands are so full they cannot receive the kindness of our merciful God. Open your hands and your heart. Receive the mercy of God and do unto others as God does to us. Forgive.

❖ Consider/Discuss

- What benefit has releasing hurt and pain given you?
- What has holding on to them done in the long run?

❖ Living and Praying with the Word

Loving God, your kindness and mercy are often beyond belief. Help me to remember them in ways that lead me to treat others the way you treat me, so that your forgiving touch might bring healing to me, and through me, to others.

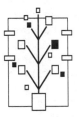

September 24, 2017

TWENTY-FIFTH SUNDAY IN ORDINARY TIME

Today's Focus: No Fair!

Sometimes God seems to act unfairly, but it is really God's generous justice in action. Perhaps having a bit more of God's generous nature would help us all be more just.

FIRST READING
Isaiah 55:6–9

Seek the Lord while he may be found,
    call him while he is near.
Let the scoundrel forsake his way,
    and the wicked his thoughts;
let him turn to the Lord for mercy;
    to our God, who is generous in forgiving.
For my thoughts are not your thoughts,
    nor are your ways my ways, says the Lord.
As high as the heavens are above the earth,
    so high are my ways above your ways
    and my thoughts above your thoughts.

PSALM RESPONSE
Psalm 145:18a

The Lord is near to all who call upon him.

SECOND READING
Philippians 1:20c–24, 27a

Brothers and sisters: Christ will be magnified in my body, whether by life or by death. For to me life is Christ, and death is gain. If I go on living in the flesh, that means fruitful labor for me. And I do not know which I shall choose. I am caught between the two. I long to depart this life and be with Christ, for that is far better. Yet that I remain in the flesh is more necessary for your benefit.

Only, conduct yourselves in a way worthy of the gospel of Christ.

GOSPEL
Matthew
20:1–16a

Jesus told his disciples this parable: "The kingdom of heaven is like a landowner who went out at dawn to hire laborers for his vineyard. After agreeing with them for the usual daily wage, he sent them into his vineyard. Going out about nine o'clock, the landowner saw others standing idle in the marketplace, and he said to them, 'You too go into my vineyard, and I will give you what is just.' So they went off. And he went out again around noon, and around three o'clock, and did likewise. Going out about five o'clock, the landowner found others standing around, and said to them, 'Why do you stand here idle all day?' They answered, 'Because no one has hired us.' He said to them, 'You too go into my vineyard.' When it was evening the owner of the vineyard said to his foreman, 'Summon the laborers and give them their pay, beginning with the last and ending with the first.' When those who had started about five o'clock came, each received the usual daily wage. So when the first came, they thought that they would receive more, but each of them also got the usual wage. And on receiving it they grumbled against the landowner, saying, 'These last ones worked only one hour, and you have made them equal to us, who bore the day's burden and the heat.' He said to one of them in reply, 'My friend, I am not cheating you. Did you not agree with me for the usual daily wage? Take what is yours and go. What if I wish to give this last one the same as you? Or am I not free to do as I wish with my own money? Are you envious because I am generous?' Thus, the last will be first, and the first will be last."

❖ *Understanding the Word*

The reading from the book of Isaiah is from the concluding poem in the section, Chapters 40–55. Attributed to an unknown prophet whom scholars call "Second Isaiah," the author is at work in exile, among the disheartened remnant. Words of chastisement and judgment are no longer necessary. Jerusalem has already been destroyed and her people taken into exile. Today's reading is taken from the longer poem in which God speaks through the prophet to offer solace and encouragement. "Seek the LORD while he may be found, call him while he is near" (Isaiah 55:6). The presence of God, once believed to have dwelt in the temple, is now near to the exiles. And while they may not understand God's mysterious ways, God is nonetheless merciful and forgiving.

Paul's Letter to the Philippians is believed to have been written later in Paul's life as he waits in prison. If the letter was written during his Rome imprisonment, then it is shortly before his martyrdom. Thus his words about life and death take on deeper meaning. Pondering his current predicament, Paul longs to complete his race and capture the prize of Christ (Philippians 3:14), but he recognizes that his work among the Philippians is not yet done. Until he is able to join them again, he encourages them to live in a manner "worthy of the gospel of Christ."

In today's Gospel reading, we hear a parable that is unique to Matthew and thus may give us insights into Matthew's community. The landowner goes in search of laborers throughout the day, and at the end of the day pays each the same amount, "the usual daily wage." The first laborers grumble that they are not given more. "Are you envious because I am generous?" counters the land-owner (Matthew 20:15). To this, Jesus offers a moral: "Thus, the last will be first, and the first will be last" (Matthew 20:16a). Other unique Matthean parables echo a similar theme about who belongs and who doesn't (Matthew 13:24–30; 25:1–13). Scholars propose that these parables may speak to the divisions within Matthew's community. These parables of Jesus share in common that the final judgment is God's and God's mercy and generosity are wholly gratuitous.

✢ Reflecting on the Word

My first grade teacher, Sr. Nathaniel, taught us that if someone made a death-bed confession or "perfect" act of contrition, that person would go to heaven. That didn't seem fair but it was attractive. I could do whatever I want in life, go to confession right before I die or pray the Act of Contrition, and still go to heaven. Of course I didn't consider that we never know when we'll die and more impor-tantly that the point of life in faith is to live Jesus, seek the Lord, and live God's ways throughout our lives.

Those workers, who began work in the morning, laboring under the hot sun all day, felt entitled to more money than those who came at day's end. When that did not happen, they felt cheated. Maybe they did envy the owner's generosity. They missed the point. The owner promised the usual daily wage to all, when-ever they started working. Our gracious and merciful God promises eternal life to all who enter into relationship with God, whenever we do so and even after we fall. This is pure gift. We are not entitled to it. We can be blinded by God's generosity to those we think undeserving. Envy blinds us to God's nearness at all times and keeps us from gratitude for such generous mercy.

God's justice looks more like human mercy. We can cry, "Unfair!" In the end, I'm glad that God's ways are not my ways. Would that mine were more like God's. The message is to conduct ourselves in a way worthy of the gospel we have received no matter when we receive it or how often we fall. Seek the Lord and our union with Christ will be clear.

❖ Consider/Discuss

- Have you ever felt entitled or envious? What has it gained you?
- How have gratitude and seeking God's ways transformed you?

❖ Living and Praying with the Word

Your ways are not my ways, O God, although I must admit that at times I wish they were. Help me seek to live your ways when I most resist them, so that entitlement can become gratitude and envy can be replaced with affirmation.

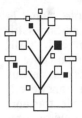

October 1, 2017

TWENTY-SIXTH SUNDAY IN ORDINARY TIME

Today's Focus: Admitting Wrongs, Saying "Yes"

One of the hardest things for us to do is to admit we've been wrong. But when we do, we often open up our lives to much affirmation.

FIRST READING
Ezekiel 18:25–28

Thus says the LORD: You say, "The LORD's way is not fair!" Hear now, house of Israel: Is it my way that is unfair, or rather, are not your ways unfair? When someone virtuous turns away from virtue to commit iniquity, and dies, it is because of the iniquity he committed that he must die. But if he turns from the wickedness he has committed, and does what is right and just, he shall preserve his life; since he has turned away from all the sins that he has committed, he shall surely live, he shall not die.

PSALM RESPONSE
Psalm 25:6a

Remember your mercies, O Lord.

In the shorter form of the reading, the passage in brackets is omitted.

SECOND READING
Philippians 2:1–11 or 2:1–5

Brothers and sisters: If there is any encouragement in Christ, any solace in love, any participation in the Spirit, any compassion and mercy, complete my joy by being of the same mind, with the same love, united in heart, thinking one thing. Do nothing out of selfishness or out of vainglory; rather, humbly regard others as more important than yourselves, each looking out not for his own interests, but also for those of others.

Have in you the same attitude
   that is also in Christ Jesus,
     [Who, though he was in the form of God,
     did not regard equality with God
     something to be grasped.
   Rather, he emptied himself,
     taking the form of a slave,
     coming in human likeness;
     and found human in appearance,
     he humbled himself,
     becoming obedient to the point of death,
     even death on a cross.
   Because of this, God greatly exalted him
     and bestowed on him the name
     which is above every name,
     that at the name of Jesus
     every knee should bend,
     of those in heaven and on earth and under the earth,
     and every tongue confess that
     Jesus Christ is Lord,
     to the glory of God the Father.]

GOSPEL
Matthew
21:28–32 Jesus said to the chief priests and elders of the people: "What is your opinion? A man had two sons. He came to the first and said, 'Son, go out and work in the vineyard today.' He said in reply, 'I will not,' but afterwards changed his mind and went. The man came to the other son and gave the same order. He said in reply, 'Yes, sir,' but did not go. Which of the two did his father's will?" They answered, "The first." Jesus said to them, "Amen, I say to you, tax collectors and prostitutes are entering the kingdom of God before you. When John came to you in the way of righteousness, you did not believe him; but tax collectors and prostitutes did. Yet even when you saw that, you did not later change your minds and believe him."

❖ Understanding the Word

Ancient Near Eastern culture, regardless of religious tradition, held a belief that the sins of the parents were visited upon their children, and indeed, the actions of the previous generation often came to bear on future ones. In today's first reading, Ezekiel is responding to just such a belief. In Ezekiel 18:2, the prophet cites the proverb, "Parents eat sour grapes, but the children's teeth are set on edge." The word of the Lord directs Ezekiel to proclaim a new moment. No longer will the community be punished for the sins of its ancestors. Rather, each individual will be held accountable. If one turns from wickedness and does what is right and just, he or she shall live (Ezekiel 18:27).

Paul offers a conditional litany ("if there is any . . . ") so as to set up his chief concern: that the Philippians be "of the same mind." As an example of such single-hearted devotion, Paul cites Christ's *kenosis* or self-emptying. Though he was "in the form of God, " Christ humbled himself, choosing human appearance, and becoming obedient even unto death. The Philippians are to have the same attitude.

Matthew portrays Jesus as a rabbi who interprets the Law in creative and merciful ways and teaches by means of parables. Today's reading is taken from a section of Matthew's Gospel in which a series of controversies is interrupted and responded to by three parables (Matthew 21:28–32, 33–46; 22:1–14). In Matthew 21:23, the chief priests and elders question Jesus' authority. Jesus turns the question back on them. If they can explain the authority of John the Baptist, then Jesus himself will explain his authority (Matthew 21:24–26). Their response, "We do not know, " sets up the parable that follows. A man has two sons who have two different responses to their father's request. Jesus likens the chief priests and the elders to the son who promises but does not deliver on his promises, while the tax collectors and prostitutes represent the appropriate response.

Once upon a time I taught a student who constantly got into trouble. Teachers even placed bets about how long it would take until he landed in jail. About a decade after he graduated from eighth grade, his sister invited me to play the organ for her wedding. After the wedding a finely dressed young man approached the organ and asked, "Mr. C, do you remember me?" I replied that I could not forget him and asked what he was doing with his life. He answered, "I'm a police officer." I must have looked stunned, because he asked, "Surprised?" "Yes," I said. "You know we placed bets about when you would land in jail." He laughed then told me, "I was about to be arrested a third time when the officer said, 'You have such great skill for getting into trouble, how about learning how to use it to help people stay out of trouble?' " The rest is history.

The son in today's Gospel who said, "No, no" learned how to say, "Yes, yes." Joe—I've changed the name to respect him—learned how to turn from wickedness to doing what is right and how to help others do so. Instead of stubbornly refusing to admit his wrongdoing, Joe emptied himself and learned obedience and freedom through what he suffered. Because of that openness he let God guide him to a just and good life thanks to an insightful arresting officer.

The tables were turned that day. My former student became my teacher. I learned to have faith in those I'd written off, as God has faith in us. God's ways are not our ways, but they certainly can become our ways.

❖ *Consider/Discuss*

- When have you said no to God's ways but then relented and did what was right?
- How has God's mercy changed how you viewed yourself or someone else?

❖ *Living and Praying with the Word*

God, our mercy, you sent Jesus to teach us the ways of humility and truth. May his example encourage us to empty ourselves of what is not your way so that we might become as merciful to others as you are to us.

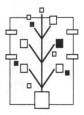

October 8, 2017

TWENTY-SEVENTH SUNDAY IN ORDINARY TIME

Today's Focus: The Error of Entitlement

There are two possible outlooks on most things in life: gratitude or entitlement. Viewing life gratefully helps us to live thankful lives, and avoid greed or jealousy.

FIRST READING
Isaiah 5:1–7

Let me now sing of my friend,
    my friend's song concerning his vineyard.
My friend had a vineyard
    on a fertile hillside;
he spaded it, cleared it of stones,
    and planted the choicest vines;
within it he built a watchtower,
    and hewed out a wine press.
Then he looked for the crop of grapes,
    but what it yielded was wild grapes.

Now, inhabitants of Jerusalem and people of Judah,
    judge between me and my vineyard:
What more was there to do for my vineyard
    that I had not done?
Why, when I looked for the crop of grapes,
    did it bring forth wild grapes?
Now, I will let you know
    what I mean to do with my vineyard:
take away its hedge, give it to grazing,
    break through its wall, let it be trampled!
Yes, I will make it a ruin:
    it shall not be pruned or hoed,
    but overgrown with thorns and briers;
I will command the clouds
    not to send rain upon it.
The vineyard of the LORD of hosts is the house of Israel,
    and the people of Judah are his cherished plant;
he looked for judgment, but see, bloodshed!
    for justice, but hark, the outcry!

PSALM RESPONSE
Isaiah 5:7a

The vineyard of the Lord is the house of Israel.

SECOND
READING
*Philippians
4:6–9*
Brothers and sisters: Have no anxiety at all, but in everything, by prayer and petition, with thanksgiving, make your requests known to God. Then the peace of God that surpasses all understanding will guard your hearts and minds in Christ Jesus.

Finally, brothers and sisters, whatever is true, whatever is honorable, whatever is just, whatever is pure, whatever is lovely, whatever is gracious, if there is any excellence and if there is anything worthy of praise, think about these things. Keep on doing what you have learned and received and heard and seen in me. Then the God of peace will be with you.

GOSPEL
*Matthew
21:33–43*
Jesus said to the chief priests and the elders of the people: "Hear another parable. There was a landowner who planted a vineyard, put a hedge around it, dug a wine press in it, and built a tower. Then he leased it to tenants and went on a journey. When vintage time drew near, he sent his servants to the tenants to obtain his produce. But the tenants seized the servants and one they beat, another they killed, and a third they stoned. Again he sent other servants, more numerous than the first ones, but they treated them in the same way. Finally, he sent his son to them, thinking, 'They will respect my son.' But when the tenants saw the son, they said to one another, 'This is the heir. Come, let us kill him and acquire his inheritance.' They seized him, threw him out of the vineyard, and killed him. What will the owner of the vineyard do to those tenants when he comes?" They answered him, "He will put those wretched men to a wretched death and lease his vineyard to other tenants who will give him the produce at the proper times." Jesus said to them, "Did you never read in the Scriptures:
The stone that the builders rejected
has become the cornerstone;
by the Lord has this been done,
and it is wonderful in our eyes?
Therefore, I say to you, the kingdom of God will be taken away from you and given to a people that will produce its fruit."

❖ Understanding the Word

Isaiah of Jerusalem was called to prophesy during a time when Israel saw mounting threats from Assyrian aggression in the eighth century B.C. Chapters 1–5 are a collection of oracles indicting Israel and Judah for their rebellion against God (Isaiah 1:2). Today's first reading depicts that rebellion in the form of an allegorical hymn about a vineyard. The vineyard represents Israel and Judah as a "cherished plant" (Isaiah 5:7). Rather than choice grapes, the vineyard produced wild ones. In response God will make of the vineyard a ruin. The people of God depicted as a vineyard is a common metaphor found throughout the prophets (Isaiah 27:2; Jeremiah 2:21; 12:10; Ezekiel 17:7; Hosea 10:1).

Paul is effusive in his joy concerning the Philippians, repeating the noun (*chara*) and the verb (*chairo*) for "joy" more than fifteen times in the four chapters. While a leadership dispute (Philippians 4:2) may have occasioned the letter, he is nonetheless pleased with the community. In today's reading, Paul concludes his letter with a *paraenesis* or exhortation to set aside anxiety and trust that God receives their prayers. Echoing Stoic moral exhortations, Paul invites them to uphold whatever is of true excellence.

The origin of the parable found in today's Gospel is debated by scholars. Matthew edited Mark's original (Mark 12:1–12), but the question is whether some form of the now highly allegorized story goes back to Jesus. The presence of a similar parable in the Gospel of Thomas may suggest that a primitive form of it does originate with Jesus. If this is the case, then Jesus has taken Isaiah's hymn of the vineyard (Isaiah 5:1–2, 7) and in an analogous setting indicted not the people of Israel and Judah as in Isaiah's day, but the Jewish religious leadership for their failure to produce fruit (Matthew 21:43). The section of woes against the scribes and Pharisees (Matthew 23:1–36) seems to confirm that Jesus directed the parable against them.

❖   *Reflecting on the Word*

When I listen to reports about what people do or do not have and how they respond to their life situations, I'm struck by the difference between those who are grateful and those who feel entitled. It seems that a sense of entitlement fills many of us and destroys the virtues of gratitude and responsibility. When I feel entitled, I often envy what others have and focus on what I do not have. Envy blinds me from seeing what I do have and keeps me from being grateful. It also feeds the need for more rather than seeing that often I have enough. I can become willing to do anything to grab more, even violence.

This is the dynamic in the Gospel parable. The tenants wanted what was not theirs. In their lust for more they become violent, even to murdering the owner's servants and son, mistakenly thinking that they would be given the vineyard. Envy, lust, and blindness yield more than wild grapes. They feed on themselves until something or someone ends that vicious cycle. The Letter to the Philippians offers an antidote: Seek whatever is true, honorable, just, pure, lovely, and gracious. Truth can lead to accepting what our gifts are and are not, and help us grow in right relationship (justice) with God, others and ourselves. Truth invites gratitude for our gifts and the ability to develop them. Truth fosters appreciation of others' gifts. Then when we mourn what we lack, we discover that we have all we need, or we find ways to seek what we need without destroying another. Pray, "Look down from heaven, and see, take care of this vine, and protect what your right hand has planted." Let it be enough.

- Have you ever felt entitled? How did that affect you?
- What helps you nurture gratitude and live the words of today's second reading?

❖ Living and Praying with the Word

Generous God, you have gifted us in many ways. How can we thank you? When envy, jealousy, or the wish for more blinds us to the gifts we have, heal us. Help us appreciate what you have given to us and affirm the gifts that you give to our sisters and brothers.

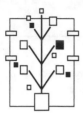

October 15, 2017

TWENTY-EIGHTH SUNDAY IN ORDINARY TIME

Today's Focus: The Abundant God

Banquets or feasts are often used in scripture to tell us something about God's reign in our midst. Called to an abundant feast, we are likewise called to be signs of that feast, and live by sharing abundantly.

FIRST READING
Isaiah 25:6–10a

On this mountain the LORD of hosts
    will provide for all peoples
a feast of rich food and choice wines,
    juicy, rich food and pure, choice wines.
On this mountain he will destroy
    the veil that veils all peoples,
the web that is woven over all nations;
    he will destroy death forever.
The Lord GOD will wipe away
    the tears from every face;
the reproach of his people he will remove
    from the whole earth; for the LORD has spoken.
    On that day it will be said:
"Behold our God, to whom we looked to save us!
    This is the LORD for whom we looked;
    let us rejoice and be glad that he has saved us!"
For the hand of the LORD will rest on this mountain.

PSALM RESPONSE
Psalm 23:6cd

I shall live in the house of the Lord all the days of my life.

SECOND READING
Philippians 4:12–14, 19–20

Brothers and sisters: I know how to live in humble circumstances; I know also how to live with abundance. In every circumstance and in all things I have learned the secret of being well fed and of going hungry, of living in abundance and of being in need. I can do all things in him who strengthens me. Still, it was kind of you to share in my distress.

My God will fully supply whatever you need, in accord with his glorious riches in Christ Jesus. To our God and Father, glory forever and ever. Amen.

GOSPEL
Matthew
22:1–14 or
22:1–10

Jesus again in reply spoke to the chief priests and elders of the people in parables, saying, "The kingdom of heaven may be likened to a king who gave a wedding feast for his son. He dispatched his servants to summon the invited guests to the feast, but they refused to come. A second time he sent other servants, saying, 'Tell those invited: "Behold, I have prepared my banquet, my calves and fattened cattle are killed, and everything is ready; come to the feast." ' Some ignored the invitation and went away, one to his farm, another to his business. The rest laid hold of his servants, mistreated them, and killed them. The king was enraged and sent his troops, destroyed those murderers, and burned their city. Then he said to his servants, 'The feast is ready, but those who were invited were not worthy to come. Go out, therefore, into the main roads and invite to the feast whomever you find.' The servants went out into the streets and gathered all they found, bad and good alike, and the hall was filled with guests. [But when the king came in to meet the guests, he saw a man there not dressed in a wedding garment. The king said to him, 'My friend, how is it that you came in here without a wedding garment?' But he was reduced to silence. Then the king said to his attendants, 'Bind his hands and feet, and cast him into the darkness outside, where there will be wailing and grinding of teeth.' Many are invited, but few are chosen."]

❖ Understanding the Word

The reading from Isaiah comes from a section of First Isaiah known as the Apocalypse of Isaiah (24—27). It envisions a future time when a city in chaos is destroyed by God, and the mountain (presumably Zion, Jerusalem's mountain) will be the site of God's salvific action. To celebrate God's victory over the tyrants, a feast of rich food and pure, choice wines (v. 6) will be provided not only for Israel, but for all people. On this mountain of Jerusalem, God will destroy death, and the reproach of God's people will be removed (v. 8). The prophet envisions a future of hope, filled with sumptuous food and drink, the absence of death, and rejuvenation of God's people. Though found within the work of Isaiah of Jerusalem (Chapters 1–39), the Apocalypse likely comes from the oracles of a later prophet in the school of Isaiah, who was writing during the Exile.

A good part of Paul's joy over the Philippian community has to do with their spiritual growth and financial support of Paul. "For even when I was at Thessalonica you sent me something for my needs, not only once but more than once" (Philippians 4:16). But Paul has maintained that he is self-sufficient, supporting himself by his own hands (1 Thessalonians 2:5–9; 1 Corinthians 9:15–18) so as not to be a burden on the local community. Hence, he writes, "I know how to live in humble circumstance." The support that the Philippians provides is deeply appreciated by Paul because it results from their affection for the apostle.

189

Matthew's Gospel is filled with more than sixty allusions to the Old Testament, evidencing the evangelist's purposeful characterization of Jesus as the fulfillment of scripture. In today's Gospel reading, Matthew has taken a parable from "Q" (a source of sayings material shared by Luke and Matthew), and inserted allegorical elements. That the kingdom of heaven is likened to a banquet picks up the image of the eschatological banquet of Isaiah and points toward the consummation of God's kingdom. But Matthew cautions that while this kingdom is already present (22:1–10), entrance into it requires scrutiny and judgment by the king (22:11–14). Scholars see the final verses as addressed specifically to Matthew's community, much as his unique parables have been elsewhere. "Many are invited, but few are chosen" (Matthew 22:14).

❖ Reflecting on the Word

A few weeks before writing this reflection, the Vatican released Pope Francis' apostolic exhortation *Amoris Laetitia* (The Joy of Love). It has caused many a reaction. One of its most powerful lines is a quote from a homily Pope Francis preached at a Mass celebrated with new cardinals in February, 2015: "The way of the Church is not to condemn anyone for ever, it is to pour out the balm of God's mercy on all those who ask for it with a sincere heart . . . For true charity is always unmerited, unconditional and gratuitous." These words sum up today's readings.

God provides for all people, friend and foe alike, on the mountain described in Isaiah. God's provident love is gracious and unconditional. The king in today's parable sends his servants out to invite to the wedding banquet whomever they find after others rejected his invitation. Someone is cast out for not wearing a wedding garment. All are invited, but we need to dress for the banquet by asking for and responding to God's gratuitous and loving balm. Our wedding garment entails clothing ourselves with gratitude, humility, and love, like Paul in the Letter to the Philippians. Paul learned how to respond with humility and gratitude to all of life's situations.

Paul's example challenges me to be grateful for what I have in abundance or want, and give God glory and praise at all times. Jesus reminds me to clothe myself with gratitude for God's generosity and mercy. Pope Francis also challenges me. Avoid condemning anyone forever. Be a vessel that pours out the balm of God's unmerited, unconditional, and gratuitous mercy so others can dress for the banquet, too.

❖ Consider/Discuss

- How do you react to the merciful love of God?
- On God's holy mountain, all peoples are provided for. Do you do the same?

❖ Living and Praying with the Word

Provident God, you set a feast rich in love, mercy, and presence every day. Open my eyes to your feast. Help me clothe myself with gratitude and generosity as I come to your table. Teach me how to feed others with your healing balm.

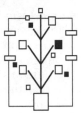

October 22, 2017

TWENTY-NINTH SUNDAY IN ORDINARY TIME

Today's Focus: Flattery Gets You Nowhere

Sometimes those who challenge Jesus begin the conversation with false praise. Now, as then, Jesus doesn't fall for insincere flattery.

FIRST READING
Isaiah 45:1, 4–6

Thus says the LORD to his anointed, Cyrus,
    whose right hand I grasp,
subduing nations before him,
    and making kings run in his service,
opening doors before him
    and leaving the gates unbarred:
For the sake of Jacob, my servant,
    of Israel, my chosen one,
I have called you by your name,
    giving you a title, though you knew me not.
I am the LORD and there is no other,
    there is no God besides me.
It is I who arm you, though you know me not,
    so that toward the rising and the setting of the sun
    people may know that there is none besides me.
I am the LORD, there is no other.

PSALM RESPONSE
Psalm 96:7b

Give the Lord glory and honor.

SECOND READING
1 Thessalonians 1:1–5b

Paul, Silvanus, and Timothy to the church of the Thessalonians in God the Father and the Lord Jesus Christ: grace to you and peace. We give thanks to God always for all of you, remembering you in our prayers, unceasingly calling to mind your work of faith and labor of love and endurance in hope of our Lord Jesus Christ, before our God and Father, knowing, brothers and sisters loved by God, how you were chosen. For our gospel did not come to you in word alone, but also in power and in the Holy Spirit and with much conviction.

The Pharisees went off and plotted how they might entrap Jesus in speech. They sent their disciples to him, with the Herodians, saying, "Teacher, we know that you are a truthful man and that you teach the way of God in accordance with the truth. And you are not concerned with anyone's opinion, for you do not regard a person's status. Tell us, then, what is your opinion: Is it lawful to pay the census tax to Caesar or not?" Knowing their malice, Jesus said, "Why are you testing me, you hypocrites? Show me the coin that pays the census tax." Then they handed him the Roman coin. He said to them, "Whose image is this and whose inscription?" They replied, "Caesar's." At that he said to them, "Then repay to Caesar what belongs to Caesar and to God what belongs to God."

❖ Understanding the Word

The redeemer of Israel, according to Second Isaiah, is not a Davidic king or even a Jewish prophet. God has anointed Cyrus, the Persian ruler (559–529 B.C.), as the instrument of God's designs (Isaiah 44:28). Cyrus is called God's anointed (Isaiah 45:1), a term that originally referred to those of Israel. In Hebrew, the word is *mashiah* (Greek *christos*) and is the root of the word "messiah." The Cyrus is anointed not only so that he might serve as a redeemer of Israel, releasing them from their Babylonian captivity. His anointing also demonstrates to those outside the covenanted people of Israel that there is none besides the God of Israel (Isaiah 45:6).

The First Letter to the Thessalonians is our oldest extant Pauline letter, likely written in the early 50s while Paul was in Corinth. In it, we see Paul following the standards of Greco-Roman letter writing. He begins with a prescript—from Paul to the church of the Thessalonians—but Paul adds his own personal touch. To the standard greetings (*chairein*), Paul incorporates the Jewish formula of *shalom*, so that that the greeting becomes grace (*charis*) and peace (*shalom, eirene* in Greek), as we see in 1 Thessalonians 1:1. He then follows with the expected thanksgiving section in which he offers prayers on behalf of the community (1 Thessalonians 1:2–10).

Following Mark's pattern, Matthew sets up a series of controversies between Jesus and the religious authorities. First, Jesus is confronted by the chief priests and the elders about his own authority (Matthew 21:23). Then the Pharisees and Herodians attempt to entrap him about the paying of imperial taxes (Matthew 22:15–22). The last group to conspire against Jesus is the Sadducees, who pose a theological question (Matthew 22:23–33). Today's reading finds Jesus defending himself against the middle group who feign respect (Matthew 22:16) but who are unmasked as "hypocrites" (Matthew 22:18), a term used by Jesus seventeen times in Matthew's Gospel. The term originally referred to an actor or one who played a part on stage. It is fittingly used here, since the Pharisees and Herodians are acting the part of interested disciples.

✤ Reflecting on the Word

Have you ever received false praise and fallen for it, only to discover that someone ultimately wanted to prove you wrong or discredit you? That happened to me while giving a workshop. One attendee did not think I was orthodox enough. She complimented me profusely and then asked a question I could not easily answer, trying to discredit me in front of a receptive crowd. I was embarrassed. Then I simply admitted that she stumped me. I would find the answer for our next session. Afterward another participant thanked me for saying honestly, "I don't know."

We see this dynamic in today's Gospel. Jesus' questioners flatter him profusely, but he doesn't allow himself to be set up. He responds quickly and truthfully, putting the ball back in their court. Everything belongs to God, so give God your all. The coin belongs to Caesar, so give the coin to Caesar. The God who remains Lord of all gave Jesus wisdom to see through the question.

A non-Jew, the Persian King Cyrus, is God's chosen leader, though he knew not the God of Israel. God gave him everything necessary to save the Chosen People, to make clear that there is no other God. The Thessalonians are also God's chosen ones, given faith, love, and hope to find true peace. The words of Isaiah and Paul speak truth to invite trust and deepened faith. They are not a set-up.

We, too, are God's chosen ones, anointed with the Holy Spirit to give God glory and honor. Our words and witness have an impact. Are they trustworthy? Do they make clear that we belong to God? Be truthful and draw others to the Lord, beside whom there is no other God.

✤ Consider/Discuss

- What difference does being God's chosen one make in what you say and do?
- How do you differentiate between words spoken in truth and words used to set you up?

✤ Living and Praying with the Word

God of all, you are great and highly to be praised. Fill me with words that proclaim my faith in you. Give me actions that show my love for you. Make my life an act of worship that proclaims you as the God of all times, peoples, and places.

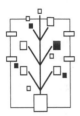

October 29, 2017

THIRTIETH SUNDAY IN ORDINARY TIME

Today's Focus: Let Me Count the Commandments

Love God. Love your neighbor. There are, essentially, two commandments—but even this short and simple list can sometimes be difficult to live out daily.

FIRST READING
Exodus 22:20–26

Thus says the LORD: "You shall not molest or oppress an alien, for you were once aliens yourselves in the land of Egypt. You shall not wrong any widow or orphan. If ever you wrong them and they cry out to me, I will surely hear their cry. My wrath will flare up, and I will kill you with the sword; then your own wives will be widows, and your children orphans.

"If you lend money to one of your poor neighbors among my people, you shall not act like an extortioner toward him by demanding interest from him. If you take your neighbor's cloak as a pledge, you shall return it to him before sunset; for this cloak of his is the only covering he has for his body. What else has he to sleep in? If he cries out to me, I will hear him; for I am compassionate."

PSALM RESPONSE
Psalm 18:2

I love you, Lord, my strength.

SECOND READING
1 Thessalonians 1:5c–10

Brothers and sisters: You know what sort of people we were among you for your sake. And you became imitators of us and of the Lord, receiving the word in great affliction, with joy from the Holy Spirit, so that you became a model for all the believers in Macedonia and in Achaia. For from you the word of the Lord has sounded forth not only in Macedonia and in Achaia, but in every place your faith in God has gone forth, so that we have no need to say anything. For they themselves openly declare about us what sort of reception we had among you, and how you turned to God from idols to serve the living and true God and to await his Son from heaven, whom he raised from the dead, Jesus, who delivers us from the coming wrath.

GOSPEL
Matthew
22:34–40

When the Pharisees heard that Jesus had silenced the Sadducees, they gathered together, and one of them, a scholar of the law, tested him by asking, "Teacher, which commandment in the law is the greatest?" He said to him, "You shall love the Lord, your God, with all your heart, with all your soul, and with all your mind. This is the greatest and the first commandment. The second is like it: You shall love your neighbor as yourself. The whole law and the prophets depend on these two commandments."

❖ *Understanding the Word*

While we tend to think of the escape from Egypt and the wandering in the wilderness as the content of the book of Exodus, the larger theme concerns the forming of a people into the people of God. In today's first reading, what it means to be a people of God is expressed in ethical behavior. "You shall not molest or oppress an alien . . . you shall not wrong any widow or orphan . . . " (Exodus 22:20–21). The basis of such behavior is Israel's own experience of oppression and alienation, and God's compassion (Exodus 22:26).

In Paul's Letter to the Thessalonians, he begins by narrating his relationship with the community. After being abused in Philippi, Paul traveled to Thessalonica, where he presented the gospel without flattery or deception (1 Thessalonians 2:3–5). The Thessalonians received the gospel because he came not in word alone "but in power and in the Holy Spirit and much conviction" (1 Thessalonians 1:5). And now the Thessalonians have become imitators of Paul, "receiving the word in great affliction," and in so doing, they have become models for all believers in Macedonia and Achaia (1 Thessalonians 1:6–7). The formerly pagan Thessalonians have turned from their idols to the "living and true God" (1 Thessalonians 1:9), and thus will be delivered from the coming wrath.

The series of controversies between Jesus and the religious leaders comes to a head in today's Gospel. "When the Pharisees heard that Jesus had silenced the Sadducees, they gathered together" (Matthew 22:34). The disparate groups against Jesus have now joined forces. In Matthew 5:17, Jesus had offered a new interpretation of the Law, and had advised his listeners that their righteousness should exceed that of the scribes and Pharisees (Matthew 5:20). Now his opponents return to questions about the Law. As Jesus had answered the rich young man (Matthew 19:18–19), he now answers the leadership. The greatest commandment is love of God and love of neighbor.

The poet Elizabeth Barrett Browning asks, "How do I love thee? Let me count the ways." Jesus is asked which commandment is the greatest. To love God with all you have and are and to love your neighbor as yourself, he answers. How do we love God? Love your neighbor. How do we love our neighbor? Love yourself with a healthy self-love. We need to ask, who is my neighbor?

The book of Exodus answers this question. All people are your neighbors, including those most in need, those alien to you or your country; widows, who had no status in that day; and orphans, who were utterly alone. Treat all people with respect and dignity, as God treated you in Egypt. In other words, imitate God by doing unto others what God has done to you. Paul gives similar advice. You imitated me by receiving the word in great affliction, with joy from the Holy Spirit. Invite others to do the same.

We struggle with how to live these words, especially when it comes to welcoming strangers, immigrants, those who harm us, or those in any kind of need. Our feelings run deep, but the challenge from the scriptures and from the words of Pope Francis is clear: "The Church must be a place of mercy freely given where everyone feels welcomed, loved, forgiven, and encouraged to live the good life of the Gospel" (*Evangelii Gaudium*, par. 114). The Pope set an example by bringing three immigrant families to live at the Vatican, another challenge. We need good judgment. St. Francis de Sales gives practical advice: Put others in your place and yourself in theirs, then treat the other the way you would like to be treated. That's how we love God, neighbor, and self.

❖ Consider/Discuss

- Who is the alien, widow, orphan, or person in need whom you have trouble seeing as your neighbor? Why?
- When has God's love for you surprised you and helped you love in a similar way?

❖ Living and Praying with the Word

You have loved me, God, even when others have not. Help me remember that bountiful love so that I can do unto others as you have done to me. Help me see the stranger and alien with the eyes I use to see my brother or sister and with which you see all of us as your children.

November 1, 2017

ALL SAINTS

Today's Focus: Pay Attention!

The Beautitudes are more than a mere grocery list of whom God favors. They are an index of signs, giving us information about where we should look for God's action in the world.

FIRST READING
Revelation 7:2–4, 9–14

I, John, saw another angel come up from the East, holding the seal of the living God. He cried out in a loud voice to the four angels who were given power to damage the land and the sea, "Do not damage the land or the sea or the trees until we put the seal on the foreheads of the servants of our God." I heard the number of those who had been marked with the seal, one hundred and forty-four thousand marked from every tribe of the Israelites.

After this I had a vision of a great multitude, which no one could count, from every nation, race, people, and tongue. They stood before the throne and before the Lamb, wearing white robes and holding palm branches in their hands. They cried out in a loud voice:
"Salvation comes from our God, who is seated on the throne,
and from the Lamb."
All the angels stood around the throne and around the elders and the four living creatures. They prostrated themselves before the throne, worshiped God, and exclaimed:
"Amen. Blessing and glory, wisdom and thanksgiving,
honor, power, and might
be to our God forever and ever. Amen."
Then one of the elders spoke up and said to me, "Who are these wearing white robes, and where did they come from?" I said to him, "My lord, you are the one who knows." He said to me, "These are the ones who have survived the time of great distress; they have washed their robes and made them white in the Blood of the Lamb."

PSALM RESPONSE
Psalm 24:6

Lord, this is the people that longs to see your face.

SECOND READING
1 John 3:1–3

Beloved: See what love the Father has bestowed on us that we may be called the children of God. Yet so we are. The reason the world does not know us is that it did not know him. Beloved, we are God's children now; what we shall be has not yet been revealed. We do know that when it is revealed we shall be like him, for we shall see him as he is. Everyone who has this hope based on him makes himself pure, as he is pure.

When Jesus saw the crowds, he went up the mountain, and after he had sat down, his disciples came to him. He began to teach them, saying:

"Blessed are the poor in spirit,
    for theirs is the Kingdom of heaven.
Blessed are they who mourn,
    for they will be comforted.
Blessed are the meek,
    for they will inherit the land.
Blessed are they who hunger and thirst for righteousness,
    for they will be satisfied.
Blessed are the merciful,
    for they will be shown mercy.
Blessed are the clean of heart,
    for they will see God.
Blessed are the peacemakers,
    for they will be called children of God.
Blessed are they who are persecuted for the sake of righteousness,
    for theirs is the kingdom of heaven.
Blessed are you when they insult you and persecute you and utter every kind of evil against you falsely because of me. Rejoice and be glad, for your reward will be great in heaven."

❖❖ Understanding the Word

The book of Revelation, from which our first reading is taken, is the only complete apocalyptic work in the Bible. The literary genre uses coded language and dramatic images to convey a message about the final days or coming *eschaton* (end of the world). In today's reading, the visionary John sees two groups of people. The first numbers 144,000 and is taken from all the tribes of Israel. These are sealed by God, so are protected from the coming destruction. The second is a great multitude from every nation, race, people, and language. Dressed in white robes and carrying palm branches, they are the faithful who stand before the throne of God and encourage those on earth to continue to persevere. The "great distress" likely refers to the sporadic Roman persecution of Christians.

The reading from First John shares with Revelation the same eschatological worldview. God's kingdom is dawning, but it will not come to completion until Christ's return (1 John 3:2). Because of God's love, the believers can now be called "children of God," but what they shall become is yet to be revealed. First John appears to be a sermon addressed to the same community for whom the Gospel of John was written, hence a similar use of vocabulary, images (love, John 3:16 and 1 John 3:1; children of God, John 1:12, and 1 John 3:1–2), and theological understanding.

The Gospel is from Matthew's Sermon on the Mount (Matthew 5 — 7:29), in which Jesus teaches the crowd new expectations of righteousness and warns against false prophets, false disciples, and faulty foundations. The sermon opens with a series of nine beatitudes. The term *makarios* in Greek means "blessed" or "happy" and is frequent in wisdom literature and the psalms. The first beatitude specifies that it is the poor in spirit who receive the kingdom of heaven. The same beatitude found in Luke is not so specific (Luke 6:20). Matthew may have meant that the pious poor or any of those in his community who have complete dependence on God are blessed. The Beatitudes in general promise a time of reversal. Those who mourn will be comforted, the meek will receive land, the hungry and thirsty will be fed, etc. These blessings will be realized when the kingdom of heaven (Matthew's preferred term) comes in its fullness.

✤ Reflecting on the Word

Recently I began taking a medication that might interact poorly with another medication I take. The pharmacist said to pay attention to any changes I experience and call my doctor if they persist. Her words reminded me about how important it is to pay attention, especially to what I can take for granted too often.

The Beatitudes are about paying attention. Attend to others: comfort those who mourn, show mercy, make peace, and work for righteousness. Respond to their needs. Learn from them how to make clear that we are children of God and followers of Jesus. Attend to how you relate to others. Become meek or humble and so faithful to living Jesus that people treat you like people treated him. Some followed him, while others insulted and persecuted him. Being attentive can cost us in the eyes of others. It cost him. And pay attention to your heart. Your heart's desires lead you closer to or away from God. They make clear whether or not you depend upon God alone or place your trust in someone or something else.

The Beatitudes also help us know God's desires for us. They help us pay attention to God. When we pay attention to the life of the Spirit, to our inner life, to the needs of others, to those who are examples of holy living to us and to the world in which we live, we are better able to see God present in our midst. We live as children of God. We become for our day and time what Jesus was for his, the visible presence of God. The saints were the visible presence of Jesus Christ in their day and time. Pay attention to the Divine Physician. Call on him in prayer and become a saint in the making today.

✤ Consider/Discuss

- How do you pay attention to God's presence within and around you?
- Which of the Beatitudes do you live easily and which do you most resist?

✤ Living and Praying with the Word

Loving God, I am grateful that you have made me your child and that you sent Jesus to show us your ways. Fill me with your Spirit so that I pay attention to you and to life, in ways that make clear that I desire to rest in you alone.

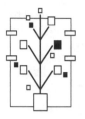

November 5, 2017

THIRTY-FIRST SUNDAY IN ORDINARY TIME

Today's Focus: Learn It, Live It

Today's Gospel passage is likely the source of the maxim "Practice what you preach." Though this saying has been around a long time, we still have trouble doing it.

FIRST READING
*Malachi
1:14b — 2:2b,
8–10*

A great King am I, says the LORD of hosts,
    and my name will be feared among the nations.
And now, O priests, this commandment is for you:
    If you do not listen,
if you do not lay it to heart,
    to give glory to my name, says the LORD of hosts,
I will send a curse upon you
    and of your blessing I will make a curse.
You have turned aside from the way,
    and have caused many to falter by your instruction;
you have made void the covenant of Levi,
    says the LORD of hosts.
I, therefore, have made you contemptible
    and base before all the people,
since you do not keep my ways,
    but show partiality in your decisions.
Have we not all the one father?
    Has not the one God created us?
Why then do we break faith with one another,
    violating the covenant of our fathers?

PSALM RESPONSE
Psalm 131:1

In you, Lord, I have found my peace.

SECOND READING
*1 Thessalonians
2:7b–9, 13*

Brothers and sisters: We were gentle among you, as a nursing mother cares for her children. With such affection for you, we were determined to share with you not only the gospel of God, but our very selves as well, so dearly beloved had you become to us. You recall, brothers and sisters, our toil and drudgery. Working night and day in order not to burden any of you, we proclaimed to you the gospel of God.

And for this reason we too give thanks to God unceasingly, that, in receiving the word of God from hearing us, you received not a human word but, as it truly is, the word of God, which is now at work in you who believe.

GOSPEL
Matthew
23:1–12

Jesus spoke to the crowds and to his disciples, saying, "The scribes and the Pharisees have taken their seat on the chair of Moses. Therefore, do and observe all things whatsoever they tell you, but do not follow their example. For they preach but they do not practice. They tie up heavy burdens hard to carry and lay them on people's shoulders, but they will not lift a finger to move them. All their works are performed to be seen. They widen their phylacteries and lengthen their tassels. They love places of honor at banquets, seats of honor in synagogues, greetings in marketplaces, and the salutation 'Rabbi.' As for you, do not be called 'Rabbi.' You have but one teacher, and you are all brothers. Call no one on earth your father; you have but one Father in heaven. Do not be called 'Master'; you have but one master, the Christ. The greatest among you must be your servant. Whoever exalts himself will be humbled; but whoever humbles himself will be exalted."

❖ Understanding the Word

The book of Malachi appears to have been written during the fifth century B.C. after the exiles had returned to Jerusalem. The author's name may be "Malachi" (1:1) or the name may be a pseudonym based on the meaning of *malachi* as "my messenger" (3:1). Despite God's love of Israel (1:2 5), the people respond poorly, failing to tithe (3:6–11) and providing defiled food for sacrifice (1:7). The blame for such behavior is placed on the priests who "have turned aside from the way and have caused many to falter" by their poor instruction (2:8). In the verses not included in today's reading, the prophet is graphic in his portrayal of God's displeasure: "I will rebuke your offering; I will spread dung on your faces" (2:3).

Paul continues his description of his relationship with the Thessalonians, reminding them that he and his coworkers were "as a nursing mother" toward them, sharing not only the gospel but also "our very selves" (1 Thessalonians 2:7–8). Paul's use of the plural "we" demonstrates that he means to include those who were also sending them out on mission, Silvanus and Timothy. It is not only Paul who supports himself; Silvanus and Timothy also seem to be self-sufficient. The refusal of the apostle and his team to receive financial support may have led some to accuse Paul of being "less than an apostle," since he did not take full advantage of his rights (1 Corinthians 9:15–18). But Paul answers that his financial independence means he can proclaim the gospel without burden (1 Thessalonians 2:9).

The Gospel is best read as a bookend to Jesus' earlier announcement that the disciples' righteousness must surpass that of the scribes and Pharisees or they would not enter the kingdom of heaven (Matthew 5:20). In today's reading, Jesus returns to the theme of appropriate behavior for religious leaders. The scribes and Pharisees "have taken their seat on the chair of Moses," so disciples are to do and observe what they are told but not follow their example. The teachings of the scribes and Pharisees are not the subject of Jesus' condemnation.

Their behavior is. "For they preach but they do not practice" (Matthew 23:3). Jesus accuses them of burdening people by their scrupulous interpretation of Torah (Matthew 23:4), performing works in order to be seen (Matthew 23:5), and seeking honor and status (Matthew 23:7). To their self-aggrandizement, Jesus responds, "Whoever exalts himself will be humbled; but whoever humbles himself will be exalted" (Matthew 23:12).

❖ Reflecting on the Word

During the time I was in ministry in Grand Rapids, Michigan, the Dominican Sisters there built two homes in a neighborhood that would blend privately built homes with homes built by Habitat for Humanity. We went to view the construction and met one of our neighbors. I introduced myself. The family's mother commented, "Your home is being built for you. We have to help build ours." The words stung. It wasn't until we shoveled her walk and driveway and cut her grass that our deeds invited her to see us as true neighbors.

Jesus tells his hearers to respect the scribes and Pharisees, but not to follow their example. Their deeds did not match their words, so do as they say, not as they do. How often has a parent, teacher or pastor said that and later regretted it? Jesus, who humbled himself, lived what he taught. So follow his example. Pope Francis does the same. He tells church leaders to smell like the sheep and he lives those words. We are to pay attention to and be with people, like the nursing mother in the second reading who cares for her children. If we do as we say, others will want to do as we say and do, too.

Malachi's message is similar. Listen to God's commandments, take them to heart and live them, or experience the Lord's curse rather than God's blessing. We are all children of one God, so show no partiality. These words are difficult, because if I'm honest, some people are my favorites and others are my nemeses. But we are to do as God does. God loves us all like a nursing mother who cares for all her children. Humble yourself. Serve all. Smell like the sheep of the flock, be blessed, and be a blessing.

❖ Consider/Discuss

- How do your deeds match your words of faith? Give concrete examples.
- To whom do you easily offer service and to whom do you begrudge it? How?

Living and Praying with the Word

You love us with the care of an attentive parent, O God. Through Jesus you chose to smell like your sheep. Help our deeds match our words and empower us to attend to one another as a nursing mother cares for her children.

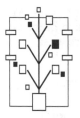

November 12, 2017

THIRTY-SECOND SUNDAY IN ORDINARY TIME

Today's Focus: Ready, Set . . . Sleep

Everyone in today's Gospel reading fell asleep. The real difference is that one group—though asleep—was prepared and ready to go whenever it was time to wake up!

FIRST READING
Wisdom 6:12–16

Resplendent and unfading is wisdom,
    and she is readily perceived by those who love her,
    and found by those who seek her.
She hastens to make herself known in anticipation of their desire;
    whoever watches for her at dawn shall not be disappointed,
    for he shall find her sitting by his gate.
For taking thought of wisdom is the perfection of prudence,
    and whoever for her sake keeps vigil
    shall quickly be free from care;
because she makes her own rounds, seeking those worthy of her,
    and graciously appears to them in the ways,
    and meets them with all solicitude.

PSALM RESPONSE
Psalm 63:2b

My soul is thirsting for you, O Lord my God.

In the shorter form of the reading, the passage in brackets is omitted.

SECOND READING
1 Thessalonians 4:13–18 or 4:13–14

We do not want you to be unaware, brothers and sisters, about those who have fallen asleep, so that you may not grieve like the rest, who have no hope. For if we believe that Jesus died and rose, so too will God, through Jesus, bring with him those who have fallen asleep. [Indeed, we tell you this, on the word of the Lord, that we who are alive, who are left until the coming of the Lord, will surely not precede those who have fallen asleep. For the Lord himself, with a word of command, with the voice of an archangel and with the trumpet of God, will come down from heaven, and the dead in Christ will rise first. Then we who are alive, who are left, will be caught up together with them in the clouds to meet the Lord in the air. Thus we shall always be with the Lord. Therefore, console one another with these words.]

Jesus told his disciples this parable: "The kingdom of heaven will be like ten virgins who took their lamps and went out to meet the bridegroom. Five of them were foolish and five were wise. The foolish ones, when taking their lamps, brought no oil with them, but the wise brought flasks of oil with their lamps. Since the bridegroom was long delayed, they all became drowsy and fell asleep. At midnight, there was a cry, 'Behold, the bridegroom! Come out to meet him!' Then all those virgins got up and trimmed their lamps. The foolish ones said to the wise, 'Give us some of your oil, for our lamps are going out.' But the wise ones replied, 'No, for there may not be enough for us and you. Go instead to the merchants and buy some for yourselves.' While they went off to buy it, the bridegroom came and those who were ready went into the wedding feast with him. Then the door was locked. Afterwards the other virgins came and said, 'Lord, Lord, open the door for us!' But he said in reply, 'Amen, I say to you, I do not know you.' Therefore, stay awake, for you know neither the day nor the hour."

❖ Understanding the Word

The book of Wisdom, written in the mid-first century B.C., attempts to answer the perennial question, why do the wicked prosper while the good suffer? The author, whom tradition holds is Solomon, personifies Wisdom as a woman who is found by those who seek her (Wisdom 6:12). That Wisdom is found "sitting by his gate" shows that insight from wisdom is neither lofty nor beyond human comprehension. By definition, wisdom in ancient Near Eastern understanding resulted from reflection on human experience in order to find the underlying order of life. Thus wisdom "graciously appears to them in the ways"—the paths of ordinary life.

The primary concern of the Thessalonians and likely their reason for seeking Paul's advice may have been the deaths of believers in the community (1 Thessalonians 4:13). The founding premise of Paul's proclamation was the imminent return of Jesus in the *parousia* (Second Coming). This urgency is what drove his apostolic efforts and likely spurred membership. But the faithful among the Thessalonians were dying, and Jesus had not returned. Paul answers their concerns by assuring that those who have fallen asleep will be the first to be raised when the Lord returns.

As we near the end of the season of Ordinary Time, the Gospel readings focus more on the coming reign of God. In today's parable, unique to Matthew, Jesus emphasizes the importance of vigilance. The maidens, like the Matthean community, are to be prepared even if the bridegroom should be delayed. When those who did not prepare rightly run out of oil, we would expect the others to "share." But this parable is not about compassionate response to those without. It is a call to personal preparation and personal responsibility, lest the believers find themselves knocking at the closed door. "Therefore, stay awake, for you know neither the day nor the hour" (Matthew 25:13). The parable served to encourage those in Matthew's community who may have grown weary awaiting the Lord's return.

When I taught music I carefully constructed my lesson plans to be as prepared as humanly possible for anything that might happen in class. That helped me stay on track when a student tried to avoid work or more singing. I could go with the flow. We can't be prepared for every eventuality, but if we show up to life in a thoughtful, reflective manner, we will be ready to face whatever comes, even death.

The wise virgins were as ready as they could be. Their lamps had enough oil so that the delay in the bridegroom's arrival and falling asleep did not keep them from greeting him with light and accompanying the wedding party into the hall. The foolish virgins had not prepared as well. Their lamps went out. They were left behind. We can learn much from these women. Be ready. Take time to reflect on life in the light of God's Word, the witness of Jesus, the liturgy we celebrate, the teachings of the Church, and trusted mentors. There we will find wisdom. Socrates said, "The unexamined life is not worth living." The examined life, however, is well worth living and can continually open our eyes to God's presence, even if we've fallen asleep or wandered away.

So ready yourself with the oil of reflection. Trim the wick of your life with truth to rekindle the Christ light we promised to keep burning brightly. Make time every day for thanksgiving by showing Jesus to others. Ask forgiveness for the times when your eyes were closed or you chose another way. That's how to stay awake and be ready at all times, for we know not the day or hour of the Lord's return.

❖ Consider/Discuss

- Where do you find the wisdom you need to live your faith clearly?
- How do you ready yourself to meet the Lord each and every day?

❖ Living and Praying with the Word

Wisdom of God, be with me. Open my eyes to see you present in the events of my life. Fan the flame of faith alive in my heart and help me to live in ways that welcome you at all times.

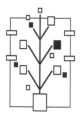

November 19, 2017

THIRTY-THIRD SUNDAY IN ORDINARY TIME

Today's Focus: All Good Gifts

Everyone has been given some gift or gifts by God. What differentiates us is the degree to which we use those gifts so they flourish and become of even greater use to those around us.

FIRST READING
Proverbs 31:10–13, 19–20, 30–31

When one finds a worthy wife,
    her value is far beyond pearls.
Her husband, entrusting his heart to her,
    has an unfailing prize.
She brings him good, and not evil,
    all the days of her life.
She obtains wool and flax
    and works with loving hands.
She puts her hands to the distaff,
    and her fingers ply the spindle.
She reaches out her hands to the poor,
    and extends her arms to the needy.
Charm is deceptive and beauty fleeting;
    the woman who fears the LORD is to be praised.
Give her a reward for her labors,
    and let her works praise her at the city gates.

PSALM RESPONSE
Psalm 128:1a

Blessed are those who fear the Lord.

SECOND READING
1 Thessalonians 5:1–6

Concerning times and seasons, brothers and sisters, you have no need for anything to be written to you. For you yourselves know very well that the day of the Lord will come like a thief at night. When people are saying, "Peace and security," then sudden disaster comes upon them, like labor pains upon a pregnant woman, and they will not escape.

But you, brothers and sisters, are not in darkness, for that day to overtake you like a thief. For all of you are children of the light and children of the day. We are not of the night or of darkness. Therefore, let us not sleep as the rest do, but let us stay alert and sober.

GOSPEL
Matthew
25:14–30
or 25:14–15,
19–21

Jesus told his disciples this parable: "A man going on a journey called in his servants and entrusted his possessions to them. To one he gave five talents; to another, two; to a third, one—to each according to his ability. Then he went away. [Immediately the one who received five talents went and traded with them, and made another five. Likewise, the one who received two made another two. But the man who received one went off and dug a hole in the ground and buried his master's money.]

"After a long time the master of those servants came back and settled accounts with them. The one who had received five talents came forward bringing the additional five. He said, 'Master, you gave me five talents. See, I have made five more.' His master said to him, 'Well done, my good and faithful servant. Since you were faithful in small matters, I will give you great responsibilities. Come, share your master's joy.' [Then the one who had received two talents also came forward and said, 'Master, you gave me two talents. See, I have made two more.' His master said to him, 'Well done, my good and faithful servant. Since you were faithful in small matters, I will give you great responsibilities. Come, share your master's joy.' Then the one who had received the one talent came forward and said, 'Master, I knew you were a demanding person, harvesting where you did not plant and gathering where you did not scatter; so out of fear I went off and buried your talent in the ground. Here it is back.' His master said to him in reply, 'You wicked, lazy servant! So you knew that I harvest where I did not plant and gather where I did not scatter? Should you not then have put my money in the bank so that I could have got it back with interest on my return? Now then! Take the talent from him and give it to the one with ten. For to everyone who has, more will be given and he will grow rich; but from the one who has not, even what he has will be taken away. And throw this useless servant into the darkness outside, where there will be wailing and grinding of teeth.'"]

❖ *Understanding the Word*

In the patriarchal world of the ancient Near East, gender roles were steadfast and carefully guarded. In today's first reading from the book of Proverbs, the expectations and behaviors of the ideal wife are described. Primarily, she is to bring honor to her husband (Proverbs 31:12), attend to the making of clothes for the family (Proverbs 31:13), and care for the poor and needy (Proverbs 31:20). Honor, care of family, and care of neighbor are hallmarks of the faithful Israelite, which Proverbs describes here in terms of a woman's duties.

The concern to which Paul responds in his First Letter to the Thessalonians is best understood in light of eschatology, or concern about the end-times. Paul and the early Christians believed that Jesus' return was imminent. That eschatological urgency drove the apostles and preachers to spread the word of repentance far and near. When Jesus returned he would judge the living and the dead and their actions would decide their fate. But a generation of believers was now dying, and Jesus had not returned. The Thessalonians rightly asked Paul "When?" to which he responds, "When you least expect—like a thief in the night." The eschatological urgency leads to an eschatological anxiety that should shape the actions of believers.

Whereas the parable of the ten maidens in Matthew 25:1–13 spoke of preparation for the end-time, today's Gospel reading focuses on the "in-between time." Jesus describes a situation in which a person has left his possessions in the hands of his servants and departed on a journey of unknown duration. Each servant is given responsibilities according to his or her abilities (Matthew 25:15). Upon his return, the master evaluates how well each servant lived up to his or her responsibilities. To the first two, the master offers commendation: "Well done, my good and faithful servant" (Matthew 25:21; 23). However, the third servant failed in his task, resulting in condemnation, "You wicked, lazy servant!" (Matthew 25:26). Jesus' summation—"For to everyone who has more will be given . . . but from the one who has not, even what he has will be taken away" (Matthew 25:29)—seems uncharacteristically harsh. But as Matthew is emphasizing to his community, entrance into the reign of heaven is not a guarantee for believers. Everyone is expected to prepare according to their ability.

❖ Reflecting on the Word

I was the executor of my grandfather's estate. Our attorney commented on how faithfully my grandfather saved money. He also noted that, having lost everything in the 1929 crash, my grandfather would only make the safest investments. Grandpa feared losing everything again.

Fear kept the third servant in today's parable from taking the risks needed to grow what he'd been given. The master chided him for being lazy. How often have life experiences kept us from taking the steps and risks needed to develop the gifts that we've been given, whether of time, talent, or treasure? Fear can be a powerful force. On the other hand, the worthy wife took those risks. She was industrious and generous to the Lord and to all people. When the Thessalonians did not experience Jesus' immediate return, Paul encouraged them to keep using and developing the gifts that God gave them. Live as children of the light, alert, sober, and ready whenever the Christ returns.

Like the Thessalonians, we await the return of the Lord. Like the servants in the parable, God has given us many gifts and the means to develop them. St. Augustine's rule for community life advises that we give according to our ability and take according to our need. Ability and need change depending upon age and circumstance. However, when we find the courage to admit our need, name our ability, and develop the gifts that God has given us, we will live in the light that readies us to meet Christ in all life's conditions. It is the Spirit who frees us from fear. Remain in the Spirit and multiply the gifts God has given. Then we can hear God say, "Well done, my good and faithful servant."

❖ *Consider/Discuss*

- What are the gifts that God has given to you? Name some of them.
- How do you make your gifts grow to give God thanks? What holds you back?

❖ *Living and Praying with the Word*

Generous God, you bless us in many ways. Help me to multiply your gifts to me in your service as a sign of my gratitude. Where fear holds me back, give me courage and freedom to move ahead.

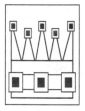

November 26, 2017

OUR LORD JESUS CHRIST, KING OF THE UNIVERSE

Today's Focus: Caring for the Least among Us—Christ

It is an upside-down view of kingship that today's feast presents to us: we see royalty in the least and the lowly, and pay honor by giving aid to them.

FIRST READING
Ezekiel 34: 11–12, 15–17

Thus says the Lord GOD: I myself will look after and tend my sheep. As a shepherd tends his flock when he finds himself among his scattered sheep, so will I tend my sheep. I will rescue them from every place where they were scattered when it was cloudy and dark. I myself will pasture my sheep; I myself will give them rest, says the Lord GOD. The lost I will seek out, the strayed I will bring back, the injured I will bind up, the sick I will heal, but the sleek and the strong I will destroy, shepherding them rightly.

As for you, my sheep, says the Lord GOD, I will judge between one sheep and another, between rams and goats.

PSALM RESPONSE
Psalm 23:1

The Lord is my shepherd; there is nothing I shall want.

SECOND READING
1 Corinthians 15:20–26, 28

Brothers and sisters: Christ has been raised from the dead, the firstfruits of those who have fallen asleep. For since death came through man, the resurrection of the dead came also through man. For just as in Adam all die, so too in Christ shall all be brought to life, but each one in proper order: Christ the firstfruits; then, at his coming, those who belong to Christ; then comes the end, when he hands over the kingdom to his God and Father, when he has destroyed every sovereignty and every authority and power. For he must reign until he has put all his enemies under his feet. The last enemy to be destroyed is death. When everything is subjected to him, then the Son himself will also be subjected to the one who subjected everything to him, so that God may be all in all.

GOSPEL
Matthew 25:31–46

Jesus said to his disciples: "When the Son of Man comes in his glory, and all the angels with him, he will sit upon his glorious throne, and all the nations will be assembled before him. And he will separate them one from another, as a shepherd separates the sheep from the goats. He will place the sheep on his right and the goats on his left. Then the king will say to those on his right, 'Come, you who are blessed by my Father. Inherit the kingdom prepared for you from the foundation of the world. For I was hungry and you gave me food, I was thirsty and you gave me drink, a stranger and you welcomed me, naked and you clothed me, ill and you cared for me, in prison and you visited me.' Then the righteous will answer him and say, 'Lord, when did we see you hungry and feed you, or thirsty and give you drink? When did we see you a stranger and welcome you, or naked and clothe you? When did we see you ill or in prison, and visit you?' And the king will say to them in reply, 'Amen, I say to you, whatever you did for one of the least brothers of mine, you did for me.' Then he will say to those on his left, 'Depart from me, you accursed, into the eternal fire prepared for the devil and his angels. For I was hungry and you gave me no food, I was thirsty and you gave me no drink, a stranger and you gave me no welcome, naked and you gave me no clothing, ill and in prison, and you did not care for me.' Then they will answer and say, 'Lord, when did we see you hungry or thirsty or a stranger or naked or ill or in prison, and not minister to your needs?' He will answer them, 'Amen, I say to you, what you did not do for one of these least ones, you did not do for me.' And these will go off to eternal punishment, but the righteous to eternal life."

❖ Understanding the Word

Frequently in the prophetic literature, shepherds represent the leaders of Israel (Isaiah 56:11; Jeremiah 2:8; Ezekiel 34:7). In today's first reading from Ezekiel, God is dismissing the shepherds of Israel who allowed the sheep to be plundered (Ezekiel 34:8). Instead God will take on this role, searching for and examining the sheep. The oracle of Ezekiel presents the actions of God as compassionate and intimate. "The lost I will seek out . . . the sick I will heal" (Ezekiel 34:16). But God as shepherd will also deal rightly with those who are "sleek and strong" (Ezekiel 34:17), perhaps the very ones who have "fattened themselves on the sheep."

Paul frequently compares Christ with Adam as he attempts to explain to new believers the effect of Christ's salvation. In Romans Chapter 5, Adam initiates the "pattern of trespass," but Christ's gift brings acquittal. In today's second reading from First Corinthians, Paul explains that death came through Adam, but now through Christ all live. In fact, Christ represents the beginning, the "firstfruits" of the coming reign of God. Like many early Christians, Paul held a particular view of eschatology (end-times) that saw Christ's resurrection as the beginning of the Reign of God. Christ's return would then usher in the fullness of God's reign.

"When everything is subjected to him," then Christ himself will be subjected to God (1 Corinthians 15:28).

This coming of Christ that Paul describes is presented in narrative form by Matthew. "When the Son of Man comes . . . all the nations will be assembled before him" (Matthew 25:31–32). This assembly sets the stage for the final judgment, which Jesus describes as being like a shepherd who separates his sheep from his goats. The parallel with today's first reading is intentional. As God served as Israel's compassionate and just shepherd, so too will Jesus as the Son of Man come in glory to sit in judgment over this world. Though the goats seem to represent those who are later "accursed" (Matthew 25:41), there is nothing inherently "bad" about the goats. They simply represent a distinction. Even today in the Middle East, sheep and goats are herded together. The criteria for judgment are the actions of mercy on behalf of the "least." To care for the "least" is to care for Jesus.

❖ Reflecting on the Word

When I meet someone in need, on a street corner or a roadway island, or when approached for assistance, my heart is tugged. When does my giving help and when does it enable unhealthy behavior? How do I respect the dignity of my sister or brother in need? How do I make a good judgment without becoming judgmental?

Both those who are blessed and cursed ask Jesus, "Lord, when did we see you hungry or thirsty or a stranger or naked or ill or in prison, and not minister to your need?" How often have I said and heard, "If Jesus came and asked, I'd gladly give." But isn't that the point of the story? Christ is the one asking when our sisters and brothers in need ask and knock on the door of my heart and that of our collective humanity. Whatever we do for one of the least of our sisters and brothers, we do for Jesus.

Some African peoples exemplify this in the concept of *ubuntu*. When some children were told that the first child to win the race to a basket of fruit would get all the fruit, all the children joined hands and ran together. Asked why they did that, they answered: "*Ubuntu*. How can one of us be happy if all the others are sad?" How can one of us be satisfied if many of our sisters and brothers have nothing? The picture of that race helps me begin to understand Jesus' words. He is the King we honor today, the Shepherd who calls us to care for his flock. The questions remain, but by doing what we can to care for and pay attention to our sisters and brothers, we join hands. We care for and pay attention to Christ and he is seen in us. *Ubuntu!*

❖ Consider/Discuss

- Where have you seen the face of Christ in a sister or brother in need?
- How do you live these corporal works of mercy and love to see and be Jesus?

❖ Living and Praying with the Word

O God, you are my shepherd. I do not always see the face of your Son in my sisters and brothers, the other members of your flock. Free me from being judgmental, even when I need to make good judgments. Help me care for and pay attention to Jesus by joining hands with all my sisters and brothers.

A Dominican Sister of Sinsinawa, Laurie Brink is an Associate Professor of New Testament Studies at Catholic Theological Union in Chicago. Brink investigates the ancient social, religious, and cultural world out of which early Christianity emerged. Having worked as a senior staff member for the Combined Caesarea Expedition in Israel, she seeks to integrate archaeological research and biblical exegesis. Her recent scholarship has focused on the role of the Roman military in the spread of Christianity. Her monograph, *Soldiers in Luke-Acts: Engaging, Contradicting, and Transcending the Stereotypes* (Mohr Siebeck, 2014), demonstrates that Luke intentionally characterizes Roman soldiers as good disciples. She is also researching and writing a book on the biblical foundations of friendship. Brink is an associate editor of *The Bible Today*, and has recorded two lecture series (Acts of the Apostles and Philippians) for Now You Know Media.

Author, *Understanding the Word*

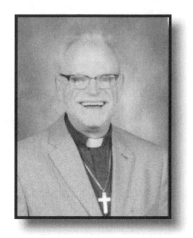

Fr. Paul H. Colloton, O.S.F.S., D.Min., is a member of the Oblates of St. Francis de Sales, Wilmington-Philadelphia Province and serves as the associate pastor for Immaculate Conception Parish, Elkton, Maryland, and St. Jude Mission, North East, Maryland. For a little over thirteen years Fr. Paul served as the Director of Continuing Education for the National Association of Pastoral Musicians (NPM). His nearly 45 years experience in pastoral ministry includes service as a liturgist, musician, spiritual director, presider, preacher, clinician, retreat director, author, and minister to and with people living with HIV/AIDS.

Author, *Reflecting on the Word*
      Consider/Discuss
      Living and Praying with the Word

Notes